Enterprise Architecture for Business Success

Authored By

Inji Wijegunaratne,
George Fernandez &
Peter Evans-Greenwood

Bentham Science Publishers Ltd.
Executive Suite Y - 2
PO Box 7917, Saif Zone
Sharjah, U.A.E.
subscriptions@benthamscienc.org

CONTENTS

contd…..

Section 3: The EA 'Project'

contd.....

contd…..

contd.....

contd.....

Foreword

Enterprise Architecture today is laden with frameworks, techniques, and processes. There are numerous flavours of these instruments available to the practitioner. Some, such as TOGAF and the Zachman frameworks are relatively well known, as are US Government frameworks (*e.g.* FEAF, DODAF). Some have publicly available reference material, while some others – consulting companies, authors in the field – have proposed their own versions.

But a fundamental question is often neglected: *How does the Enterprise Architect, working in a complex corporate environment actually deliver value to the enterprise?* Everything else is secondary to this point. The authors have taken this theme as the central focus of this eBook. As the title suggests, they have presented a very practical guide to deliver successful Enterprise Architecture outcomes.

The authors start with a hypothetical example, presenting some key ideas that are discussed in depth later on. Chapter 4 sets the scene by defining the terms and introducing the structural elements of their approach. In the next three chapters the reader is taken through the various stages of an EA "program". Following a chapter that talks explicitly to EA delivering value, the eBook ends with a set of case studies from the authors' experience. Several important points are made in this process:

- What does the label enterprise architecture actually mean? It defines several facets of meaning behind this term
- The importance of aligning the enterprise architecture cycle with the business cycle – of planning, implementing and operating; and within this, the alignment of enterprise architecture development with business strategy and objectives.
- In the initial key stages of business planning – where direction setting occurs – essential business skills are required. Understanding the business, communicating in "business speak", and taking the IT cue from business imperatives; are more important skills in these vital early stages than heavyweight frameworks and elaborate architecture detail.
- The responsibilities of an enterprise architect must change and expand to cover much more than the traditional technical/IT domain. These include the ability to make your voice heard in senior and executive management circles, facilitating business and IT alignment, periodically assessing performance of the IT estate as well as assessing the benefits of business/IT initiatives.

The authors' prescription for successful enterprise architecture resonates strongly with my own experience in managing the enterprise architecture function in large and complex organisations. In my own experience running Enterprise Architecture teams I have seen my EA team move from purely IT driven technical architecture standards to more strategically aligned business capability driven architecture. EA function should assist the business achieve their strategies by enabling enterprise wide business capabilities to reduce costs and optimise the investment spend. This can only be achieved by working closely with business stakeholders and developing business capability roadmaps that can evolve the business capability improvements over time. The eBook talks about Enterprise Architecture work aligning with the corporate investment planning cycle.

This is critical to ensure investments can be aligned and sequenced to evolving the most critical business capabilities to support the business strategies.

Established EA practitioners as well as to those intending to work in or starting out in EA would find this eBook useful as a practical guide and a source of resource material.

Chris Tisseverasinghe
Head of Enterprise Architecture
National Australia Bank
Australia

Preface

Many books have been written on Enterprise Architecture (EA). However, despite all the attention that EA has received over the last few years, there is little help for the EA professional on successfully running an EA programme. The literature is full practical yet general advice—'understand the limitations', 'identify bottlenecks', 'communicate with the business'—but provide little direction on how to achieve these worthy goals.

If you are an enterprise architect faced with the prospect of using EA to deliver value to the business, then how do you structure your programme of work? How do you set the scope? Where do you start? What problems are you likely to find? Can you avoid them? What tools can you use? How do you communicate with the business to ensure that they are engaged and support you for the duration?

Frameworks such as TOGAF propose a sequence of steps appropriate to conduct EA, but these processes alone do not provide sufficient practical guidance to an EA team. And failed EA projects keep accumulating.

Successful EA projects—whether small, medium, or large—do not aim simply to apply a framework or technique. Instead they work with the business to interpret their strategy and make sure that IT helps them achieve their goals. Most importantly, the business is always kept in the loop and engaged as a partner, rather than being lectured to on what IT should do for them.

Frameworks are valuable tools as they provide us with a mechanism to ensure consistent quality across complex engagements, but they are not enough to navigate the treacherous waters of a sizeable organisation. Based on our experience we developed an approach and collection of tools that EA practitioners should able to apply to their own work to establish, refine, control and manage EA successfully. We present here a model for undertaking an EA exercise based on a cycle of alignment, elaboration and governance that can be naturally blended with the standard EA frameworks.

The phrase 'Enterprise Architecture' means different things to different people. Is it the content of EA? Is it what an enterprise architect does? Does it encompass *all* architecture? Is it the process of running an EA programme or practice? Behind fuzziness surrounding the expression, there lies a deeper malaise; fuzziness around *what the enterprise architect needs to do – how they can make a difference*.

The position of an enterprise architect is a privileged one, but all too often this privilege is wasted by pushing a favourite technology barrow; taking refuge in visually appealing diagrams; or becoming the organisational change police. *How an EA adds value in his or her position is unanswered for many organisations*.

The title of this eBook includes the term 'Success'. In our view, 'successful' EA must help a business achieve the goals the business has set for itself; the means is provided by the tools and techniques used to achieve these goals. We establish realistic, grounded objectives for EA and focus on helping IT use EA to deliver benefits to the business that it is a part of, while ensuring that the exercise enjoys continued support of all stakeholders. Although we focus on delivering business benefits, we do not set business strategy: by and large the strategic goals of the enterprise is a given, though IT may work together with the business to clarify strategic drivers. In this, we depart from the traditional approach of IT and make IT, *via* EA, an active participant throughout the business planning process.

Our motto can be expressed as:

To be successful and maintain stakeholder support, the enterprise architect must: • Communicate in business terms, and not technical jargon • Deliver value *via* tangible, demonstrable business benefits • Provide timely and pragmatic solutions that work within the business's time and resource constraints

How to do this is the main focus of this eBook.

AUTHORS' NOTES

Diagrams in the eBook are labelled either as "Figures" or "Images". Please do not strive too hard to find a qualitative difference between the two sets – there isn't any; it was simply a quirk of the labelling process.

The cover design rather tenuously alludes to 'Business Success' - enterprise architecture looking outward into the business, rather than inward into IT systems.

ACKNOWLEDGEMENTS

Between 2008 and 2012 the authors were involved in delivering a set of lectures in enterprise architecture for the Master's degree course in EA at RMIT University in Melbourne, Australia. Teaching to others and having them comprehend your reasoning and perspective is by far the best way to grow one's own insight and understanding. These lectures were instrumental in integrating and shaping our collective experience in EA into a cohesive whole, developing insights, and in turn providing the benefits of these insights to future clients. We are grateful to RMIT University for affording us the opportunity.

We convey our appreciation to the management of the Journal for Enterprise Architecture for permitting us to include a previously published paper in the Case Studies Chapter of this eBook.

Last but not least the authors thank their spouses and families for the forbearance and tolerance they exhibited as we frittered away many evenings ruminating upon this eBook.

CONFLICT OF INTEREST

The authors confirm that this eBook content has no conflict of interest.

Inji Wijegunaratne, George Fernandez & Peter Evans-Greenwood
E-mails: injiwije@gmail.com, drgeorgefernandez@gmail.com & pevansgreenwood@gmail.com

Author Biographies

Inji Wijegunaratne

Inji is an experienced enterprise architect possessing over 25 years well-rounded IT experience. He undertook his first enterprise architecture assignment in 1998 for a utilities company in Australia. He has since consulted to enterprises in many industry verticals – including finance, insurance, health insurance, fast moving consumer goods, and gaming – in IT strategy, planning and enterprise architecture development. In addition, Inji has served in IT architecture management positions for firms in health insurance and utilities.

Inji has worked for several IT consulting organisations in Australia including Logica, Deloitte Consulting, IBM, and Capgemini; he is currently with Infosys Australia. Inji lectured on enterprise architecture at RMIT University in Melbourne, Australia, for the Master's degree course on Enterprise Architecture between 2008 and 2012. He holds Doctoral and Master's degrees from London University and a Bachelor's degree from the University of Essex, UK.

George Fernandez

Associate Professor George Fernandez completed a Master of Science (Mathematics) at the University of Buenos Aires. After moving to Australia, he completed a PhD in Computer Science at Swinburne University of Technology (Melbourne). George has more than 30 years of experience in Computing and Information Systems, working in academia, private industry and government organisations. He is an experienced manager, with extensive educational and organisational leadership, demonstrated ability to lead and coordinate Higher Education (HE) units, and a proven capacity to establish, foster and maintain high quality Teaching and Learning and Research activities in a HE setting. Until recently he was the Head of School, Information Technology and Engineering at the Melbourne Institute of Technology. He works now as an independent consultant.

George is an active researcher in the area of Distributed Computing, Enterprise Architecture and Enterprise Integration, and often presents technical seminars in academic and industry forums. Among others, he has been Visiting Professor at The Institute in Princeton, Texas at Austin, Western Washington and University 1 "La Sapienza" in Rome. George has been Chair, Committee Member and referee for many international conferences and journals. He has graduated close to 20 postgraduate (Master and PhD) students.

In the 1990s George focused on e-learning, an area in which he developed a number of software tools for Flexible/On-Line course delivery. As a consequence, in 2000 he received an Australian Award for University Teaching in this category. He is very involved in student-centred learning, often presenting seminars about this type of subject delivery to professors and educators in the US, Europe and the Asia-Pacific region.

Peter Evans-Greenwood

Peter is advisor & futurist at the intersection between business and technology. During his career he has worked in Asia, Australia, Europe and the US, lived in Silicon Valley through boom and bust, and held leadership roles in global organisations such as Deutsche Post DHL, as well as startups and research and development labs. These days he works as a strategic advisor on both business and technology sides of the fence. An avid writer, blogger and public speaker, music lover and coffee addict, his biggest thrills are his family and that buzz one gets from helping clients to achieve the impossible.

Publications by the Authors

Aguilera N., Fernandez G., Fitz-Gerald G.: "Addressing Different Cognitive Levels For On-Line Learning", Proceedings of the 19th Annual ASCILITE Conference, 8th - 11th December 2002, Auckland, New Zealand.

Fernandez G., Bevinakoppa S., "Student-Centred Blended Learning for a Mixed Student Cohort", 7th WSEAS International Conference on Circuits, Systems, Signal and Telecommunications (CSST '13), Milan 9th to 11th Jan 2013, pp. 77-81

Fernandez G., Fitz-Gerald G.: "A Bold Mathematics Course to Support a New Civil Infrastructure Program: RMIT's Experience", Proceedings of the Ninth Asian Technology Conference in Mathematics (ATCM2004), Singapore, Dec 13-17, 2004, pp 103-111, ISBN 0-9763064-0-9.

Fernandez G., Fitz-Gerald G.: "E-assessment: why, what for, and how", Invited Paper to the ATCM2005 (Advanced Technology Council in Mathematics) Conference 2005, Special CD Edition, December 2005.

Fernandez G., Fitz-Gerald G.: "Towards an Automated Web Tutor Environment", Proceedings of the International Conference on Computers in Education (ICCE2004), Nov 30-Dec 3, 2004, Melbourne, Australia, pp 79-87,

Fernandez G., John S., Netherwood G.: "Objective-Based Teaching of Science and Engineering With an On-line Student-Centred Environment", Proceedings of the 12 AAEE Conference, QUT, Brisbane Australia, Sept 26-28, 2001, pp 332-337.

Fernandez G., Rossi P.: "Estimating Dynamic Aspects of Distributed Software Quality", Proceedings of the Argentine Symposium of Software Engineering, September 2002, pp 46-59.

Fernandez G., Rossi P.: "Measuring Distributed Software Quality: a First Step", Proceedings of the Argentine Symposium of Software Engineering, September 4-8, 2000, pp 19-27.

Fernandez G., Shi W.: "Security Architecture and Services for Enterprise Integration", Proceedings of the 3rd ACIS SNPD '02 (Information Security and Privacy), Madrid, Spain, June 2002, pp 409-415.

Fernandez G., Sivadas M., "GeM: Supporting Database Access in a Virtual Enterprise", Proceedings of the 6th Workshop on Enabling Technologies (WETICE'97): "Information Infrastructure for Global and Virtual Enterprises", MIT, Cambridge, Massachusetts, USA, 18-20 June 1997

Fernandez G., Sterbini A., Temperini M.: "Component-based Automated e-Learning" Proceedings of the Fourth IASTED International Conference on Web-Based Education, WBE 2005, Grindelwald, Switzerland, February 21 - 23, 2005

Fernandez G., Sterbini A., Temperini M.: "Learning Objects: A Metadata Approach", Proceedings of the IEEE Region 8 Eurocon 2007 Conference, Fitting E-Learning To The Learner's Needs, September 9-12, 2007, Warsaw, Poland.

Fernandez G., Sterbini A., Temperini M.: "On The Specification Of Learning Objectives For Course Configuration" Proceedings of the The Sixth IASTED International Conference on Web-based Education-WBE 2007, Chamonix, France, March 14 – 16, 2007.

Fernandez G., Wijegunaratne I., "A Cooperative Approach to Distributed Applications Engineering", Proc. Asian'96 WORKSHOP, Coordination Technology for Collaborative Applications, Dec 5 1996

Fernandez G., Zhao L., Wijegunaratne I., "A Pattern Language for A Federated Architecture", Proceedings of the First Asia Pacific Conference in Pattern Languages of Programs, Melbourne, May 2000.

Fernandez G., Zhao L., Wijegunaratne I.: "Patterns for a Federated Architecture", Journal of Object Technology, Vol.2, No 1, Jan-Feb 2003, pp. 135-149.

Fernandez G.: "WebLearn: A CGI-Based Environment for Interactive Learning", Journal of Interactive Learning Research, Vol 12, Numbers 2/3, 2001, pp 265-280.

Fernandez, G, Liang G., Mo J., McGovern J., "An Object Oriented Intelligent CAD/CAM Interface", Technical Report 1/92, Department of Mathematics and Computing, Phillip Institute of Technology, Melbourne, Australia, 1992

Fernandez, G., "Weaving Cloud Services into the Enterprise", The 9th WSEAS International Conference on Remote Sensing (REMOTE'13), Budapest, Hungary, Dec 10-12, 2013

Fernandez, G., Bevinakoppa, S., "Heat Maps: Evidence-Based Addressing of Generic Graduate Attributes", Proceedings of the AAEE2013 Conference, Gold Coast, Qld, Australia, Dec 8-11, 2013.

Fernandez, G.: "Cognitive Scaffolding for a Web-based Learning Environment", Proceedings of the 2nd International Conference on Web Learning ICWL'2003, Melbourne, Australia, 18-20 August 2003, pp. 12-20.

John S., Netherwood G., Sudarmo, Fernandez G: "Learning Taxonomy Analyses Of Student-Based Activities Using The Lego Mindstorms System", Proceedings of the 13 AAEE Conference, Canberra, ACT, September 2002.

Johnson J., Fernandez G., "Re-engineering Relational Normal Forms in an Object-Oriented Framework", Proceedings of the OOIS'97 Conference, the 4th International Conference On Object-Oriented Information Systems, Brisbane, Australia, Nov 1997

Land F, Le Quesne P, Wijegunaratne I, "Effective Systems: Overcoming the Obstacles" in the Journal of Information Technology, vol 4(2), June 1990.

Land F, Le Quesne P, Wijegunaratne I, "Implementing Systems Standards in a Merchant Bank: an IPSE at Mbank", in K Legge, C Clegg, and N Kemp (Eds), Case Studies in Information Technology, People, and Organisations, NCC Blackwell 1991.

Liang G., Fernandez G., and Mo J., "Intelligent CAD Data Recognition For An Object-Oriented CAD/CAM System", Proceedings of the International Conference on Data and Knowledge Systems for Manufacturing and Engineering, Hong Kong, May 1994.

Mo J., Fernandez G., and Liang G., 1993 "An Object-Oriented Framework for Intelligent Manufacturing from Computer-Aided Design Features", Proceedings of the Computers and Engineering Conference, ASME, Houston, Texas, February 1993.

Paul Taylor, Peter Evans-Greenwood & James Odell (April 2005), Agents in the Enterprise, In the proceedings of the Australian Software Engineering Conference.

Paul Taylor, Peter Evans-Greenwood & James Odell (September 2005), The Genesis of a Pattern Language for Agent-Based Enterprise Systems, In the proceedings of Integration of Software Engineering and Agent Technology (ISEAT)

Peter Evans-Greenwood, Peter Williams (2014), Setting aside the burdens of the past: The possibilities of technology-driven change in Australia, Deloitte

Peter Evans-Greenwood (2012), The New Instability, Exacting

Peter Evans-Greenwood, Peter Williams, Ian Harper (2012), The Future of Exchanging Value, Deloitte

Peter Evans-Greenwood (2008), Product Meta-Models, Align Journal

Peter Evans-Greenwood (January 2007), SOA *vs.* Web 2.0, Information Management & Consulting

Peter Evans-Greenwood (2007), Supporting Dynamic Business Logic, Capgemini

Peter Evans-Greenwood (2006), CapITalise: A game for the whole company, Capgemini

Peter Evans-Greenwood (2006), SOA. Next generation procurement, SRM Research 2006-2007: Business Insights, Capgemini

Peter Evans-Greenwood (December 2006), Agent Technologies Discussion Paper, Open Group

Peter Evans-Greenwood, Mark Stason (June 2006), Beyond Composite Applications, Business Integration Journal

Rossi P., Fernandez G.: "Definition and Validation of Design Metrics for Distributed Systems", Proceedings of Metrics 2003 (9th International Software Metrics Symposium), Sydney, Australia, 3-5 September 2003.

Rossi P., Fernandez G.: "Design Measures for Distributed Information Systems: an Empirical Evaluation", Proceedings of the First International Workshop on Software Audits and Metrics (SAM '2004) (Sixth International Conference on Enterprise Information Systems (ICEIS 2004)), Porto, Portugal, April 13-14, 2004.

Savitri Bevinakoppa, George Fernandez, "Mapping Learning Outcomes Onto Assessment Tasks", 3rd International Conference on Circuits, Systems, Control And Signals (CSCS '12), Barcelona, Spain, October 17-19, 2012, pp 116-121

Sivadas M., Fernandez G, "GeM and WeBUSE: Towards a WWW-Database Interface", Proc. Asian'96 WORKSHOP, Coordination Technology for Collaborative Applications, Dec 5 1996

Slamkovic R., Fernandez G., McGovern J.: "Dynamic Adaptive Marshalling A Dynamic Solution to Middleware Heterogeneity", Proceedings of the Argentine Symposium of Software Engineering, September 2003.

Slamkovic R., Fernandez G., McGovern J.: "TUBE: Automated Protocol-Level Middleware Interoperation", 19th Australian Software Engineering Conference, ASWEC2008, March 25-28, 2008, Perth, Australia.

Slamkovic R., McGovern J., Fernandez G.: "The Ubiquitous Broker Environment (TUBE) An Architecture for Protocol-Level Systems Integration", Proceedings of the Argentine Symposium of Software Engineering, September 2002, pp 22-31.

Tari Z., Fernandez G., "Security Enforcement in the DOK Federated Database System", Database Security X: Status and Prospects, P Samarati & R Sandhu (eds.), Chapman & Hall, 1997, pp 23-42.

Tari Z., Yetongnon K., Savnik I., Cheng W., Fernandez G., "The DOK Project: Towards the Integration of Heterogeneous and Distributed Multimedia", Databases Int Conf. on Information, Systems, Analysis and Synthesis (ISAS), Orlando, 1996, pp. 852-860

Wijegunaratne I., and Fernandez G, Distributed Applications Engineering, Springer-Verlag, UK (Nov 1998).

Wijegunaratne I., Evans-Greenwood P., Fernandez, G.: "EA Heavy and EA Light-Two Examples of Successful Enterprise Architecture", Journal of Enterprise Architecture, December 27, 2011, Volume 7, Number 2.

Wijegunaratne I., Fernandez G., "A Federated Application Architecture for the Enterprise", Proc. World Multiconference on Systemics, Cybernetics and Informatics ISAS/SCI'97, July 7-11, 1997, Caracas, Venezuela, pp 402-409

Wijegunaratne I., Fernandez G., Valtoudis J., "A Federated Architecture for Enterprise Data Integration", Proceedings of the Australian Software Engineering Conference, Canberra, Australia, 29-30, April 2000, pp 159-167.

Wijegunaratne I., Socic M, Chow B, "An Architecture for Client/Server Application Software" Australian Computer Journal, May 1994.

Wijegunaratne I., Yale Y., "An Extended Enterprise Model for Enterprise Transformation Strategy" 11th International Society for Business Innovation and Technology Management Conference,Tsinguha University, Beijing, China, May 17-19, 2013

Wong F., Fernandez G., McGovern J.: "CONFER: Groupware for Building Consensus in Collaborative Software Engineering", Proceedings of the 8th AUIC (Australasian User Interface Conference), Ballarat, Victoria, Australia, January 30th to February 2nd, 2007.

Wong F., McGovern J., Fernandez G.: "Managing Consistency and Conflict in Real-Time Collaborative Software Engineering", Proceedings of the Argentine Symposium of Software Engineering, September 2003.

Zuluaga C., Morris E.J.S., Fernandez G.: "Cost-Effective Development and Delivery of 100% Online IT Courses", Proceedings of the 19th Annual ASCILITE Conference, 8th - 11th December 2002, Auckland, New Zealand.

1

CHAPTER 1

Background

Abstract: This chapter introduces the subject by surveying the scene: a brief account of the origins and growth of the discipline is presented, some definitions of the term "Enterprise Architecture" and some representative answers to the question, "why Enterprise Architecture?" are introduced, as are a set of terms related to enterprise architecture.

Keywords: A modern enterprise, EA state of play, what is EA, why EA.

1.1. Origins and Growth

Enterprise Architecture (EA) has its roots in earlier technology planning practices such as Strategic Information Systems Planning, the work of James Martin and Clive Finkelstein [1] and others in Information Engineering, and the early work of John Zachman [2] that led to his eponymous Zachman framework. Since then EA has become a formidable presence in the IT industry. Efforts by individuals such as Zachman, industry bodies such as the Open Group, governments and allied entities—US Federal Government, US Department of Defence among others—as well as IT consulting companies all have contributed to this expansion. Table **1.1** lists some of these contributions.

Table 1.1. Existing EA approaches of the last 15 years.

Creator	Contribution
John Zachman	The Zachman Framework
The Open Group	The Open Group Architecture Framework (TOGAF) and associated models
US Federal Government	Federal EA Framework and Reference Models (FEAF/FEA-RMs)
US Department of Defence	Department of Defence Framework (DODAF)
Private Companies, Consulting Firms	Gartner Group, Meta Group, Capgemini, Object Watch

EA has become a common tool used by large, complex organizations in all sectors to integrate strategic, business, and technology planning:

Public Sector: Mandated in law for U.S. Federal agencies. EA's presence is reflected by the US public sector frameworks (FEAF, TEAF) that exist. Individual States of the U.S. now require agencies to have formal IT architectures though

Inji Wijegunaratne, George Fernandez & Peter Evans-Greenwood

there is limited use at the local level. South Korea has adopted EA nationally, while Canada has adopted of the use of EA at the provincial level.

Private Sector: Many major companies in the U.S. use EA, though for obvious reasons their artefacts are not available in the public domain. Most Fortune 500 companies have some form of EA practice.

Non-Profit Sector: Tight budgets and a strong desire for collected donations to flow directly to core activities as resulted in slow adoption of EA by the non-profit sector.

Academic Sector: EA is becoming more pervasive with an increasing number of universities developing enterprise-wide architectures, though again most artefacts are not publicly available.

Military Sector: EA is required by the U.S. Department of Defence (DOD Directive 5000); all IT-related programs must use the 'DOD Architecture Framework' (DODAF) for design and documentation, as well as DOD's extended version of the Federal EA Reference Models to report the status of major and mission-critical IT programs each year.

By way of commencing this discourse, let us now look at some definitions.

1.2. The Enterprise

The meaning of the terms 'organisation' and 'enterprise' has evolved over time, driven by advances in technology. Large, geographically dispersed organisations—such as the Ottoman Empire, the British Empire, and the Dutch East India Company—existed in the past, but in the past an 'enterprise' was generally understood as an institution defined *via* strong lines of authority, structure or geographical boundaries. Today though, advances in modern technology have made possible for many types of entities to interact with each other in many different ways, rendering the concept of an enterprise to be much more flexible and its boundaries more amorphous.

'Enterprise' may mean any of the following:

- A single commercial or operating entity: such as Amazon.com, Microsoft, Apple
- A group of operating entities under the same ownership or control: *e.g.*, G.E.

- A collection of agencies under the same loose control structure, such as the agencies under a State or Federal Government
- A collection of organizations that collaborate to achieve common goals: *e.g.*, a network of hospitals
- Consequentially the definition of 'enterprise' also needs to be appropriately loose:

An enterprise is characterized by common activity and goals where information and other resources are exchanged [3]

Enterprise is any collection of organizations or people related things that has a common set of goals/principles and a single bottom line [4]

1.3. What Is Enterprise Architecture?

The word 'architecture' is used throughout this eBook. Although originally in use in a building context – such as 'the science, art, or profession of designing and constructing buildings, bridges' – over the past 15 years of so the term has been adopted by IT to mean 'the organizational structure of an information system' [5]. Putting the two terms together we get, not surprisingly, 'enterprise architecture'.

How have people defined this term?

Representation of the functioning enterprise (*Zachman*)

The fundamental organization of a system embodied by its components, their relationships to each other and to the environment and the principles guiding its design and evolution (*ANSI/IEEE Std*)

Formal description of a system, the structure of components, their interrelationships to each other and to the environment, and the principles guiding its design and evolution over time (*TOGAF*)

A set of principles, rules, standards and guidelines expressing a vision and implementing concepts and containing a mixture of style, engineering and construction principles (*Cap Gemini, Ernst & Young*)

A holistic expression of the enterprise's key business, information, application and technology strategies and their impact on business functions and processes (*Meta Group*)

A discipline for proactively and holistically leading an enterprise's responses to disruptive forces by identifying and analyzing the execution of change toward desired business vision and outcomes. EA delivers value by presenting business and IT leaders with signature-ready recommendations for adjusting policies and projects to achieve target business outcomes that capitalize on relevant business disruptions. EA is used to steer decision making toward the evolution of the future state architecture. (*Gartner*)

It is about understanding all of the different elements that go to make up the enterprise and how those elements interrelate. *(Institute for Enterprise Architecture Development)*

An enterprise architecture is a description of the goals of an organization, how these goals are realized by business processes, and how these business processes can be better served through technology. *(ObjectWatch, Roger Sessions)*

In reading through these definitions we may think why, in defining 'enterprise architecture' we often make explicit references to IT or information systems. Initially, the term enterprise architecture originated within the realm of IT, and not the broader disciplines of Management, Organisation Behaviour or Organisational Design. The definitions above making references to IT or information systems betray these origins. This is an important point, and we will talk about it again later in the eBook.

1.3.1. Architecture Terminology

EA frameworks typically provide a classification scheme to categorize and order the various EA artefacts. For example, TOGAF [6] posits four architecture domains, below, and Zachman define a six by six matrix.[1]

EA components of TOGAF:

- **Business Architecture:** includes strategy and key business processes, governance and organizational strategy.

---

[1]We discuss EA frameworks, including TOGAF and Zachman in later chapters.

- **Data Architecture**: the logical and physical structure of the data assets.
- **Application Architecture:** involves the structure of the applications, their interactions, the services they offer, and their relationships to the business processes.
- **Technology Architecture:** describes the logical software and hardware capabilities of the IT infrastructure, middleware, networks, communications, processing, standards, *etc.*

The term 'Architecture' used in IT possesses other connotations as well:

- **IT Architecture:** General term applied to architecture in general; typically includes EA, domain, solution, data, application, technology, *etc.*
- **Domain Architecture:** The architecture of a particular domain; *e.g.* integration, Customer Relationship Management (CRM), analytics, Business Intelligence.
- **Solution Architecture:** The architecture pertaining to a single solution, generally in the context of a project, *e.g.* the solution architecture for the CRM implementation.
- **Infrastructure Architecture:** Depending on context could have the same scope as Technology Architecture above, encompassing hardware, middleware, network, security; deployment topologies; or can be narrower in scope, focusing on hardware, networking, and communications. The term can be used in an enterprise, solution, or domain context.

1.4. Why Enterprise Architecture?

John Zachman is one of the pioneers of Enterprise Architecture, and this is what he has to say:

> *"It is my opinion that this issue of Enterprise Architecture is not well understood in the ranks of general management who see Enterprise Architecture as just an IS or IT issue, nor in the ranks of IS management who see it as taking too long and costing too much, nor in the ranks of academia who tend to focus on what they perceive constitutes current market demand, typically a promising technology. My opinion is, Enterprise Architecture may*

well be the "Issue of the Century." ... I know I have a rather radical view of this, but my observation would be the whole reason you want people with technical skills in your Enterprise is not for building and running systems. Anybody can build and run systems, the employment of the technology. The reason you want these kinds of people in your Enterprise is because they have the capability of engineering and manufacturing your Enterprise for you. That's the reason for their being, NOT simply for building and running systems." (John Zachman, 2004) [7]

A survey undertaken a few years ago by Infosys to ascertain the state of EA in organisations according to CIOs, Chief Architects, Business managers and IT managers, yielded these results on the perceived objectives and benefits of EA [8]:

Objective	% who included the objective	% who perceived benefits
Enable business and process flexibility	100%	68%
Simplify technology and applications portfolio	63%	32%
Better align business and IT	63%	57%
Reduce IT cost	46%	72%
Enable business and process change	50%	60%
Improve customer satisfaction	46%	61%

A Gartner survey reported the following as the primary driver for EA [9] (values out of 5):

Objective	Score
Reduce Technology Cost	3.84
Service Oriented Architecture	3.61
Reduce project or service redundancy	3.66
Technical Adaptability	3.65

What is the view of the authors on what constitutes enterprise architecture? We continue the discussion in Chapter 2, and present our views in Chapter 3.

CHAPTER 2

What is the Problem with EA?

Abstract: This chapter presents our view of the problems with "Enterprise Architecture" as it is commonly understood and conducted today. We sow the seeds of our perspective of Enterprise Architecture, planting its roots in the business of the enterprise. We argue that EA conducted as an IT exercise focusing mainly on technical aspects is often the reason for the lack of success of EA engagements, and that in order to succeed, the EA team needs to deliver *value* to the business at the *speed* that the business needs.

Keywords: Aligning business and IT, EA and business outcomes, engineering the enterprise, the problems of EA, the Zachman framework.

The surveys and discussion of the previous chapter serves to underline that Enterprise architecture has evolved from an arcane and esoteric niche, shaped by pioneers such as Zachman, to become a part of mainstream IT in the early part of the 21st century. Enterprise architects are now common in most substantial organisations; according to a study by the Institute for Enterprise Architecture Developments (IFEAD) 66% of the respondents considered enterprise architecture an important element of their strategic governance processes [10]. Another study among Swiss and German companies revealed that 38 from 51 companies interviewed were either implementing enterprise architecture models or using enterprise architecture models [11]. Numerous frameworks exist—Zachman, TOGAF, FEAF, DODAF—and many consulting organisations have also developed their own framework or methodology.

How successful has EA been in improving the operations of businesses that have adopted it? Even though the theoretical benefits of EA are widely discussed, there is evidence to show that the adoption rate of enterprise architecture and its reported benefits are not uniformly promising [12]. What are the reasons for this lack of success?

Let us start with Zachman's definition of enterprise architecture, "A representation of the functioning enterprise" [13]. All functioning enterprises possess some kind of architecture that can be represented as a series of layers along the lines that Zachman defines[1]. The enterprise architect can reasonably assume that the challenge in a functioning enterprise is to uncover and represent

[1]We talk about the Zachman framework in Chapter 4.

Inji Wijegunaratne, George Fernandez & Peter Evans-Greenwood

this structure; that is, to capture and maintain architectural artefacts of the enterprise to express and represent these states. This approach, however, conceals a trap.

> *The elephant*
>
> *"See – we have this elephant in this room. We have been trying to get the elephant to move* ***over there****. So much so that, for six months we had a here a team of people advertising themselves as elephant-movers. They took a lot of trouble and undertook an analysis in great detail. Then they gave us a great deal of information on the anatomy and physiology of the elephant and said that in their considered opinion the elephant would look better, not* ***over there****, but in this other corner. In the meantime the elephant has lurched across the room and damaged these walls – see. We've now gotten rid of the elephant mover team. Can you help us? We really want to move the elephant* ***over there*** *as soon as possible..."*

The task of accurately describing an enterprise and the way it works is a complex and difficult undertaking. Indeed, given the size, complexity, and dynamic nature of modern organizations it may even be infeasible in many instances. It is easy for the enterprise architecture team to become caught up in producing enterprise representations that do not provide tangible benefits to the business and senior IT stakeholders. A common consequence of this is for enterprise architects to experience significant confusion and frustration when their efforts run into problems with stakeholders or sponsors unable to see the value in what the architects are doing.

An enterprise architects' position is typically a high profile one, visible to senior business and IT stakeholders. Expectations are typically high, and a perception that they are not delivering can form relatively quickly.

In the mid-1990s, one of the authors had occasion to meet a team enterprise data architects in a UK-based multinational. A small group, they were housed in a location away from mainstream IT and were working hard on developing an enterprise data model. They had been working on the data model for some years, ensconced in their cocoon. It was hard to identify a stakeholder or a beneficiary of their output. Looking back, we cannot help thinking that in today's world of tight budgets and short business cycles, a group such as this would have met their corporate demise relatively swiftly, perhaps in a matter of months.

This focus on creating an EA representation of the enterprise confuses the end with the means; EA contains many tools, constructs, and techniques to classify and show relationships and connections between categories. However, these techniques to *represent* content do not in themselves answer the question of *what* you represent, or *what you need to* represent.

A related issue with EA today is that more often than not, EA is conducted mainly as an IT exercise, its output driven by technologists using technical criteria to evaluate from among alternatives and select a preferred outcome. These choices are frequently justified on the basis that they are 'architectural decisions'. This tendency is aided and abetted by parts of the literature. See for example TOGAF ADM: an *architectural* vision is first conceived and then elaborated upon.

This mind-set is misguided. IT serves the business and the enterprise architect must help IT serve the business: for a business manager intent on increasing sales by 20%, talk of service orientation, XML, the Cloud, the merits of this vendor's technology over that vendor's, is not particularly interesting. Unless the architect's tune changes, the business managers' patience or, more significantly, the funding provided by the manager, will run out. When visiting clients, we have often found the ruins of EA teams who were 'in ivory towers' and had since been disbanded.

Zachman again:

> *"Anybody can build and run systems, the employment of the technology.* ***The reason you want these kinds of people in your Enterprise is because they have the capability of engineering and manufacturing your Enterprise for you.*** *That's the reason for their being, NOT simply for building and running systems* [14]; (Authors' highlight)

Although the origins of enterprise architecture are in IT, the scope of EA is wider than purely the technology and its deployment and use. The term 'enterprise' in EA is often interpreted in a very narrow sense; but as Zachman states, *the true calling of the enterprise architect is to engineer the enterprise;* in other words, *help the senior executives of the enterprise navigate the increasingly choppy and treacherous waters of the competitive seas.*

Zachman's aim is laudable but ambitious. Because of their background and expertise, many enterprise architects to focus on a lesser aim: *how to configure and shape the enterprise's information technology and systems to support the enterprise in its journey along the direction that the business executives have chosen for the company*. If he or she does this well today, tomorrow their brief could well be wider[2].

To summarise, very often in our experience we find that [3]:

- a typical EA exercise is often driven by IT and by technologists with a focus on content representation
- often the direction depicted in the EA exercise ('the target state') is based primarily on technologists' views on what is good for the company, technology preferences, and other 'architectural considerations', rather than the satisfaction of strategic business drivers: choices and benefits are communicated in technical IT terms, rather than business terms
- EA development is assumed to be a heavyweight exercise, consuming many expensive resources over long periods of time and producing voluminous content

Producing visually appealing diagrams with colourful boxes and arrows does not in itself add value. Neither do pages of detailed technical content not grounded in providing the outcomes the business is asking for. The time and money spent creating artefacts that do not serve any business purpose becomes, in the eyes of stakeholders, an unnecessary expense. *Business will invest in EA if it is apparent to them that it helps deliver a better business outcome*[4]. What would be even more attractive would be a situation *where EA activity is actually embedded in a wider*

---

[2]Although EA originated in the realm of IT, it has begun to move outside the IT area and to emerge as a strategic tool at the corporate level. In some quarters EA has begun to be perceived by managers and stakeholders as an important tool for corporate decision-making (Infosys survey 'Win in the flat world', 2007).
However, although in EA we may aspire to encompass a whole-of-organization strategy, we believe that in terms of EA maturity and acceptance by the business we are still some way off from that objective. Instead, our more realistic objective for EA is to enhance the relationship between business strategy and enterprise IT, so that IT initiatives have a direct mapping to organisational drivers and objectives, there is clear communication between the two areas, and IT delivers value to the business.

[3]The case studies in Chapter 9 contain some supporting material and analyses.

[4]There are three fundamental ways to improve business (see the case studies for a discussion).

- Create a new product/service/market: more business.
- Create new interactions between customers and the company: better business.
- Change the cost of production/operation: cheaper business.

business value producing exercise – i.e. aligning IT with business aims and goals and helping to shape and deliver them.

Alignment here is not confined only to purpose, but it extends to the time dimension as well. Businesses are under increasing pressure to act quickly to take advantage of narrowing windows of opportunity and find the IT delivery cycle frustratingly long. Indeed, this malaise is often evident in EA activity itself, with EA models and documents often losing relevance, overtaken by business events, before they can be used. In other words, *IT—and therefore EA—must deliver at the speed that the business needs*.

Much has been written on enterprise architecture, but there is very little help for the enterprise architect on how to run a successful enterprise architecture programme in this manner. Guiding the enterprise architect on the practicalities of implementing a successful EA programme, delivering business-aligned output in a timeframe acceptable to the business, is the focus of this eBook.

CHAPTER 3

EA Imperatives, Drivers and Objectives

Abstract: EA is about enterprise evolution and, as such, it has been often compared with the evolution of a city. This is quite appropriate as—similarly to enterprises—cities are complex and dynamic organizations that need to respond to a changing environment.

In this chapter we provide an analogy for an enterprise architecture exercise by way of planning the future of a city, introducing, through this setting, some key concepts that we elaborate upon later, for instance the levels of detail relevant to each stage of the planning process. We draw upon the learnings from this example to propose a 3-stage approach to conduct an EA exercise: Align, Elaborate and Govern.

Keywords: EA and the evolution of a city, EA drivers, EA imperatives, EA objectives.

3.1. The City of Melbourne

Imagine yourself in Melbourne in Australia (or any other similar large city anywhere in the world) in 1994. You have been invited to a six-day high-powered workshop to develop a plan for the city for the next 20 years. The State Government has provided the workshop with the following overarching drivers:

- sustain population growth
- sustain economic development
- make the city an attractive place for business and leisure activity
- fully utilize non-productive land assets

3.2. Melbourne Workshop

3.2.1. Day 1: What Needs to Be Done to Achieve the Objectives

Day 1 of the workshop involves a good deal of discussion; by the end of the day the participants agree that to satisfy each high-level driver or objective, the following have to be accomplished.

- Sustain population growth:

Inji Wijegunaratne, George Fernandez & Peter Evans-Greenwood

  - Open up new outer suburbs in the larger metropolitan area.
  - Provide the new suburbs with amenities, schools, hospitals, sports and shopping precincts.
  - Provide the necessary infrastructure: electricity, gas, water, local and interconnecting roads.
  - Establish scalable transport connectivity: public transport (rail, trams, buses), and highways to link the new suburbs to the rest of the city.
  - Investigate amenities and infrastructure of established suburbs and renew them where appropriate
- Sustain economic development:
  - Provide incentives for businesses to locate to Melbourne: tax and other incentives, establish business precincts.
  - Provide incentives for existing businesses to stay.
  - Provide mechanisms for maintaining skilled labor pipeline: *e.g.* with industry-tailored education and apprenticeships.
- Make the City of Melbourne an attractive place for business and leisure activity:
  - Improve sports facilities adjacent to the city to attract significant events.
  - Capture and retain high profile sporting and business events.
  - Give incentives to develop leisure activities in the city: restaurants, cinemas, theatre and music.
  - Improve public transport for business (*e.g.* trucks) and leisure.
  - Create and maintain parks.
- Fully utilize non-productive land assets:

- Identify non-productive land assets in and around Melbourne Central Business District.

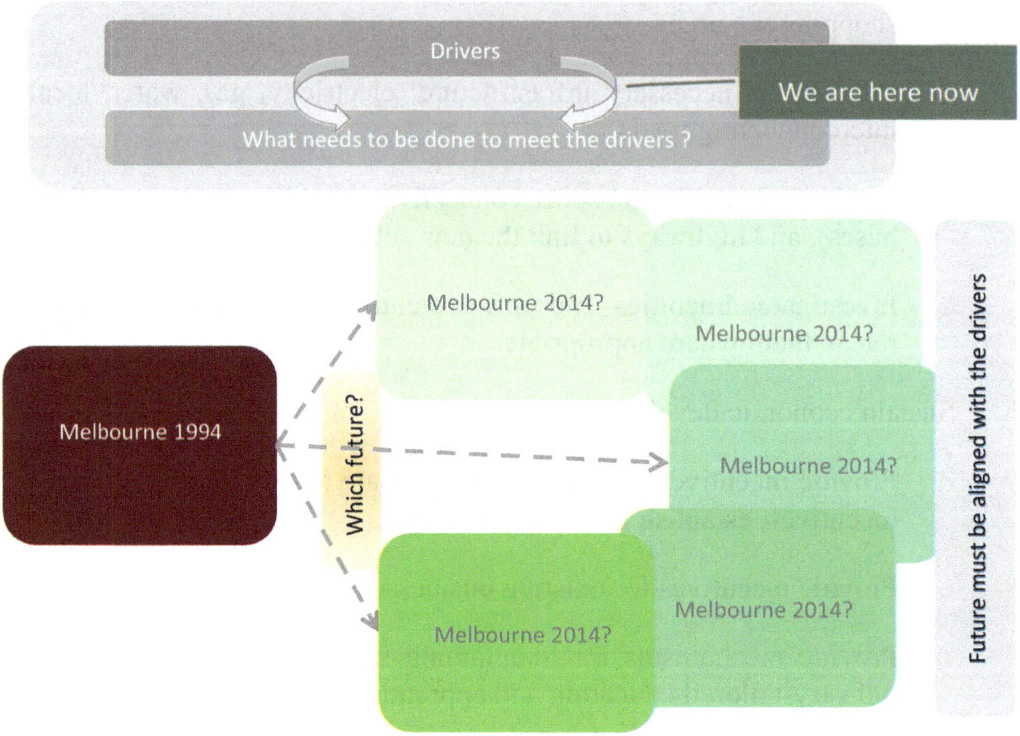

Fig. (3.1). Drivers for the evolution of Melbourne.

> Reflect:
>
> There were many possible futures for the city in 2014 when we started. We used the drivers and objectives to paint us a desired future. The initial analysis is characterised by **extensive breadth** and very **shallow depth**, at a very **high level**. We used very little detailed knowledge of the city in 1994. We also know very little about the shape of the city in 2014 (Fig. **3.1**).

3.2.2. Day 2, 3: Objectives/Initiatives

- More detail is fleshed out on the shape of the city on the second day of the workshop.

- The attendees break out into four groups, with each responsible for tackling one driver. Each group is given the task of expanding upon the outcomes of Day 1 and identifying, at a high level, specific initiatives needed to address each bullet point developed on day 1. Specialists in town planning, utilities, education, health, *etc.*, are available to the workgroups as resources to answer questions and provide information, but not to direct, coerce, or veto the group's outcomes.

- By day 3's end each specific initiative that is identified has to be presented typed in a single A4 sheet of paper containing the scope, ball-park cost and effort, and the benefits.

- Sustain population growth (Image **3.1**)

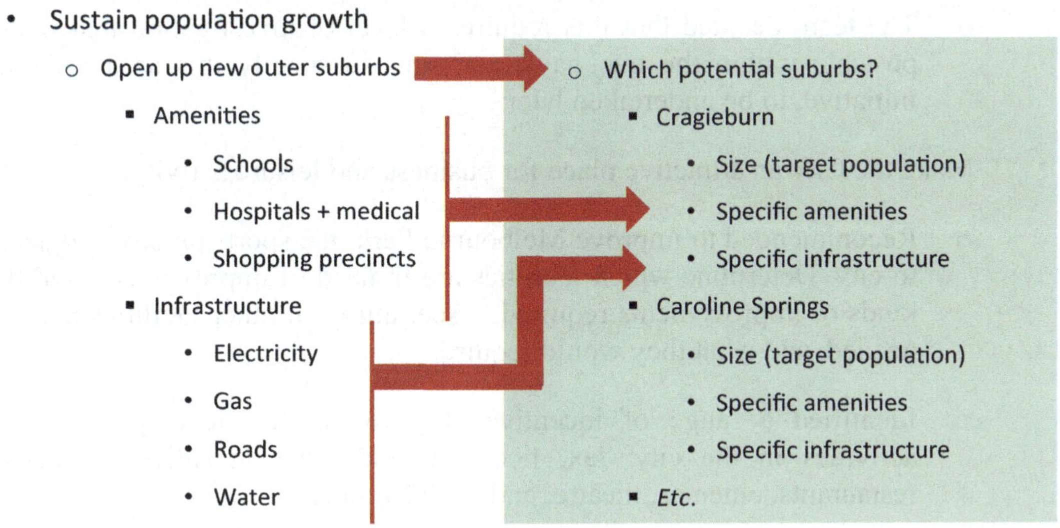

Image (3.1).

- Identified outer suburbs to be earmarked for development, the broad target population in each, and the mix of residential *vs* industrial areas.

- For each suburb:

  - At a very high level, identified the amenities, schools, hospitals, sports and shopping precincts for each suburb – broadly how many and where they should be located

  - Schools: how many primary/secondary/technical schools

    - Hospitals and other medical facilities
    - Shopping precincts
  - Infrastructure:
    - Electricity, gas and water requirements and connectivity
    - Roads and transport connectivity: interconnecting roads in and out of the suburb, the different modes of transport – trams, railways
- Investigate amenities and infrastructure of established suburbs and renew them where appropriate:
  - The team decided that this requires a level of investigation that is not possible within the two days, and thus to specify this as a separate initiative, to be undertaken later.
- Make the City an attractive place for business and leisure activity:
  - Recommended to improve Melbourne Park, the sports precinct adjacent to city. Determine which facilities are in need of improvement, and the kinds of improvements required. Ascertain what other facilities may be needed, and what they would require.
  - Identified a range of incentives to provide for developing leisure activities in the city: tax, licensing and other incentives attractive restaurants, cinemas, theatre, and music venues.
  - Improve public transport: identified five of the most critical issues with public transport and ways to remedy them.
  - Capture and retain high profile sporting and business events: targeted specific national and international events, including retaining the Australian Open and the Australian Grand Prix in Melbourne.
  - Create and maintain parks: Identified three areas for development as new parks, of the parks currently in the CBD and inner suburbs, identified four parks in need of improvement and the kinds of improvements required.

- Fully utilize non-productive land assets:
  - o Identified the following areas for development:
  - The Melbourne Docklands area
  - Queen Victoria hospital site in Melbourne *etc.*;
- Sustain economic development:
  - o New business:
  - Identified three specific industries to attract to Melbourne. For each industry type, Identified tax and other incentives for businesses to locate to Melbourne
  - o Existing business
  - Identified five potential business precincts and amenities to be provided
  - Identified specific incentives for existing businesses to stay
  - o Mechanisms for maintaining skilled labor pipeline
  - Identified the main types of skills needed (based on the work already done on business, population growth) For the skill areas, identified.
  - o Technical and Further Education requirements for industry-tailored education
  - o Requirements for apprenticeships
  - o Needs for adult education and training
- **End day 3**

We now begin to see the change initiatives forming and taking shape. Still, the outcome is a very high level view, with an initial list and very high-level descriptions of the initiatives that aim to achieve the stated objectives. These are not yet in any sequence or order of precedence (Fig. **3.2**).

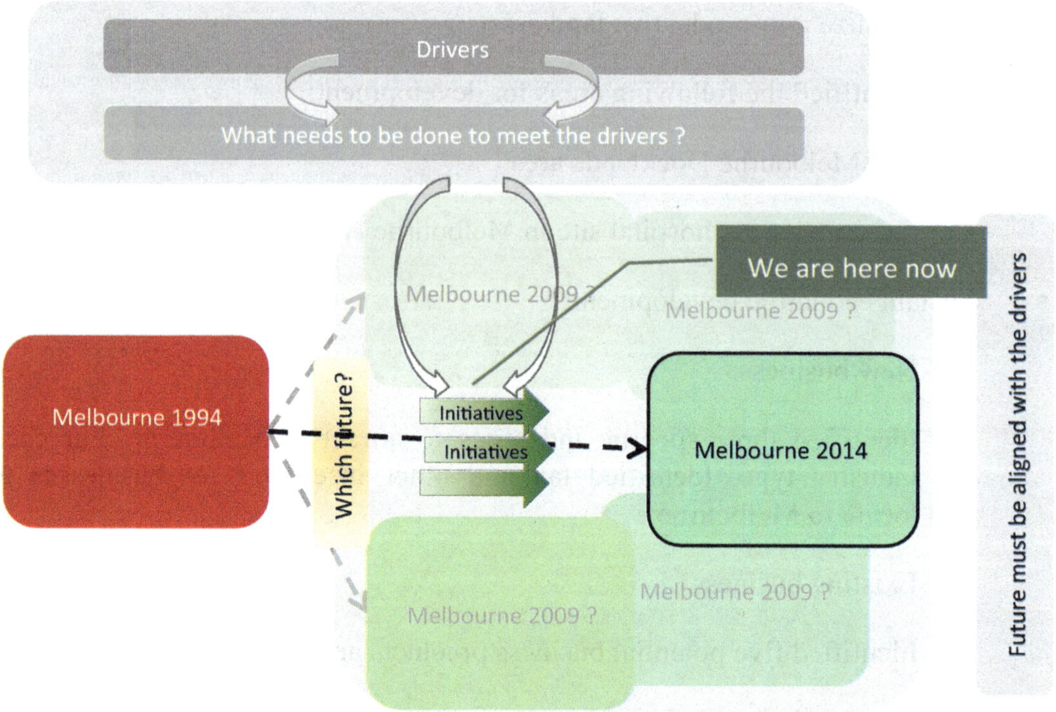

Fig. (3.2). Initiatives at high level.

> Reflect:
>
> How much knowledge did we use on the detail of Melbourne in 1994? Somewhat more than Day 1, but still at a very high level.
>
> What do we know about your city in 2014? A future, the collective outcomes of the identified initiatives, is now taking shape.

3.2.3. Days 4, 5, 6: Consolidation, Target and Roadmap

The outcome of Day 3 is a list of initiatives linked to the objectives. Days 4, 5, and 6 are dedicated to consolidate and sequence the initiatives.

- What are the similar initiatives that can be grouped together into work streams?
  - We need to take a macro view where necessary and determine any characteristics and needs at may emerge at the macro level – for

example the outer suburbs may coalesce into a few growth corridors – any emergent characteristics or needs?

- o We need now to group similar initiatives such as the provision of water, sewerage, gas and electricity, so that work streams can be identified. We may rationalize instances of the same or very similar initiative that cropped up in multiple work groups; we will also retain the identity of each initiative, but group them into work streams.

- What are the dependencies and precedence requirements?
- What is the sequence? The sequencing is broadly determined by the dependencies as well as the importance or value of the initiatives.

Again, specialists are available for consultation and advice.

Although lacking detail and granularity, a vision of the city in 2014 is consolidating and taking shape.

3.2.4. Workshop: End of Day 6

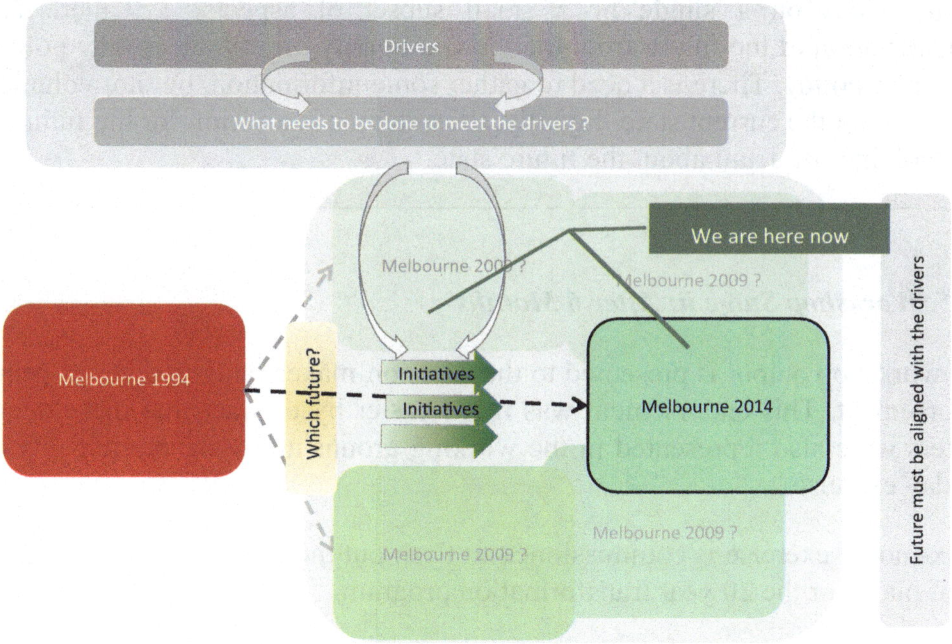

Fig. (3.3). Roadmap at high level.

The 6-day workshop has produced a high level roadmap for the transformation of the city (Fig. **3.3**). The outcomes and deliverable are shown in the table:

Outcomes	Deliverables
Changes traceable to drivers/objectives	
List of consolidated initiatives	1 page each, high level value, cost, duration
High level Gantt chart	
High level representation of the city in 2014	3 or 4 pages of diagrams and text

Reflect:

Given a set of drivers, the workshop determined what the specific objectives are, and then how to 'best' satisfy them through initiatives. 'Best' is established by reaching a consensus among the stakeholders—participants of the workshop—about the identification and prioritisation best aligned with the objectives. In other words, one future, out of many, is selected by consensus based on alignment to the given objectives.

The level of analysis at the workshop is broad, but shallow; also holistic, there is no focus on a single or a small subset of aspects—*i.e.* there is no consideration of the future from the viewpoint only of, say, electricity policy or transport policy. There is a need to gather some information, but not volumes of detail about the current state. Equally, the outcome is a vision for the future, but not volumes of detail about the future state.

3.2.5. Workshop Stage ii: After 6 Months

The workshop output is presented to the decision-makers and receives in-principle endorsement. This endorsement was made easier by the fact that these decision-makers were also represented in the working groups and were participants in the six-day exercise.

A six-month exercise is commissioned to flesh out the output to present a detailed set of plans for the 20 year transformation program.

Reflect:

How much detail of your city in 1994 is needed for this? Significant detail, compared to the first round: Existing infrastructure and amenities blueprints, planning codes, costs, legal and other constraints, *etc.*

How much detail of Melbourne 2014 have we captured now? Significant detail, compared to the first round: Target populations of new suburbs, new and updated facilities—schools, hospitals, highways, roads in built-up areas, *etc.* Similar detail for the transformation programme—the specific projects, their precedence relationships, costs, triggers for commencement, *etc.*

3.3. Summary

Reflect:

Can you characterise the process we went through in the example into stages?

How many stages can you discern?

How did you identify each stage? What are the defining features of each stage?

There are actually three stages, two of which we encountered in this Chapter:

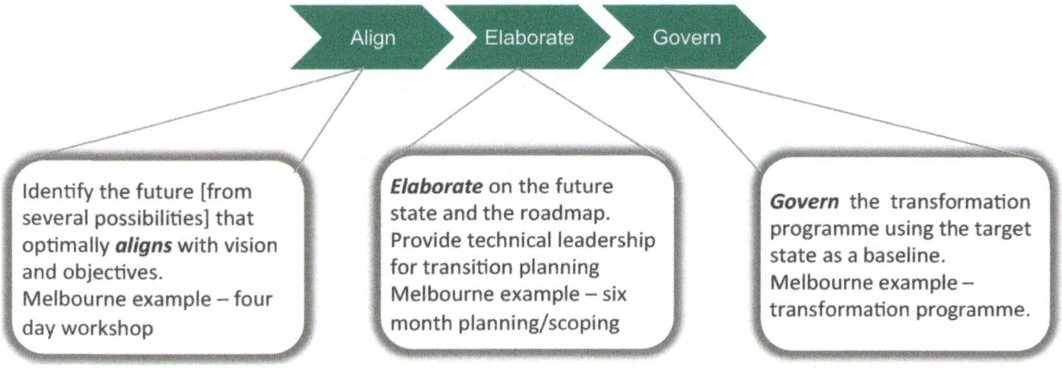

Fig. (3.4). The three stages.

As we will see, this is the form (Fig. **3.4**) that we will apply to manage Enterprise Architecture.

We deliberately used the hypothetical example of the evolution of the City of Melbourne, which is far removed from the familiar world of IT, to illustrate certain key features without getting mired in technology or EA terminology. We are not the first to use city planning as inspiration for Enterprise Architecture (see for example [15]). The 'City' is an attractive analogy for several reasons.

- The size and complexity of a modern city has parallels with the size and complexity of a modern enterprise.
- In both cases we are dealing with a live, dynamically changing entity, which will not stop evolving while we run the project.
- Like cities, enterprise should preserve existing assets of value and provision infrastructure to accommodate new developments in the long run.

CHAPTER 4

The Architecture of EA

Abstract: This chapter dissects the structure of Enterprise Architecture, not be delving into detail, but by "stepping back". We describe the various facets of the term "Enterprise Architecture": Context, Content and Process. We then analyse options for the scope of EA, from an ideal (or idealistic) scope of EA at one end, to the typical IT-driven EA at the other. We propose a pragmatic and achievable scope and approach to EA between these two ends, based on the strategic fit of business and IT.

Each of the three stages introduced in Chapter 3— Align, Elaborate and Govern—is then discussed under this new light.

Keywords: Business and IT misalignment, communication misalignment, EA stages: Align, Elaborate and Govern, enterprise evolution, pragmatic EA, scope of EA, strategic fit of Business and IT, time misalignment, value misalignment.

4.1. Enterprise Evolution: The Needs of the Business

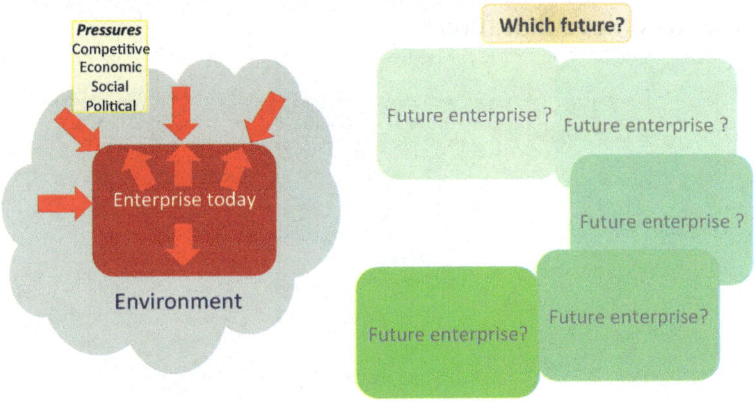

Fig. (4.1). Enterprise evolution: which future?

Enterprises need to evolve. Imperatives for evolution are always present, emanating from both internal and external factors (Fig. **4.1**).

Pressures from the inside and outside the enterprise fuel the need for change. For example:

- Competition: the pressure to remain competitive, the need to be flexible, the need to react quickly to changes.

Inji Wijegunaratne, George Fernandez & Peter Evans-Greenwood

- Economic: the pressure to reduce operational costs.
- Social: becoming 'green', or 'socially responsible'.
- Regulatory: responding to new or changed anti money-laundering or statutory reporting regulations.

Obviously not all the imperatives have the same importance, urgency or potential impact on the enterprise.

Starting from a single point there are many possible futures for the enterprise. How do we select which one to pursue? Generally, planners in the organization assess these internal and external pressures for change, and articulate key aims and objectives for the future. These are the drivers for change.

A particular future begins to emerge when we work out what needs to be done to satisfy these drivers and, at a very high level, how. This process of *alignment* with the drivers should place a *value* on a particular future, and so *prioritize* certain changes above others. A particular future will then begin to emerge and, at a very high level, how to achieve that future.

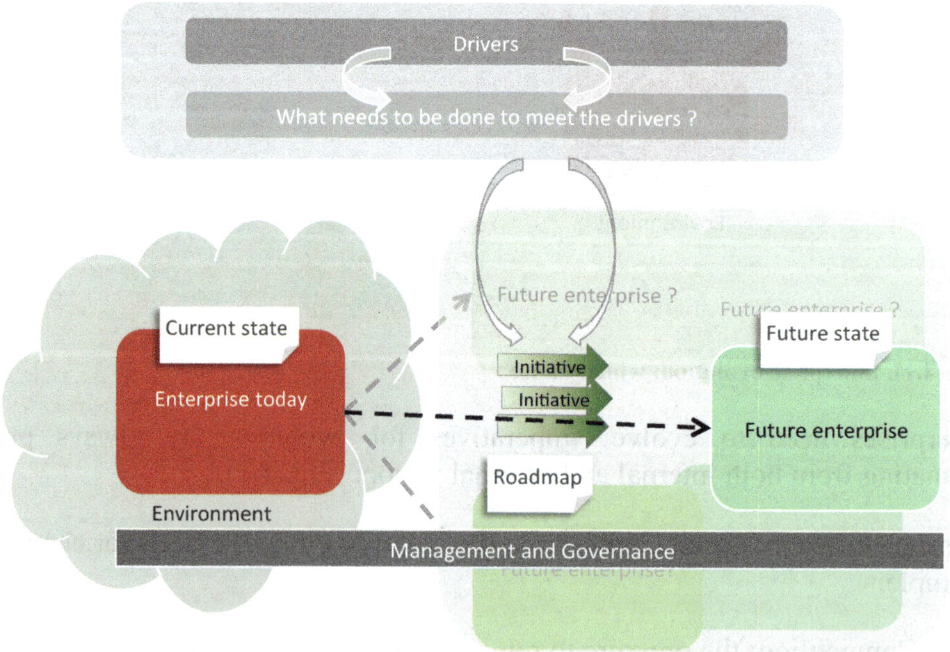

Fig. (4.2). Enterprise evolution: getting to the future.

In the language of Enterprise Architecture, we have a current state, a future state, and a roadmap to get from current to future (Fig. **4.2**). Depending on business intentions, the envisaged future may involve very significant changes from the current state, or only relatively minor ones.

4.2. Scope of Enterprise Architecture: How Can IT Help?

What do we mean when we talk of Enterprise Architecture? In Chapter 1 we surveyed the current state of play, but what we described masked a fundamental issue: we mean different things at different times by 'Enterprise Architecture'. Enterprise Architecture is an overloaded term; it can have one or more of the meanings below (Fig. **4.3**).

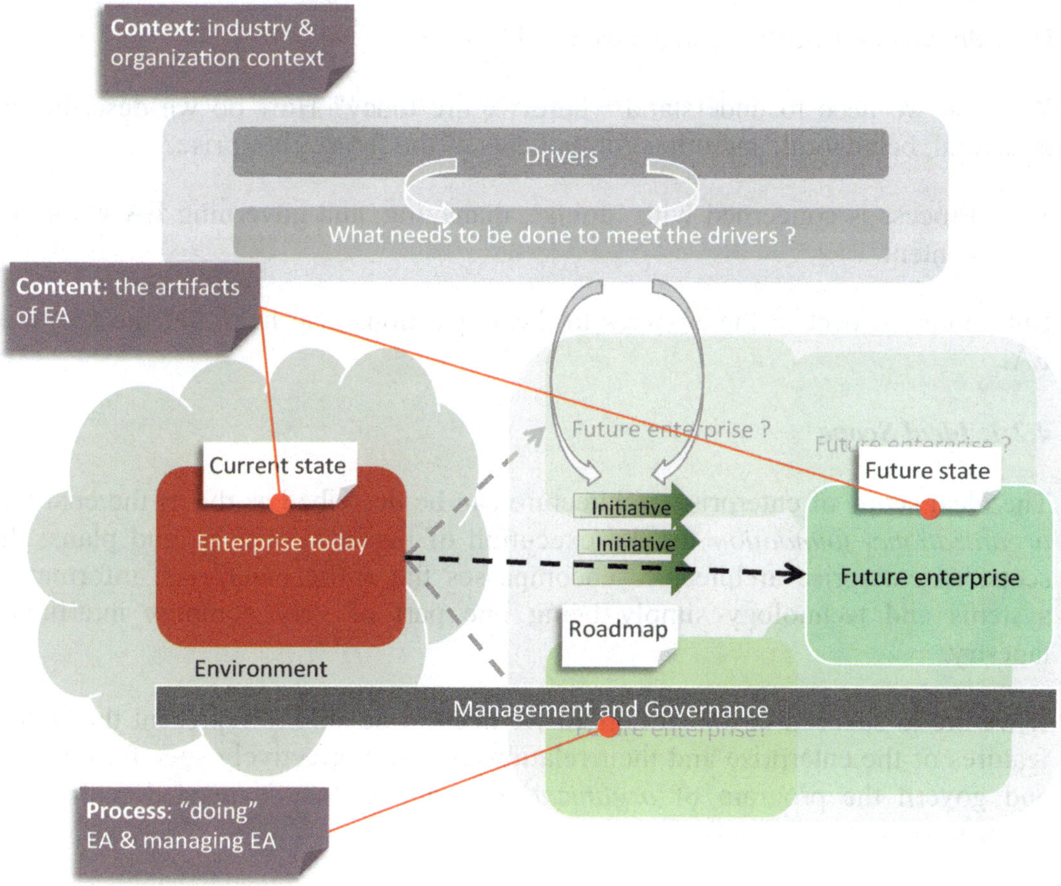

Fig. (4.3). Enterprise evolution: scoping.

- Context: Why are we doing EA?

What we have talked about is the business strategy and plans and their execution. If the planners strategies are implemented effectively and their assumptions hold, then they should carry the enterprise toward the desired future. The context of EA is therefore firmly rooted in business strategy and planning.

> *We can therefore think of enterprise architecture as an enabling foundation for the execution of business strategy and plans* (Definition influenced by [16]).

- Content: Represents the artefacts of EA, what form these take, how they are classified, what relationships do they have with one another:

How do we describe the changes we need?

What do we need to understand where we are today? How do we describe the structural, behavioral, and other components of the future enterprise?

- Process is concerned with 'doing', managing, and governing EA work and content.

But another aspect to the answers to these questions also helps fix the scope of EA.

4.2.1. Ideal Scope

The ideal scope of enterprise architecture can be described as the as the enabling *organizational foundation* for the execution of business strategy and plans: the scope of enterprise architecture encompasses the entire enterprise; information systems and technology simply being one part of very complex interlinked tapestry.

If we are to succeed in this ambition, we need to be able to represent the salient features of the enterprise and their relationships and effectively specify, manage, and govern the program of *organizational* change that is needed realize the business strategy (Fig. **4.4**).

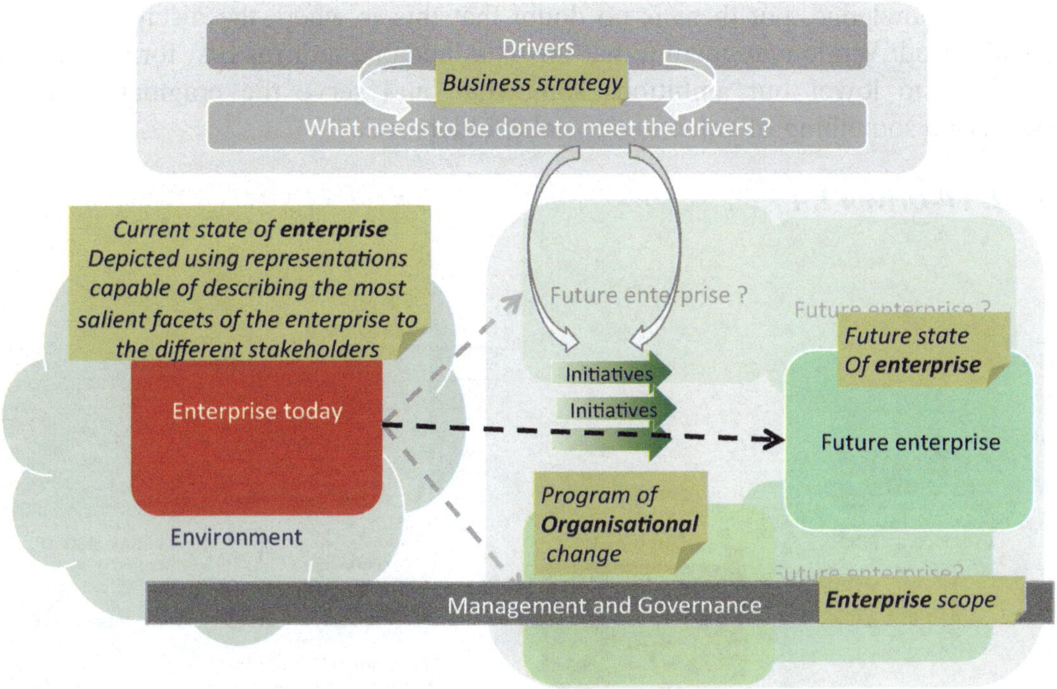

Fig. (4.4). Ideal scope of EA.

We have mentioned before that the origins of EA lie within IT and with IT practitioners. EA and allied disciplines today have created techniques for modeling and representing an enterprise, as well as the processes required to govern, manage, monitor, and report on programs of work, but all these betray their roots in information technology. Enterprise architecture today is biased towards the more restricted terrain of information technology, systems, and IT/IS projects within the enterprise. It is true that project and program management techniques are similar, if not identical; however, we do not possess the tools and techniques to create a complete representation of an enterprise. For instance: how do you represent culture, leadership, learning, motivation, or team work and their impact on, and relationships with, other elements of the enterprise? Without a doubt this is a laudable aim, but, given the current state of the discipline, this ideal is some way off. Some techniques do exist but they are scattered across several disciplines, such as organizational behavior, accounting and finance, psychology, and management theory. Pulling these together into a single framework, identifying their interdependencies, and most importantly establishing how these elements can be changed in a controlled manner and orchestrated to achieve some organizational outcome is a huge exercise. It would push the boundaries of our current knowledge, but there is no doubt that this is where the discipline of EA should head. While recognizing that this is a laudable aim for EA, for the present we need to lower our ambitions somewhat, and serve the pragmatic end of delivering something of value to our stakeholders today.

4.2.2. IT-Driven EA

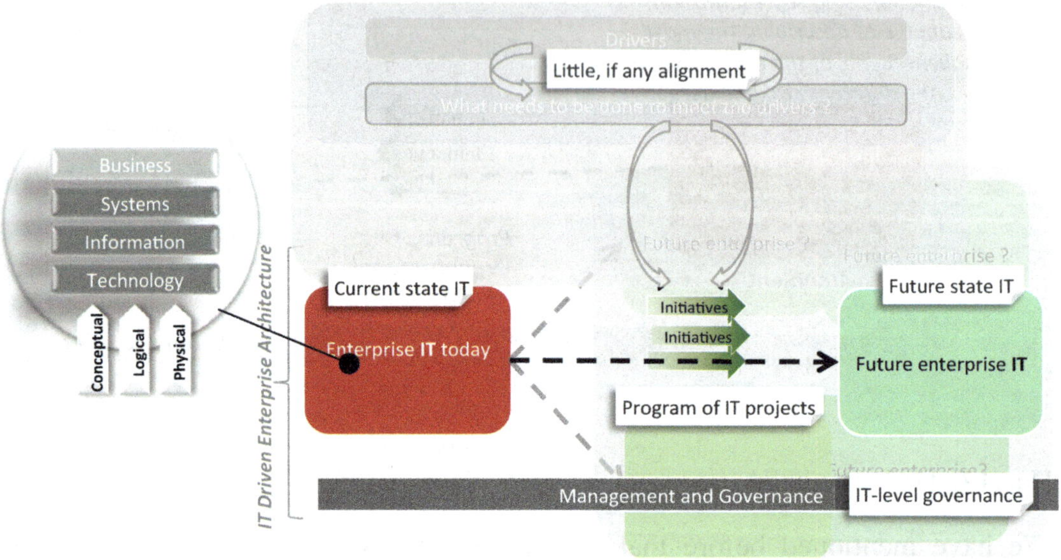

Fig. (4.5). Scope of IT-driven EA.

At the other extreme lies IT-driven EA that, unfortunately, characterizes today's mainstream EA practice (Fig. **4.5**). IT-driven EA regards enterprise architecture as essentially a *technical* exercise, with perhaps some limited attempt made to tie this to factors in the business domain. The finished artefacts concentrate on technology—Cloud, ERP, SOA are often mentioned—and technical detail, but tenuous on the link to business.

IT teams are comfortable with this output, but there is no connection or rapport with the business. This type of architecture does not translate easily into action, as there is no chain of evidence linking the proposed IT-driven changes or end state to business value. Consequently the justification of each technology change involves a considerable effort. Who would, for example, fork out ten million dollars for the implementation of infrastructure consolidation or two million dollars for single sign-on, if these were presented to the business purely as 'architectural decisions'? Moreover, Business changes often leave the target enterprise architecture and roadmap behind: for instance, what the business really needed was a single view of their customer and the ability to report on channel profitability—so obviously these initiatives (which were not on the EA radar) get funding while EA 'architectural decisions' do not.

To recap, IT driven approaches typically exhibit several shortcomings, all of which are manifestations of the lack of alignment between business and IT.

- *Value misalignment:* EA target state, roadmap, initiatives, are not traceable to business value. EA deliverables—future state and the roadmap—what business benefits do they bring? What business problems do they solve? What business objectives/drivers do they support? How do you justify the—often significant—cost of realizing the target state?

- *Language or communication misalignment:* One of the key skills of an enterprise architect is the ability to relate to and communicate with non-technical people, whether they are IT or business executives and senior management. If you produce something of value but fail to communicate value and don't take your stakeholders along the journey with you, it is as good as not producing anything at all. In particular, enterprise architects need to communicate with the business in a way that the business can understand, *by couching value and benefits in business terms, not in technical terms*.

- *Timing misalignment:* the previously mentioned time asynchrony between business and IT cycles, where Business wants results *quickly* whereas IT typically moves more slowly. Typical EA contributes to and exacerbates the problem. *Why?* Because in our experience a typical IT-driven EA exercise is a relatively heavyweight affair, consuming resources and time as the EA team flounder in the throes of current state analysis or delve into details of application, data, and technology architecture. The business may well perceive EA as the slow vanguard of the traditional slow-response IT shop.

Hark back to the Melbourne City planning example: how long did it take for the participants to craft the high-level response to the business drivers?

When EA is not value-aligned, it is very difficult to maintain alignment between enterprise architecture, approved projects, and solution architecture, as we alluded to earlier. Misaligned EA may become shelf-ware and will be overtaken by events. But there is an even worse scenario: misaligned EA may become a millstone around the neck of each IT initiative, where in the name of governance EA representatives attempt to foist misaligned EA direction and standards upon every subsequent IT initiative.

If these issues persist, the spotlight may eventually fall upon the EA function itself. The stakeholders may begin to think: "See that bunch of very expensive staff? They spend a lot of money producing things nobody needs or reads. Not only that, they delay and try to block things really important to us in the name of 'governance'". All the while the EA team, disenchanted, mumble "these guys have *no* understanding of EA".

The problem though, is that this is not a symmetrical situation, in the sense that EA stakeholders—senior IT management and the business—hold the purse strings. If you are not getting your message across, then you are misaligned in direction or content (your output is not aligned with business priorities or direction), time (you have not produced stuff in time), or communication (you have not engaged stakeholders and/or communicated value in terms that non-technical people understand). *It is up to you, the EA, to remedy the situation. Otherwise the stakeholders will, by erasing you from the IT map.*

> One of the authors has a favorite phrase that expresses the situation very well: *"Remember that Enterprise Architects are overhead on an overhead function. Therefore always focus on value to your stakeholders"*

4.2.3. Achievable EA: IT to Support the Business and Keep them Onside

We have rejected a whole-of-organisation strategy as well as an IT centric one, for different reasons: the former is an aspirational ideal, but today we don't quite possess the wherewithal to mount a successful EA design with this scope; the latter, based primarily on technologists' views on what is good for the company, technology preferences and other 'architectural considerations' rather than the satisfaction of strategic business drivers, is self-indulgent, and ultimately self-destructive.

So where do we go from here? Somewhere in between these extremes lies the ground that we advocate and explore in this eBook (Fig. **4.6**).

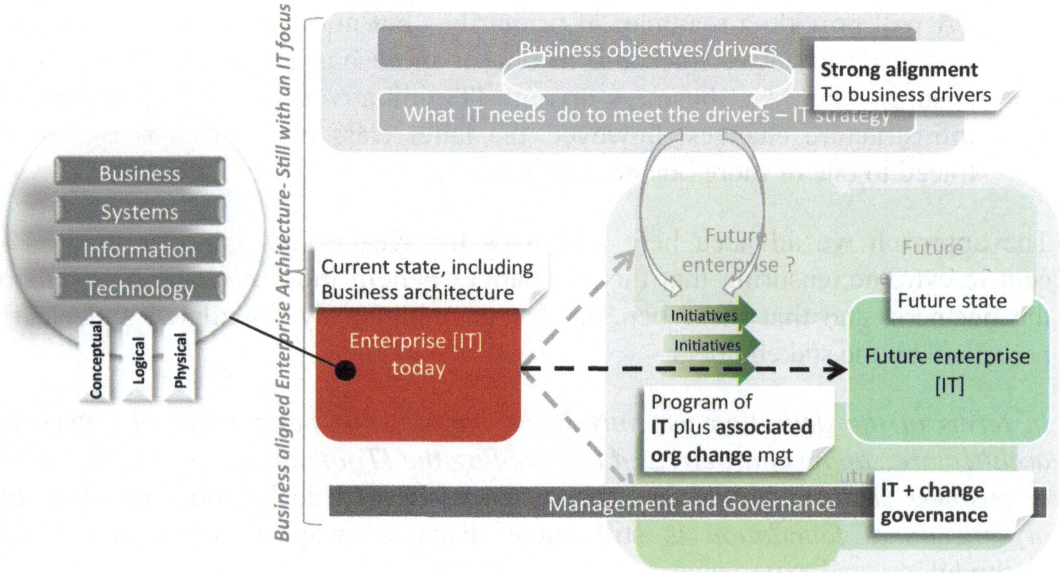

Fig. (4.6). Scope of pragmatically achievable EA.

As we said earlier "today, the focus of the enterprise architects would be on how technology and systems would support the enterprise in its journey along the direction that the executives have chosen—but if they do this well today, tomorrow their brief would be wider… our more realistic objective for EA is to enhance the relationship between business strategy and enterprise IT, so that IT initiatives have a direct mapping to organisational drivers and objectives, there is clear communication between the two areas, and IT delivers value to the business".

Accordingly, the EA approach we advocate has the following characteristics:

- EA may be primarily initiated by IT, but has a very strong business fit. There will be an explicit alignment of IT to business drivers, with IT keenly focused on providing the solutions that the business requires to achieve their objectives.
- EA is positioned so that EA activity is embedded in a wider business value-producing exercise, synchronized with the business planning cycle to readily and flexibly support the business strategy. Adjust the EA delivery cycle to deliver EA outcomes in timeframes relevant to the business timeframes.

- EA will provide a roadmap of primarily—but not exclusively—IT change, with each initiative traceable to one or more business imperatives. These changes can be business-driven IT initiatives, or IT platform or infrastructure changes; however, the latter class of changes is rigorously traced to one or more business imperatives.

The approach we advance here addresses the weaknesses inherent in the IT-centric extreme, ensuring that the IT changes benefit the fast changing needs of the business, and that these benefits are unambiguously articulated and clearly perceived by the stakeholders.

In terms of the definition we introduced earlier, this perspective of enterprise architecture can be characterized as enabling the IT foundation for the execution of business strategy and plans. As we discussed in 'Ideal Scope' enabling the *organizational foundation* is still some distance away in terms knowledge, methodology, and experience.

4.3. A Pragmatic Approach to EA: The Strategic Fit of Business and IT

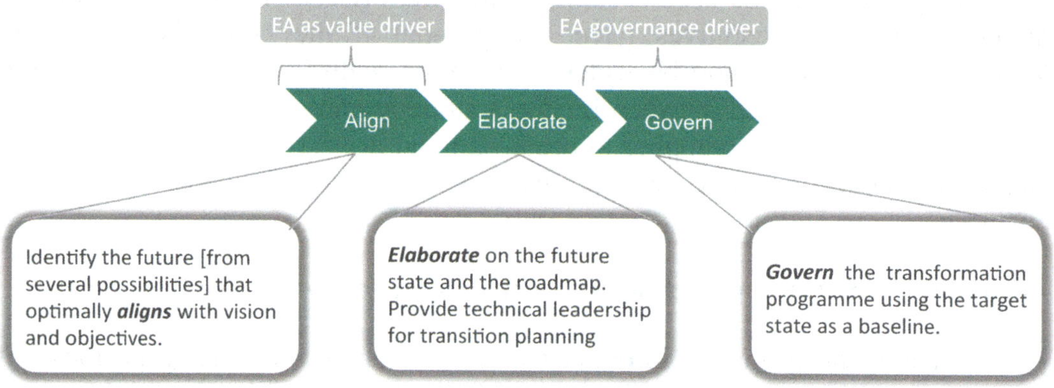

Fig. (4.7). The three stages of EA.

Based on our EA project experience, we introduce here a three-stage approach to EA (Fig. **4.7**). Each stage has its own characteristic objectives and techniques. This approach is a distinctive feature of this eBook. An overview is presented here, but a detailed discussion of each stage, how to conduct them and the appropriate methods and tools, are deferred to the chapters that follow. The first stage focuses on EA as the value driver, whereas in the last stage EA's role transitions to governance driver. Each of the three stages may be mapped to the City of Melbourne example discussed in Chapter 2, as follows:

Align ⇒ Six day workshop

Elaborate ⇒ Six month planning

Govern ⇒ Transformation program

4.3.1. First Stage: Align

Image (4.1).

4.3.1.1. Context

This first stage is critical for EA success: here we align IT's direction with business direction, in a manner that (ideally) makes IT's objectives and direction congruent with that of the business (Image **4.1**, Fig. **4.8**).

The context of the Align stage is planning: the align stage should ideally be undertaken during the business planning cycle of the enterprise. The Align stage output must synchronize with business planning output in terms of *content* (see below) and *timing*. The alignment in timing enables IT/IS investment decisions of the enterprise to be taken as part of the wider business planning and investment process.

4.3.1.2. Process

The alignment process is a relatively limited exercise, primarily circumscribed by the imperatives of the planning cycle. The level of detail of its output must be tailored to these constraints. Think about the four day workshop in the Melbourne example.

- The exercise here takes the shape of a consulting assignment, rather than an IT delivery project. The tasks undertaken are not detailed and granular, but high-level.

- The 'management' techniques needed are those of consulting assignment—rather than project management—leadership, stakeholder management, persuasion and 'selling'.

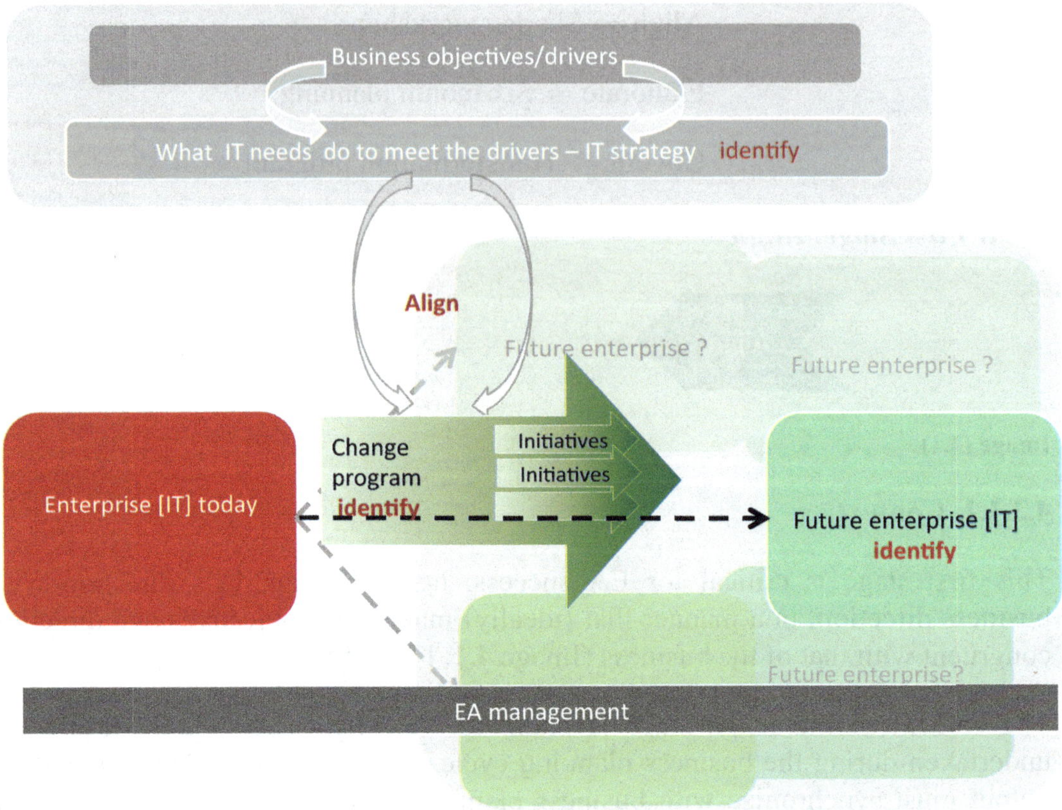

Fig. (4.8). The Align stage.

4.3.1.3. Content

This stage must identify the business drivers, and produce a set of business aligned initiatives and target at a high level. There must be explicit traceability between drivers plus the initiatives to realize them and the target that ensues. An indicative example of output may be artefacts consistent with selected cells of rows 1 and 2 of the Zachman framework[1].

Techniques appropriate (Fig. **4.9**) for the 'Align' stage are:

- Primarily alignment techniques
- Appropriate use of assessment to establish how we are performing today

[1]If you are unfamiliar with the Zachman Framework, see Section 4.4.3 Sidebar.

- Limited use of traditional EA techniques

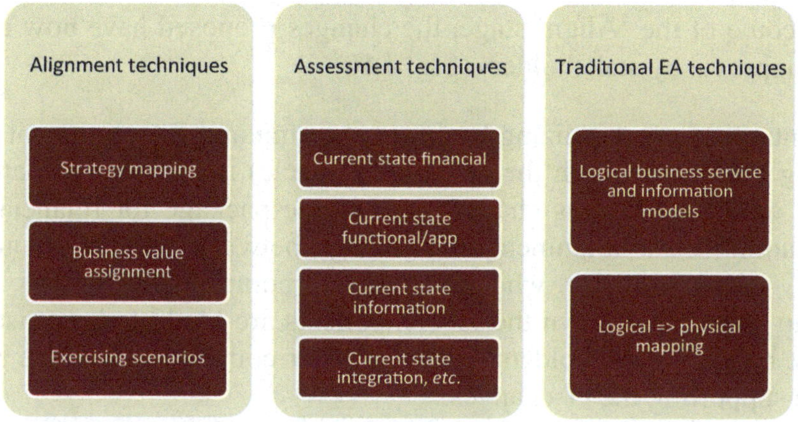

Fig. (4.9). Techniques for the Align stage.

4.3.2. Second Stage: Elaborate

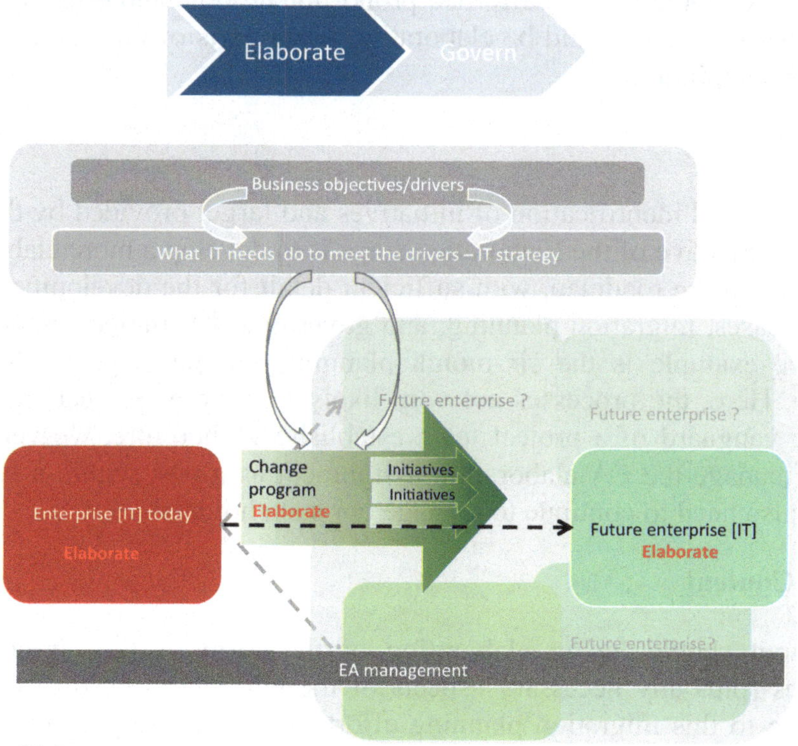

Fig. (4.10). The Elaborate stage.

4.3.2.1. Context

As an outcome of the 'Align' stage, the changes proposed have now received in-principle approval by stakeholders (Fig. **4.10**).

One advantage of synchronizing business planning and EA alignment cycles (*i.e.* embedding this stage within the IT planning cycle) is that the IT changes can be submitted with the business changes in a single package for financial approval. Now, assuming clear alignment, the linkage between the two should become abundantly clear to those who hold the corporate purse strings. Moreover, attempts to knock/pare down the IT components are likely to be resisted both by IT and the business stakeholders, since the latter community will see a clear self-interest in supporting the IT changes.

Thus the context for the 'Elaborate' stage is planning the program of change. Of course 'program of change' here does not necessarily mean a huge organizational transformation exercise; depending on the organizational circumstances, it may range from very small to very large. But whatever the scope of the change program, we would now be afforded proportionate time and effort to plan—and a part of that planning would be elaborating those parts of the EA content relevant to the change program.

4.3.2.2. Process

Given the initial identification of initiatives and target provided by the Alignment stage, the objective of the Elaboration stage is to develop a more elaborate view of the target and the roadmap, with sufficient detail for the development of detailed business cases, migration planning, and governing the implementation effort. An indicative example is the six-month planning/scoping stage in the Melbourne example. Here, the processes are very likely to have a 'project' focus, possibly with the vanguard of a project team established. Therefore, we very likely will need to manage the EA elaboration assignment as a task within a larger project; we will also need to continue to manage our stakeholders.

4.3.2.3. Content

The output should be an elaboration of the form of the target and change initiatives (plus any necessary aspects of the current state), providing technical leadership to this migration planning effort. Indicative output, for example, will be artefacts consistent with Zachman rows 2, 3 and 4. Traditional EA techniques will be used here (Fig. **4.11**). Please note that the outputs produced here are not the architectures of the solutions of the impending changing program: rather, they would be artefacts that can *govern* downstream solution architecture development and implementation.

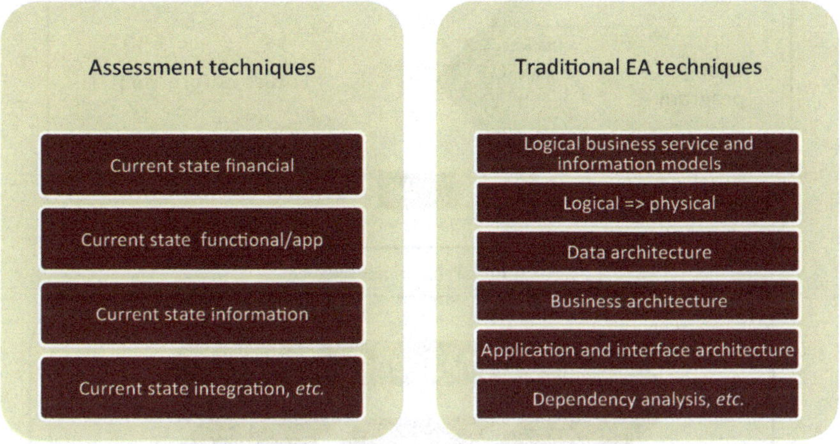

Fig. (4.11). Techniques for the Elaborate stage.

4.4. Third Stage: Govern

Image (4.2).

4.4.1. Context

Here the scene shifts to implementation (Image **4.2**). Again, the magnitude of the program of work will vary according to organizational circumstances; qualitatively though, EA's role will be the same. In EA terms, it is business as usual (BAU): Substantively, EA 'development' activity has ceased, now the focus is on using the EA baseline to govern the implementation program.

4.4.2. Process

As we stated above, the process objective is to govern the program of work (regardless of its magnitude) using the target state and the other artefacts of previous stages as a baseline.

Here again, the 'management' processes have a strong project management flavor, since we need a strong change management discipline during this stage (Fig. **4.12**). We will continue to need to manage our stakeholders.

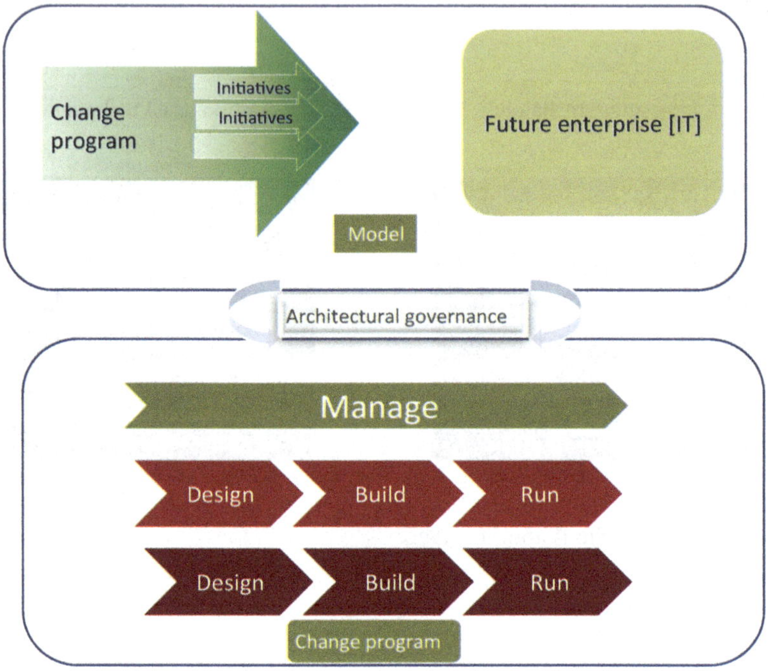

Fig. (4.12). The Govern stage.

4.4.3. Content

The output of the Elaboration stage is baselined. As we govern a change program, it is expected that the baseline itself will evolve slowly through the life of the program. Any necessary changes will be folded into the EA model under change control. The baseline will evolve in two ways:

- As solution architectures and other detailed artefacts are developed, they will add to the existing body of architectural artefacts and populate the appropriate 'cells' of the architecture repository. As part of the governance process, those responsible for EA need to (proactively, not reactively) ensure that these detailed artefacts support the direction that has been set; they also need to ensure that traceability exists between the different artefacts in the repository. The repository here can be anywhere in a spectrum between a fully-fledged model in an EA tool to a set of paper-based documents, but the same principle applies.

- The artefacts produced during Align and Elaborate stages may need to evolve as implementation progresses, taking heed of feedback from the actual path that is being treaded.

An ambiguity appears to have crept in: what we have seen at a very summary level as the discussion moved from Align to Govern, is the emergence of more and more detailed artefacts. Which of these are EA artefacts and which are not? The ambiguity arises because are two possible meanings to 'EA content'. EA content can mean:

- Enterprise architecture content as expressed, say, by the Zachman framework (Image **4.3**). Since the Zachman framework classifies *all* artefacts in the representation of a working enterprise, this representation includes everything by way of content that we have discussed thus far, from Align to Govern.
- EA content as those artefacts that the enterprise architect is responsible for creating and maintaining. As we will see, these are typically those employed in Align, as well as some of the artefacts created in Elaborate.

Sidebar: Zachman Framework

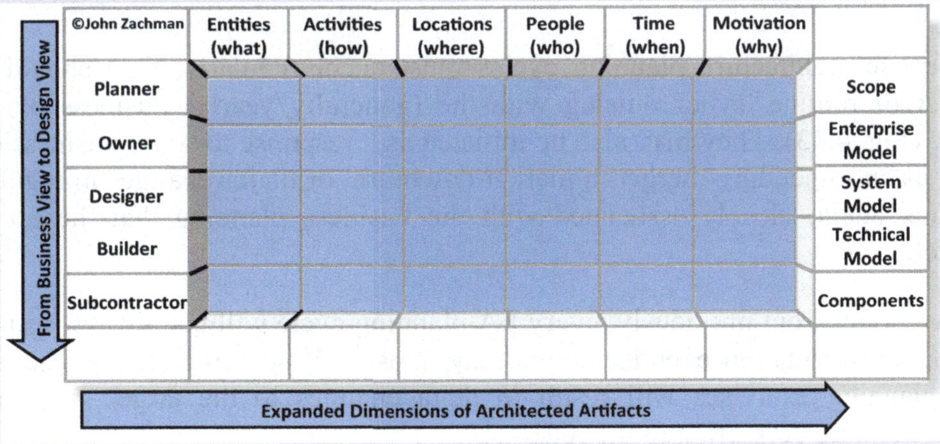

The Zachman framework ©John Zachman

Image (4.3).

Developed by John Zachman - first in 1987 and updated most recently in 2008. Premier framework on the classification of content: how various EA artefacts may be classified and how they relate to each other. The columns answer questions what, how, where, who, when, why; rows give various perspectives – strategist (planner), executive leader (owner), architect (designer), engineer (builder), technician (sub-contractor). It is an extremely useful reference framework for EA practitioners. The framework is more fully referenced in coming chapters.

4.5. EA Cycles

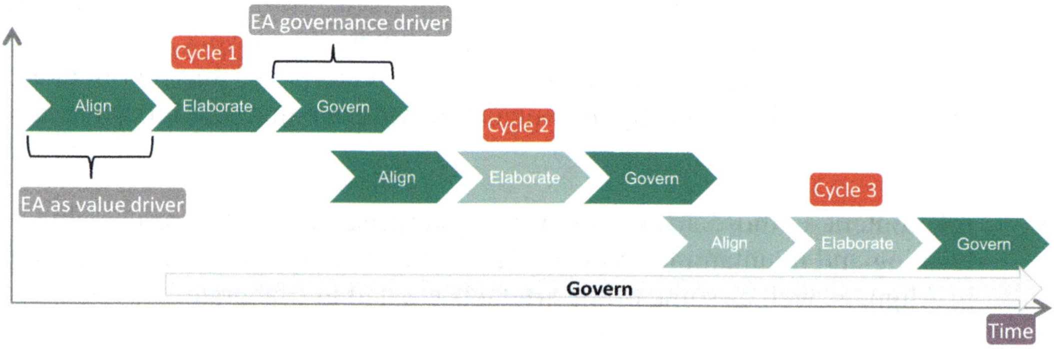

Fig. (4.13). EA is cyclic.

Enterprise architecture planning cycles must occur regularly, they should be a matter of routine, synchronising with the (generally yearly) business planning cycle (Fig. **4.13**). They may also be initiated as a response to some business event such as an impending merger, a market downturn, or major changes in regulatory regime; again, closely associated with the business planning that these events provoke.

As we pointed out previously, every EA planning cycle will not always result in a major transformation exercise; some may, most will not. In a steady state, most EA planning exercises will result in delta changes to the target stage and a corresponding correction to the roadmap.

It is also worth stating that this process will result in a gradual production of artefacts: their number and coverage will increase through time. Think back to the Melbourne example (this will be reinforced in the coming Chapters). We can be very productive in the Align stage with very little. If we have detail in the current environment, fine; if we do not, we can manage to be productive with a few key artefacts that we can produce in a short time. We will then focus on elaborating upon and governing the area of change and change impact. Pragmatically, for the time being, the detail of the stable areas is less important and can be laid aside in the time and resource constrained environment we typically face.

Gradually then, as the spotlight of business change shifts with the passage of time so does our focus – A-E-G cycles progressively encompassing more and more coverage.

This 'just in time' approach is in contrast to the typical EA exercise, which generally attempts considerable breadth and depth in one fell swoop. Our approach ensures that there is no time and energy wasted; we only focus on artefacts that make a contribution to the purpose at hand.

Finally, you will notice that this regime quite easily fits in with something about EA that we have known for a long time: that the 'target' state is aspirational but always distant. Each EA cycle will continually adjust and modify the target of the previous one, in some cases a small change, in some cases a larger one.

This is quite enough by way of preamble: the three chapters of the next Section, 'The EA Project', take us through one cycle of this A-E-G process.

Section 3: Introduction

Previously we discussed the adverse consequences of EA not aligning with business objectives and stressed the crucial importance of EA being business-driven and aligned. We examined three approaches to EA in the previous chapter, and for pragmatic reasons chose the middle one:

"In terms of the definition we introduced earlier, this perspective of enterprise architecture can be characterized as enabling *the IT foundation* for the execution of business strategy and plans."

This section, comprising Chapters 5, 6, 7, takes us through a scenario illustrating the lifecycle of a pragmatic, business-aligned EA development exercise. This scenario necessarily simplifies the picture, but it hopefully brings out the pertinent concepts clearly and concisely.

In later Sections, we briefly explore some ideas that push our boundary into the *organizational* domain; provide a few pointers to how we would go about achieving the 'Ideal Scope' and "enabling the *organizational foundation* for the execution of business strategy and plans." But before we plunge in though, let us step back and examine the big picture.

Our often-repeated theme is that "today, the focus of the enterprise architect would be on how technology and systems would support the enterprise in its journey along the direction that the executives have chosen (…) our more realistic objective for the EA is to enhance the relationship between business strategy and enterprise IT, so that IT initiatives have a direct mapping to organizational drivers and objectives, that there is clear communication between the two areas and that IT delivers value to the business".

The burden of the enterprise architect has traditionally focused on the custodianship and policing aspects of enterprise architecture. In our view this must change: the primary focus of the enterprise architect must be in *shaping* the enterprise architecture, and in doing so the enterprise architect's ambit must straddle IT strategy and planning. Indeed, we believe that the enterprise architect must be seen as the specialist not only in EA, but also in IT strategy and planning within the enterprise.

Inji Wijegunaratne, George Fernandez & Peter Evans-Greenwood

The enterprise plans, implements its plans, and operates the business while it plans and implements. IT's operating cycle must thus align with that of the business: IT must plan in accord with the business, participate in and support the changes the business implements, while operating business as usual (BAU) IT to support business operations. We contend that the enterprise architect and enterprise architecture plays a critical role here, ensuring that the two cycles operate in harmony by:

- Aligning IT's direction with the business direction.
- Elaborating on that direction so that the vision for implementation is clear.
- Helping steer the ship in the waters of implementation and operation by providing architectural and technical governance.

As the above figure illustrates, the stages of the EA cycle (align, elaborate, govern) that we introduced in Chapter 3 are nothing more than the enterprise architect's responsibilities and activities pertinent to each stage of this business/IT cycle. Let us make an even stronger statement: *these are the main meaningful, value-producing activities of enterprise architecture*. You may label the activities differently; you may describe those using different words; but in essence this is the context, the process and the content for the enterprise architect.

With this background, let us explore the EA stages in more detail.

CHAPTER 5

Alignment

Abstract: To detail the main meaningful activities of EA, in chapters 5, 6 and 7 we go through a scenario illustrating the lifecycle of a pragmatic, business aligned EA development exercise.

Chapter 5 covers the first, crucial stage of our EA lifecycle: Align. The main activities, tools, techniques and artefacts for the alignment phase are introduced.

Keywords: Architecture artefacts, business and IT alignment, business value classification, current state assessment, enterprise 'as is', Heat Maps, investment priorities, IT strategy maps, business service maps, strategy maps, The EA project.

5.1. Business-IT Alignment: Context

The context of this Align stage, as we reasoned in the Introduction to Section 3, is business/IT planning. In many ways this stage is crucially important, since it sets the scene for all that is to follow. If we get this right, we would have done our part in ensuring that IT's direction is entirely aligned and compatible with that of the business (Fig. **5.1**).

What do we try to establish in Align?

- What are the business drivers?
- What does IT need to meet/satisfy/support these business drivers?
- What concrete initiatives is the business looking at to evolve the enterprise and carry it into the future?
- What does the end state look like?

As we said before, it is our responsibility to conduct this exercise at the speed that business wants; we need to organize ourselves and the Align assignment to deliver at 'business speed'.

You are likely to find yourself in a setting like this (see "Alignment project - illustrative structure and relationships" (Image **5.1**)); the organizational structure and relationships of an alignment exercise can be complex. Keeping this large and disparate group—typically, high-level stakeholders—with possibly different

Inji Wijegunaratne, George Fernandez & Peter Evans-Greenwood

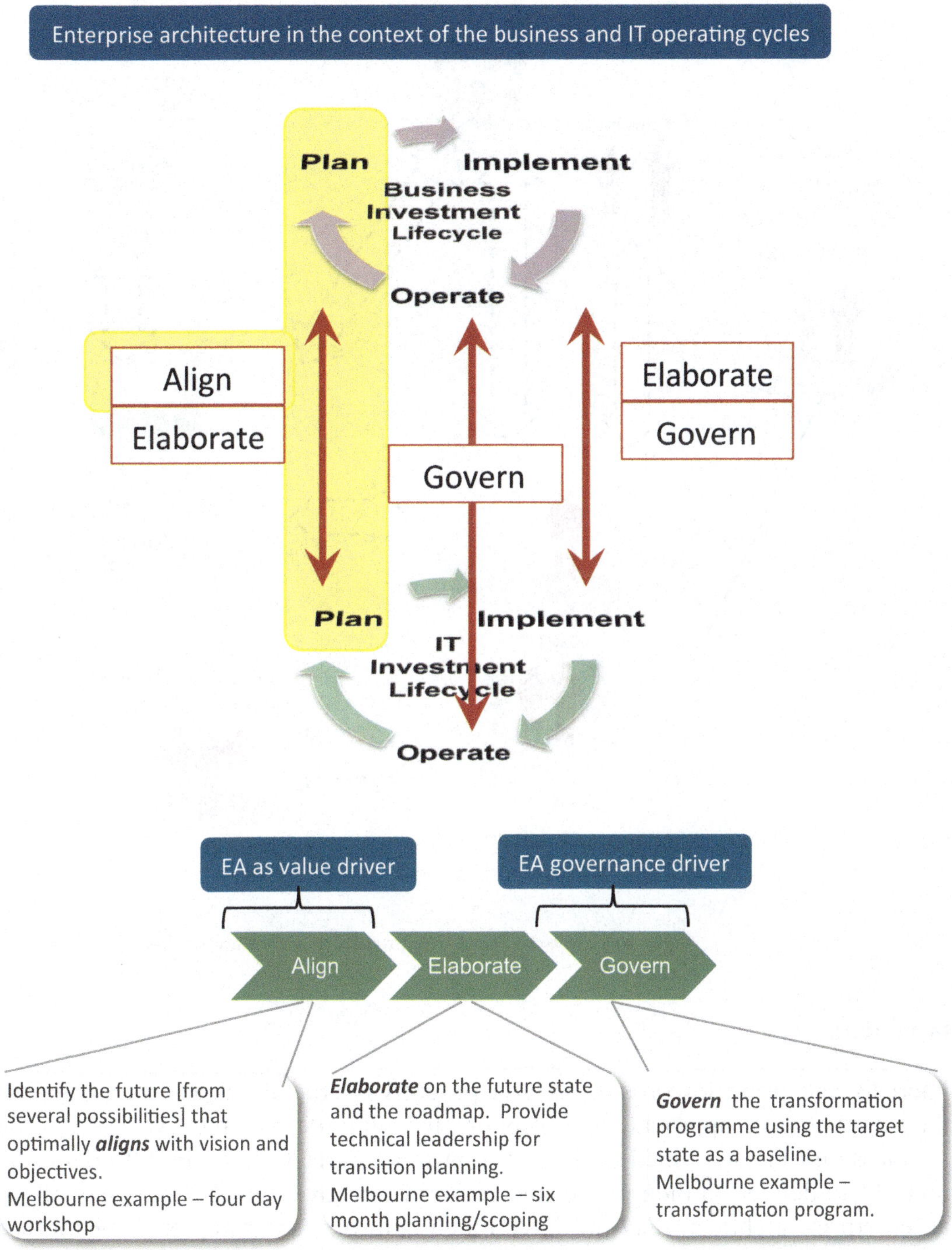

Fig. (5.1). Enterprise Architecture and the business and IT operating cycles.

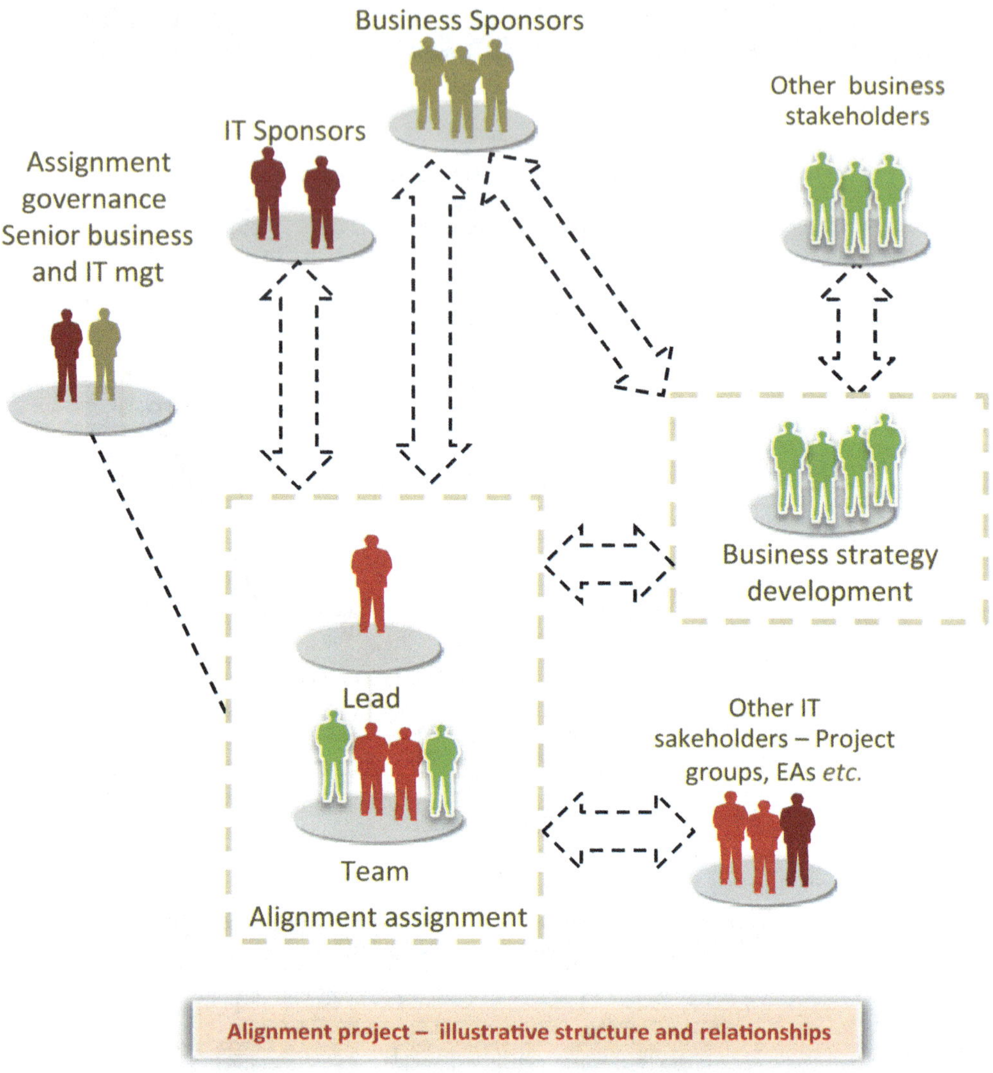

Image (5.1).

interests and priorities on-side as you proceed is crucial: if you do so, gaining their acceptance, approval, and support for your deliverables will mean that business and IT have lined up in cohesion in an agreed direction. Of course it is up to IT to deliver on their part of the commitment (over which you personally, as an enterprise architect, may not have much control – see Chapter 7 for more on this point), but, in helping unify business and IT vision, you will certainly have done your part.

It helps if the alignment team is a joint business and IT team; consider this as a consulting assignment rather than, say, a development project. Stakeholder buy-in is more important than trying to keep to an initially agreed scope; you can change tack and detail of output and overrun by a week, if the stakeholders are happy. Manage politics and stakeholder expectations; apprise stakeholders of developments, keep 'surprises' to a minimum; don't present findings and deliverables as a *fait accompli*, always involve stakeholders in the journey.

What is a typical timeframe? It depends on the circumstances: as we have said several times, it is essential to execute these activities at a speed the stakeholders require. Techniques presented in this Chapter can be employed for a six week—small—assignment for two people or a six to eight month—large—assignment for ten people. It is up to you, as the practitioner, to configure the team, the depth and breadth of the deliverables, and to manage stakeholder expectations to the needs of the circumstances.

5.2. Alignment: Process

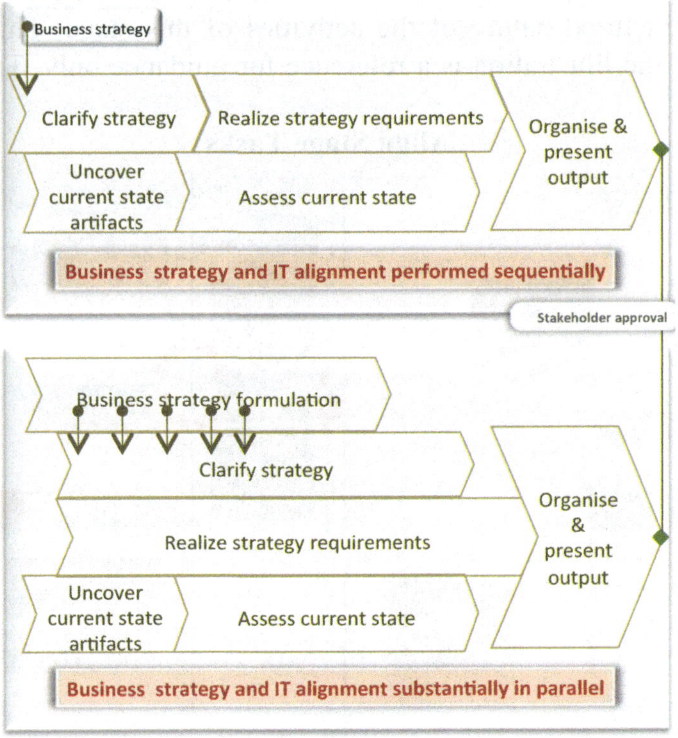

Image (5.2).

Broadly, as depicted above (Image **5.2**), you would understand and clarify the business strategy (which the business may or may not have formalized and documented), and together with business stakeholders identify ways that IT can assist in realizing these strategy requirements. At the same time the current state is assessed to uncover opportunities to support the business as well as to expose any issues standing in the way. These are then organized and presented for stakeholder buy-in.

Notice that the term 'architecture' is noticeably absent in the above description. This is intentional: the primary objective in this phase is to undertake this exercise at a pace and level of detail that the business requires (remember the six day workshop of the Melbourne example). For example the knowledge of IT SMEs (Subject Matter Experts) may suffice to accomplish the task of realizing a strategy requirement, especially if this is undertaken in a business/IT workshop format.

Image (**5.3**) shows Align stage tasks in more detail, for example the interplay between an evolving roadmap and an emerging target state in organizing and presenting the findings. But we must stress that you should be mindful of the relatively unstructured nature of the activities of this stage. This is no cookie-cutter process; the illustration is a reference for guidance only. The process must

Align Stage Tasks

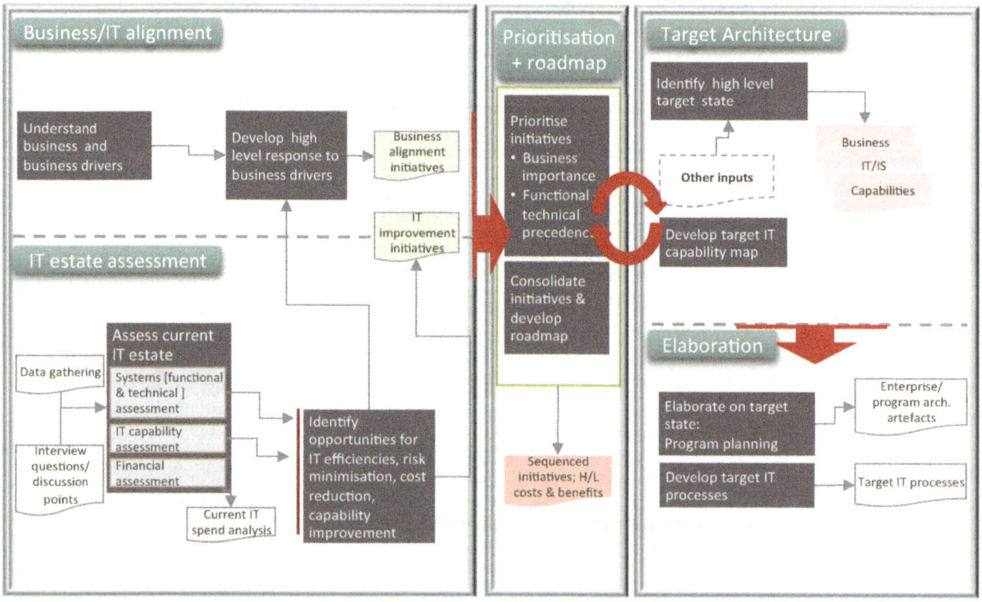

Image (5.3).

be configured to the imperatives of each situation, with a focus on the essential output—what does IT need to do to support the business drivers? How do we best identify this in a manner that carries the business (and IT) stakeholders forward? If this is done well, the time and resources for elaborating on these outcomes will come later.

5.3. Alignment: Content

5.3.1. Technique: Strategy Maps and the Different Views of an Organization

Let us first consider the strategy map (Fig. **5.2**), a technique introduced by Kaplan and Norton in:

- "Having Trouble with Your Strategy ", Kaplan & Norton, HBR, Sept-Oct 2000
- "Measuring the strategic readiness of intangible assets", Kaplan & Norton, HBR, Feb 2004

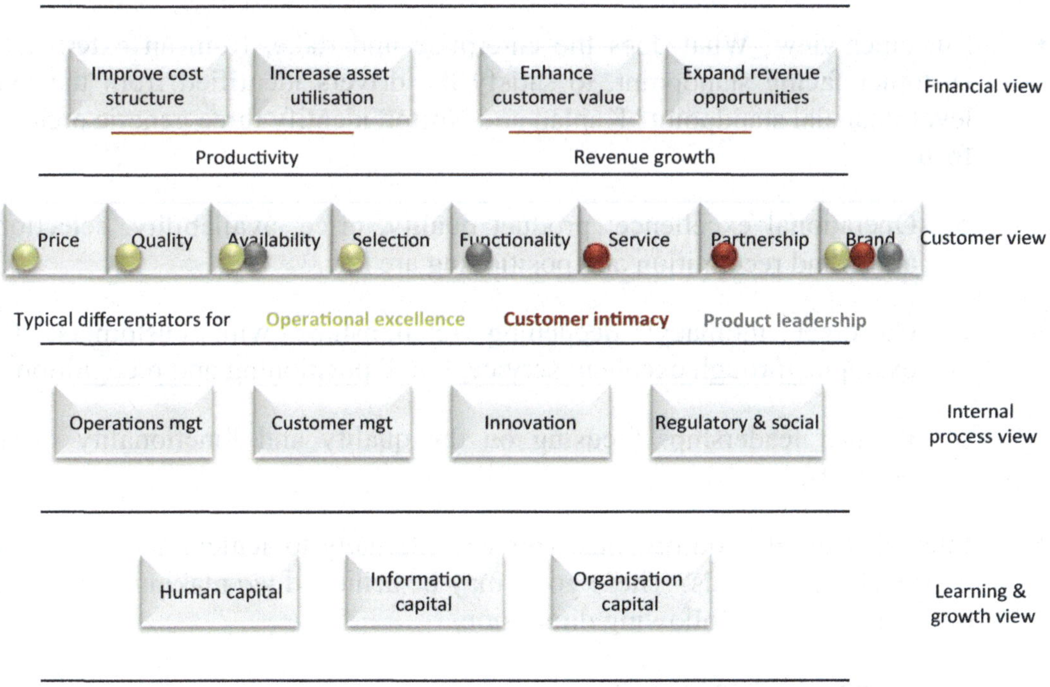

Fig. (5.2). A strategy map.

These techniques developed by Kaplan and Norton enable *structure and traceability* in strategy development. With these techniques, changes to operational and organizational assets to support strategy outcomes are clearly identified, making it easy to communicate and execute the strategy.

Carrying over from their balanced scorecard technique, a strategy map includes four different views:

- Financial view: Typically the starting point for a for-profit organization. (Other organizations—such as a University—may have different values as their top consideration.) In the general case there are two avenues to explore:
    - Increasing revenue: expanding revenue opportunities with new markets, new products, and new customers, or increasing value to existing customers by extending relationships with them.
    - Improved productivity: reducing cost by tightening direct and indirect expenses, and using assets more efficiently.
- Customer view: What does the enterprise undertake, from an external or customer facing standpoint, to satisfy the drivers identified from the top-level financial standpoint? Kaplan and Norton identify three generic areas of focus:
    - Operational excellence: product quality, price, availability, selection, and brand recognition and positioning are key.
    - Customer intimacy: deepening relationships with customers, for example, through excellent service, brand positioning and recognition.
    - Product leadership: focusing on the quality and functionality of its products.
- Internal: How do you organize yourself internally to achieve these external customer facing goals? These goals may be achieved *via* making changes to one or more of the following dimensions
    - Operations management
    - Customer management

- Innovation
- Regulatory and social

- Learning and Growth: this perspective defines the core competencies and skills, and the culture needed to support the internal processes, which in turn support the externally facing objectives that in turn support the drivers from the strategic financial standpoint.

How does this technique help us? We observe that this is a powerful technique firstly to clarify your thoughts and present them clearly and concisely; secondly, this technique establishes traceability, the linkages between separate perspectives and so assists in building a chain of evidence.

A slight modification creates a clear and concise visual representation of the outcomes of business and IT alignment.

5.3.1.1. Modified Strategy Map

We modify the strategy map representation to facilitate our EA ends, as shown in the schematic in Fig. (**5.3**). The right side vertical shows the original strategy map concept, whereas the left vertical illustrates the modified perspective. Essentially, recognizing that the Business is IT's customer, the four business strategy perspectives are collapsed into a 'customer view' for IT; the 'internal' view for IT then reflects the concrete things IT must undertake to satisfy the imperatives of the goals of IT's customers.

The figure shows the Mobil example presented in the Kaplan and Norton work. We take up their thread to produce an internal IT perspective congruent with business goals and the outcome in a modified version of the strategy map.

- Shown in the figure is a representation of the outcome of the analysis.

- What is required of IT to align with the strategy drivers is shown in the bottom two rows: The 'internal' view is a high level view of what IT needs to do; the last row contains the concrete actions.

- This layout makes the traceability between strategy directives and IT actions very clear.

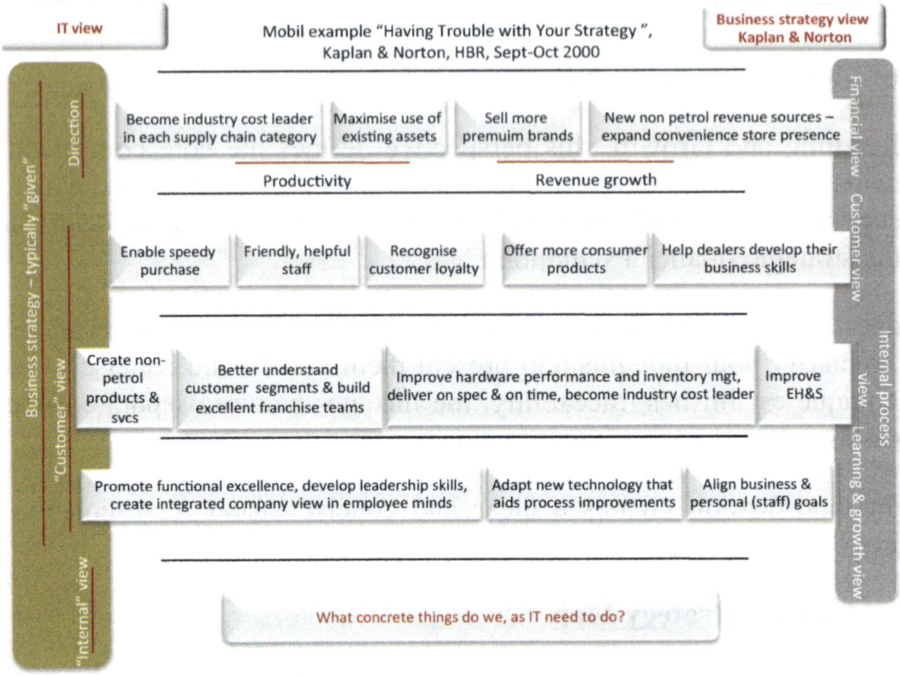

Fig. (5.3). The IT Strategy Map-derived from the general Strategy Map.

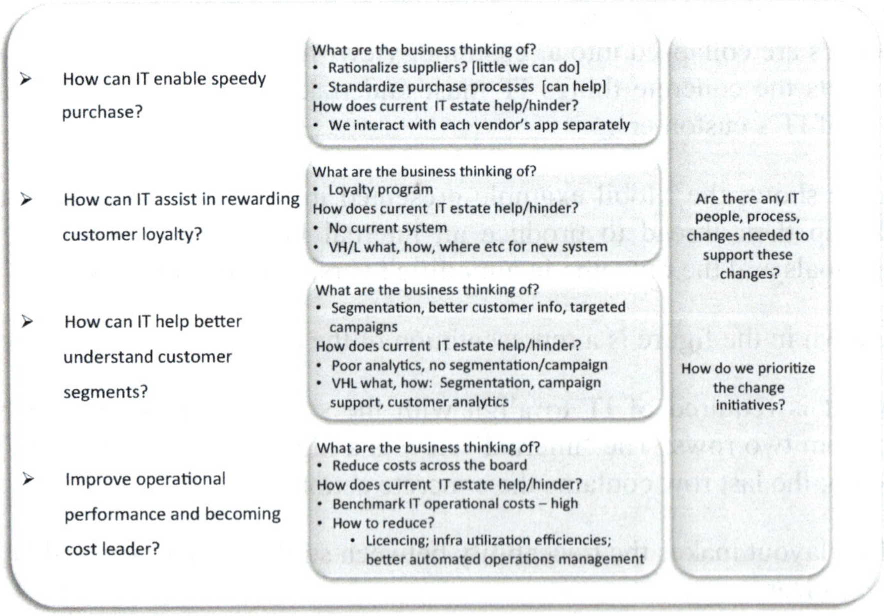

Fig. (5.4). From strategy to concrete action.

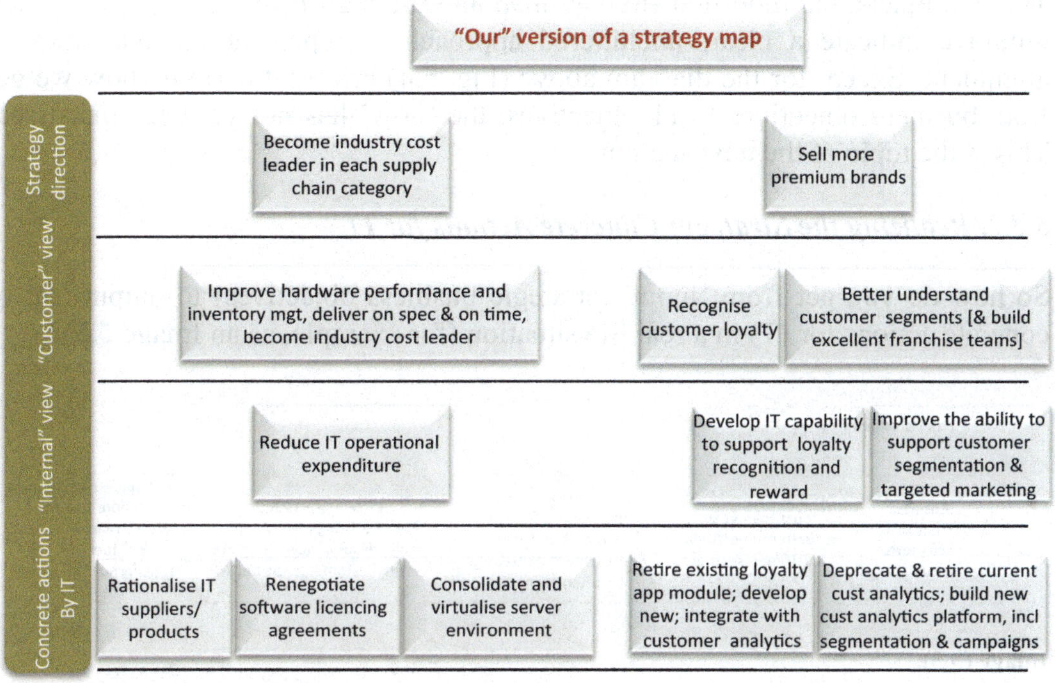

Fig. (5.5). IT version of the Strategy Map.

Each of the initiatives presented in this modified strategy map (Fig. **5.5**) is described broadly to the level of detail shown in Image (**5.4**).

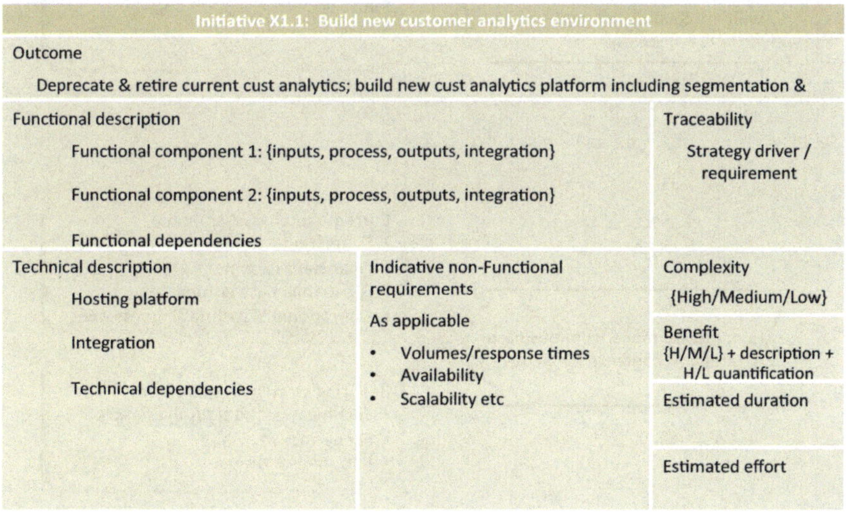

Image (5.4).

These artefacts, the modified strategy map and the high-level description of each initiative indicate a clear, uncluttered approach to represent the outcomes of alignment. Except for the diagram above (Fig. **5.4**) briefly describing how we get from business objectives to IT objectives, the 'how' has not yet been discussed. This is the topic of the next section.

5.3.2. Realizing the Strategy: Concrete Actions for IT

So how do you get from 'input' (strategic business objectives) to output (set of concrete actions for IT) in a real life situation (for example, as an Image **5.5**)?

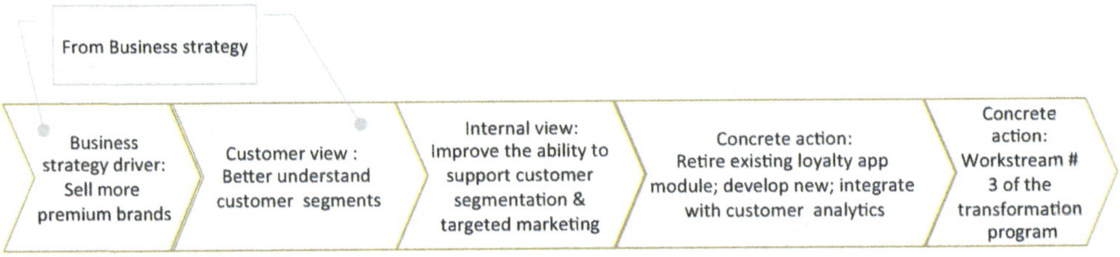

Image (5.5).

The first thing is to clarify the business strategy, if it is not apparent. Then we need to move from business strategy to concrete IT initiatives (Fig. **5.6**).

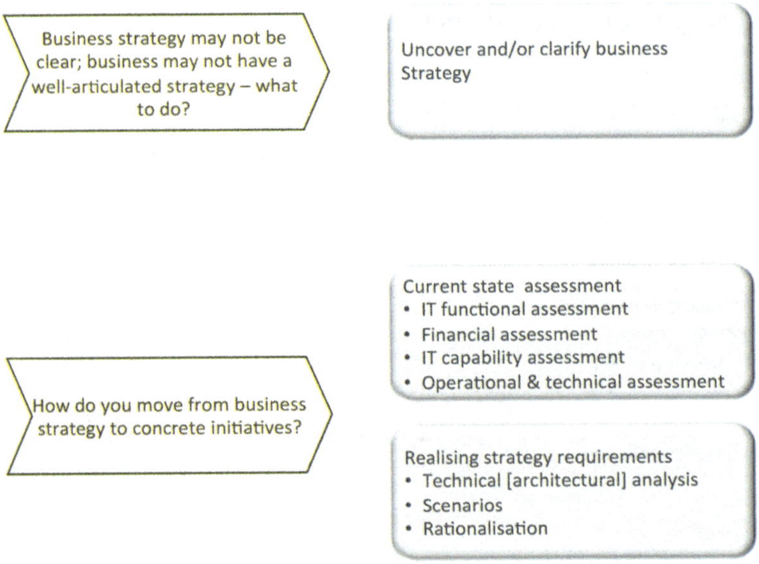

Fig. (5.6). From strategy to initiatives.

5.3.2.1. Clarifying the Business Strategy

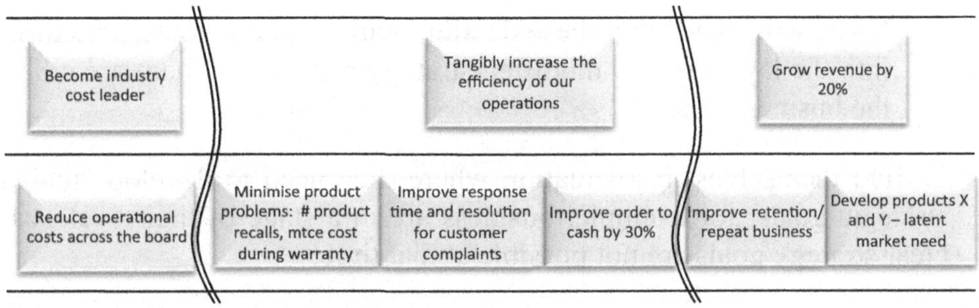

Image (5.6).

Image (**5.6**) illustrates a two-level business strategy, clearly presented and at a level that IT and the business can work together to develop concrete business driven IT initiatives to support these goals. In some situations though, this level of clarity may not exist. Let us run through some scenarios that you may encounter and suggest what you need to do in those circumstances:

- The strategic business direction is not clear
  - Help clarify business thinking; structure and organize business imperatives into a form suitable for rows 1 and 2 in 'our' strategy map
  - Socialize, agree, obtain acceptance
- Business may use another technique
  - Analyze, structure and organize business imperatives into a form suitable for rows 1 and 2 in 'our' strategy map
  - Socialize, agree, obtain acceptance. Use it for communicating with the business if the stakeholders are comfortable with this type of representation as a high-level view; else maintain it as a mapping internal to IT, to foster a business value driven discipline in IT capital works.
- Business gives IT a specific strategic imperative. For example:
  - Rationalize your IT estate
  - IT costs too much, reduce operational costs by x%

- Focus on improving our B2B capabilities.
- If you can, check that these do align with business goals, structure them into the layers of our modified strategy map; see if there are others that the business missed.

- IT find themselves in a situation where they need to develop "their own" strategic goals; for example, business are in a stage of their cycle where a clear strategy/goals are not possible at that time:

    - If this is the case, we must be very careful that this exercise is not, and is not seen to be, a purely IT-driven exercise. We may choose to wait until the business vision is clarified; if this is not possible, we need to come up with IT initiatives that do link back to levers that are attractive to the business

    - Some generally acceptable IT-driven initiatives are:

      IT cost reduction/efficiency improvement, which is an overall cost win, and should be desirable outcome under most business circumstances

      Investing to improve service levels to business. This is likely to be an overall cost burden, but should be acceptable if it results in tangible gains *via* improved business benefit realization within an acceptable timeframe

- What techniques can we use:

    - To help clarify business strategy?

      Scenarios are a very useful technique to understand and clarify business strategy. For example, exercising an appropriate set of scenarios can help in moving from the first row to the second row of a strategy map.

    - To help uncover the type of IT initiative attractive to the business in a situation where strategic business imperatives hard to discern?

      A current state assessment is a useful technique, especially analyzing how the different parts of the IT estate (of varying value to the business) are supported and the respective financial outlays incurred in supporting them (these techniques are discussed later in the Chapter).

5.3.2.2. Realising a Strategy Requirement

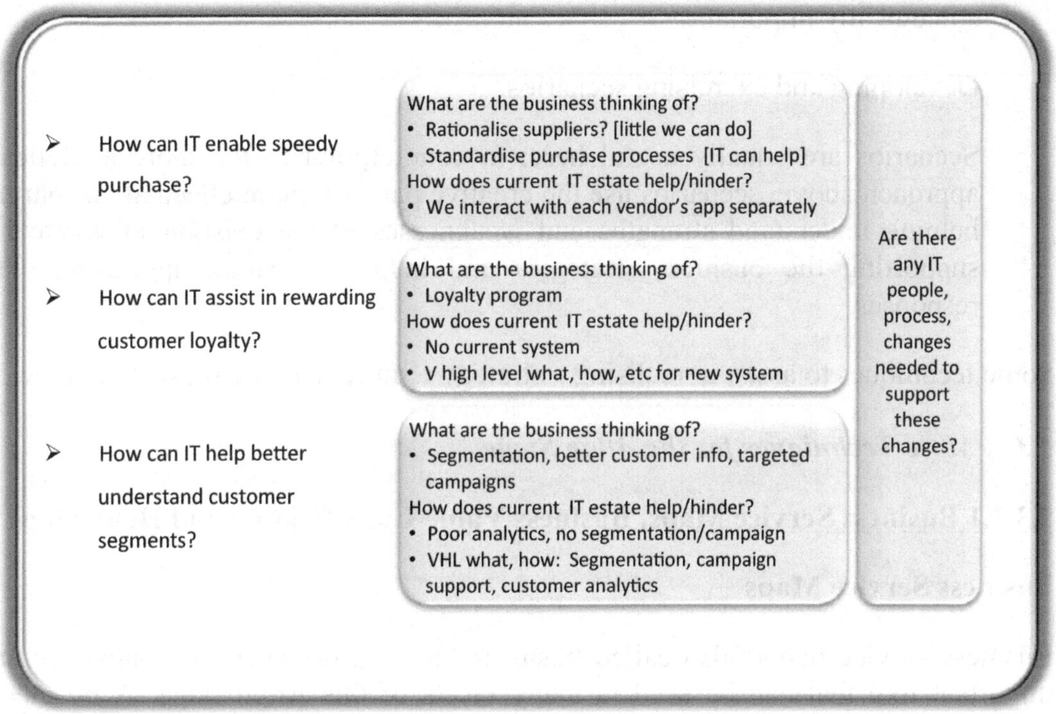

Image (5.7).

There is no magic bullet. First, for clarity, we need to understand, and if needed restate, the strategy requirement. We discussed this previously. We then need to investigate how, in cooperation with the business, IT can assist in realizing the strategy requirement (Image. **5.7**). The types of likely outcome are business initiatives supported by IT, business sponsored IT initiatives, or IT platforms – *i.e.* common functionality sharable by several business divisions such as an Internet platform or an integration platform. Some ways in which we can identify these outcomes are:

- Examining aspects of existing enterprise / domain architecture

  Not all parts of the IT estate are equally important for the business; examining the existing enterprise or domain architecture at a high level with a critical eye will help understand the relative significance of different parts of the IT estate. We can also understand how the different parts perform today, especially in relation to the emerging strategic needs—are there gaps, deficiencies? What has been the investment in IT; for example, have parts of the estate been systematically neglected, that now have become strategically important?

- Developing and exercising scenarios

  Scenarios are equally useful here; in counterpoint to the more analytical approach above, scenarios use the creative parts of the intellectual arsenal in helping understand strengths and weaknesses of the existing IT estate in supporting the business strategies and help in creating appropriate IT responses.

Some techniques to assist in realising a strategy requirement are presented below.

5.3.3. More Techniques for the Align Stage

5.3.3.1 Business Service Maps, Business Value Classification and Heat-Maps

Business Service Maps

Business service maps (also called business function or capability maps) are an important tool that can be used in many facets of this Align stage. A business capability or service is simply a set of similar activities (requiring similar skills and people); not in itself an end-to-end business process but called into play in executing a business process. A business service map is the set of such functions that represent the activities of a business division or the entire enterprise.

Here is a fragment of a business services map for the insurance industry (Fig. **5.7**); this map does not belong to any particular insurance company, but is a generic one that depicts business services of a typical insurance operation. Such a *reference* artefact used as a starting point can accelerate the development of a business services map for a given enterprise.

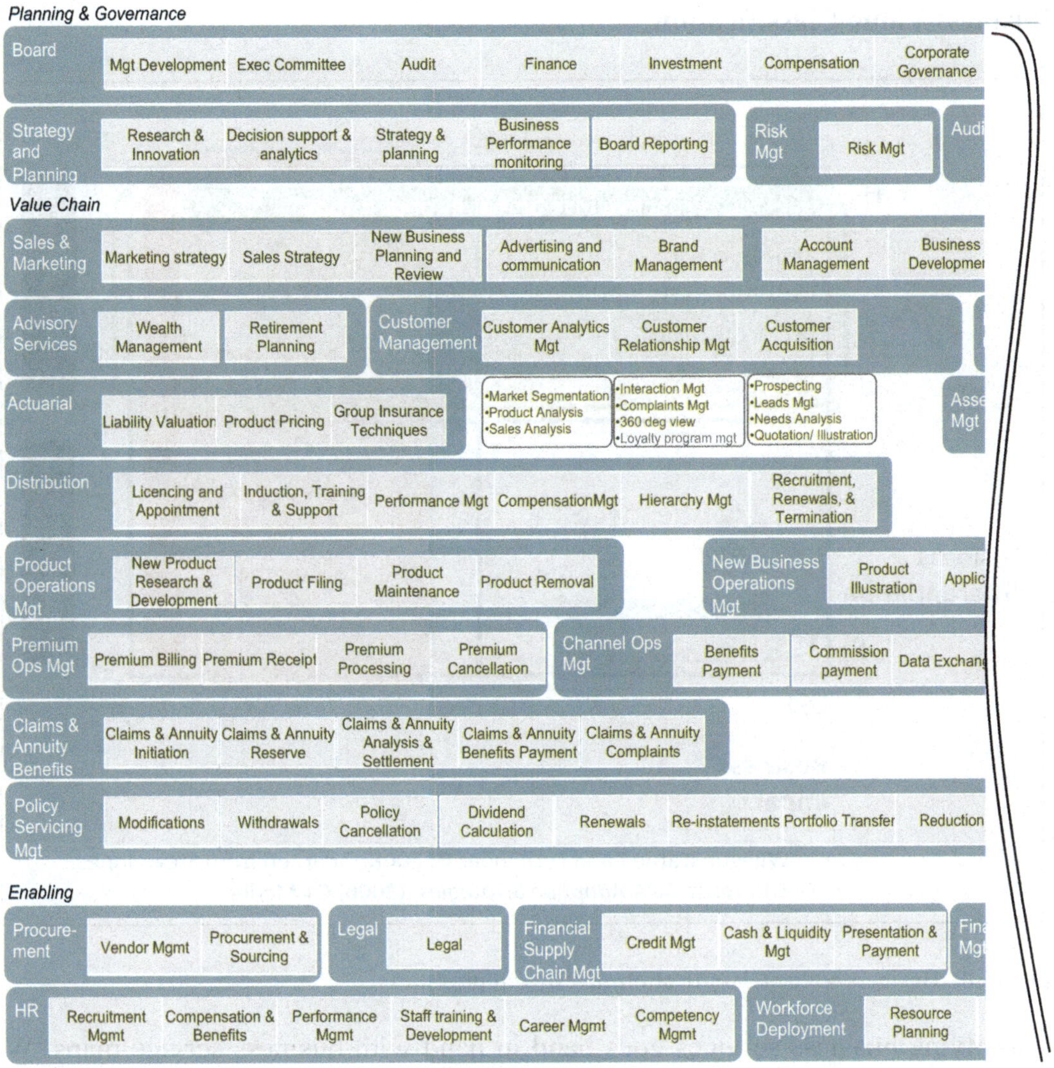

Fig. (5.7). Business services map for an insurance company.

Level 1 of the map is each row of the map, *i.e.* Sales and Marketing, Advisory Services, *etc.*; level 2 each rectangle, Marketing Strategy, Wealth Management, *etc.* This map expands out into Level 3 for some business services; *e.g.* each bulleted line item under Customer Analytics Management.

Business Value Classification

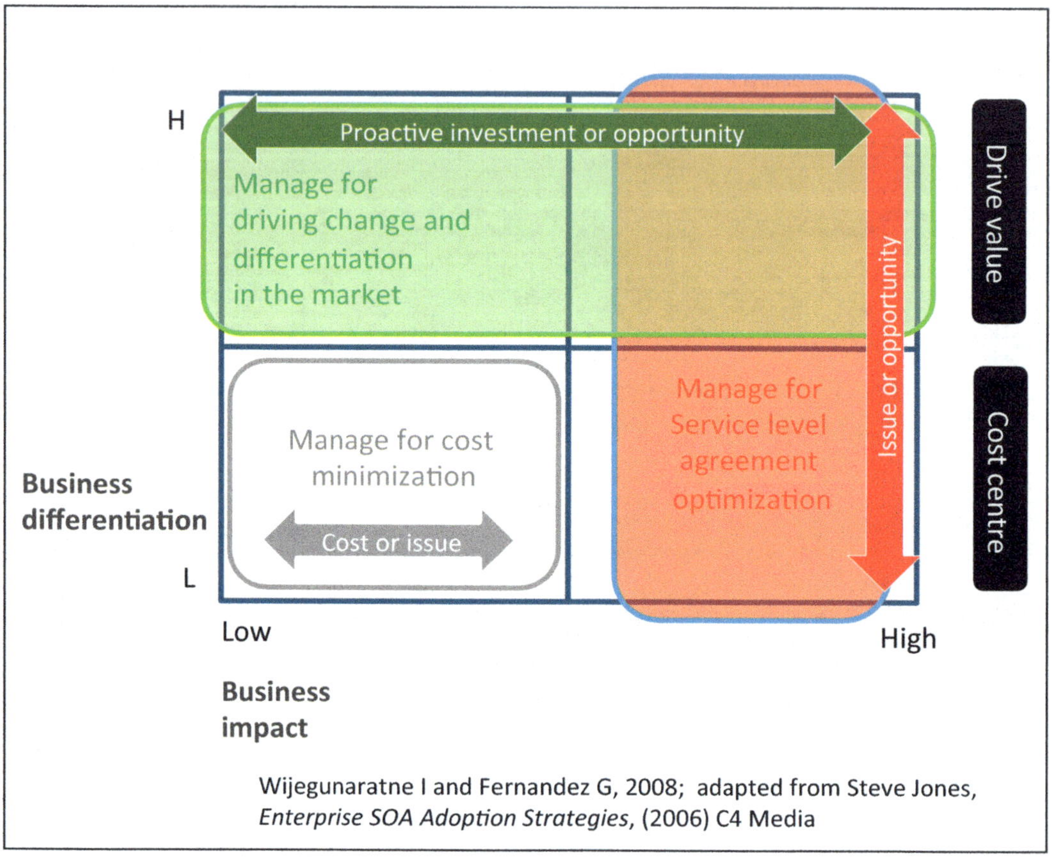

Fig. (5.8). Business Value Classification-investment priorities.

Classifying business services goes hand in hand with business service maps. We can think about business services in different ways to help shape our investments in them; business value classification helps this process (Fig. **5.8**). The above classification is one way of differentiating between business services that we have found to be useful.

- Business differentiation: ability of the business service to help the business differentiate itself

- Business impact: extent to which an unexpected outage to the business service impacts the business

For example, an outage to a business service bringing in revenue to the enterprise, *e.g.* insurance premium processing, will have a high business impact as the break will result in loss of revenue; however, it is unlikely to be a differentiator (generally, insurance companies do not compete on how they process premiums). Hence it is a low differentiating, high impact business service.

On the other hand, insurance product design is a differentiator (companies obviously compete on products), but an outage to product design will not impact the daily operation of the business significantly: hence, a high differentiating but low impact business service.

We must also mention that this characterization of a business service is (or should be) a deliberate act by the enterprise. An insurance company may for example make a conscious decision to make a differentiator out of the way it processes premiums—it may see a competitive opportunity there.

A sample heat mapped fragment of a business services map is shown in Fig. (**5.9**). Each business service is overlaid with a coloured circle identifying its significance (HDLI => high differentiation low impact, HDI => high differentiation and impact, and so on).

How does this classification scheme help us?

Many IT divisions do not possess a clear picture of how the business values different parts of the organization; indeed the business themselves may not have a clear metric for the relative value of their business services. In such an environment IT investment decisions tend to be driven by factors such as the current budget and the cost of the proposed change, or the influence of the business sponsor, but not on the strategic or operational business value of the proposed change.

This framework provides a way to structure and prioritise strategic as well as operational investment decisions. The four quadrants give three investment perspectives:

- Market changing business services: Invest proactively, identifying and creating investment opportunities or opportunistically when an opportunity presents itself.

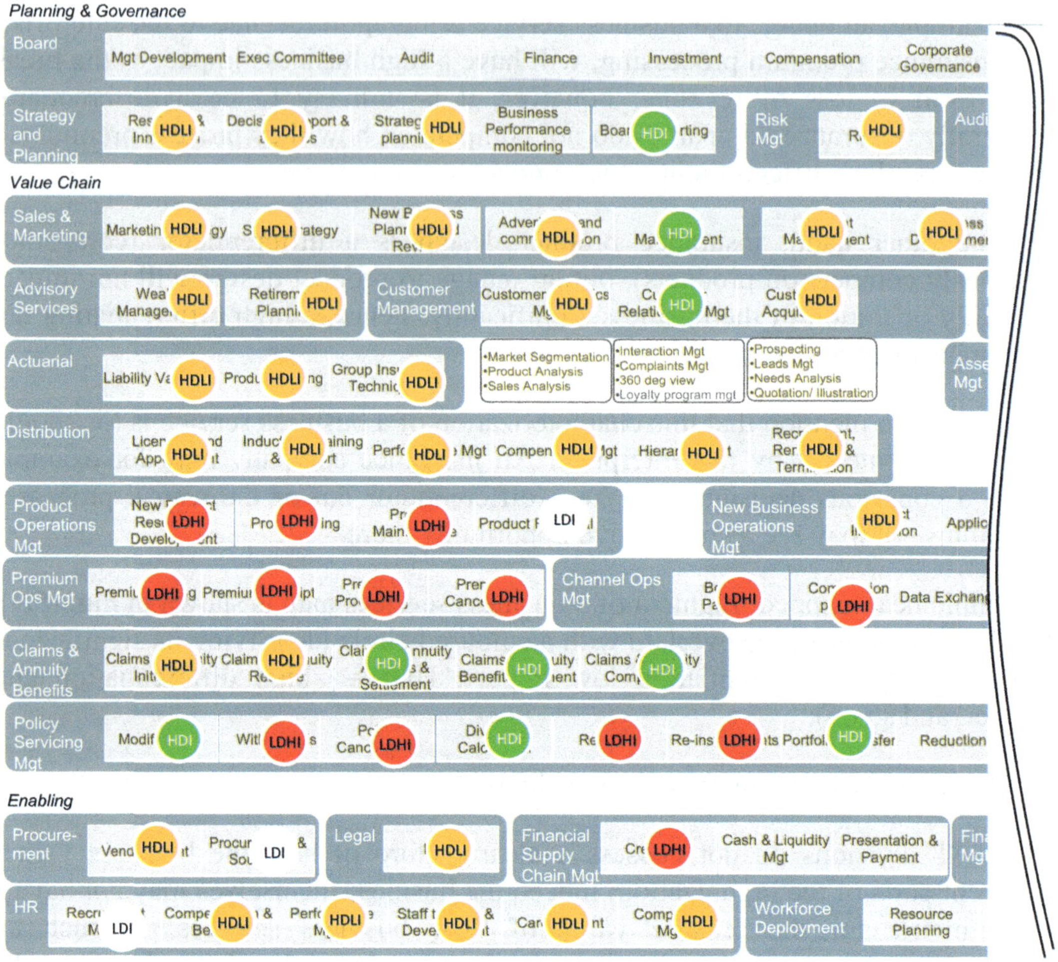

Fig. (5.9). Heat-mapped business services for an insurance company.

- Essential utilities: Invest to maintain service levels or service level agreements (based on an issue or opportunity)

- Others: Manage for cost minimization

To summarise

- Organise your company's business services in the manner of a business services map.

- Classify the business services; a heat-map is a useful way to depict the classification
- Use this to inform and guide investment decisions in the business services

Ideally this exercise should be performed by senior business managers. The business should own the business services map plus the heat-map and use these as one measure to guide investment decisions in the business services, irrespective of whether they contain an IT component or not. Pragmatically, the ownership of these artefacts may reside in a business architecture group, and/or IT plus business stakeholders may have joint ownership.

- Business and IT may then use the business services map artefacts as one input to guide their thinking in shaping business and business/IT strategic initiatives to align with the corporate strategic objectives.
- IT may use the business services map artefacts to ask the question "is the spread of IT investments and focus/attention across the IT estate consistent with the relative significance of the business services", especially in the context of a current state assessment.

5.3.3.2. Current State Assessment: The Enterprise 'as is'

Current state assessment is not a single technique. Rather, it employs a set of techniques to review and scrutinize the current performance of IT along several dimensions to formulate inferences and recommendations for improvement.

When would you undertake a current state assessment in this (align) context?

For instance

- When cost or efficiency is a strategy driver
- When IT is seen as needing to lift its game
- When IT is in a position to proactively propose improvements

Do not confuse current state assessment with sourcing, identifying, and completing existing architectural artefacts. As a prerequisite for certain elements of such an analysis we may need to source, review, and collate existing architectural artefacts, but do not spend too much effort in developing or completing them: very rarely do you get that luxury in our context here. Make do with what is there; let stakeholders know that the technical detail/granularity of the output of the align stage is conditional on the quality and detail of the existing information.

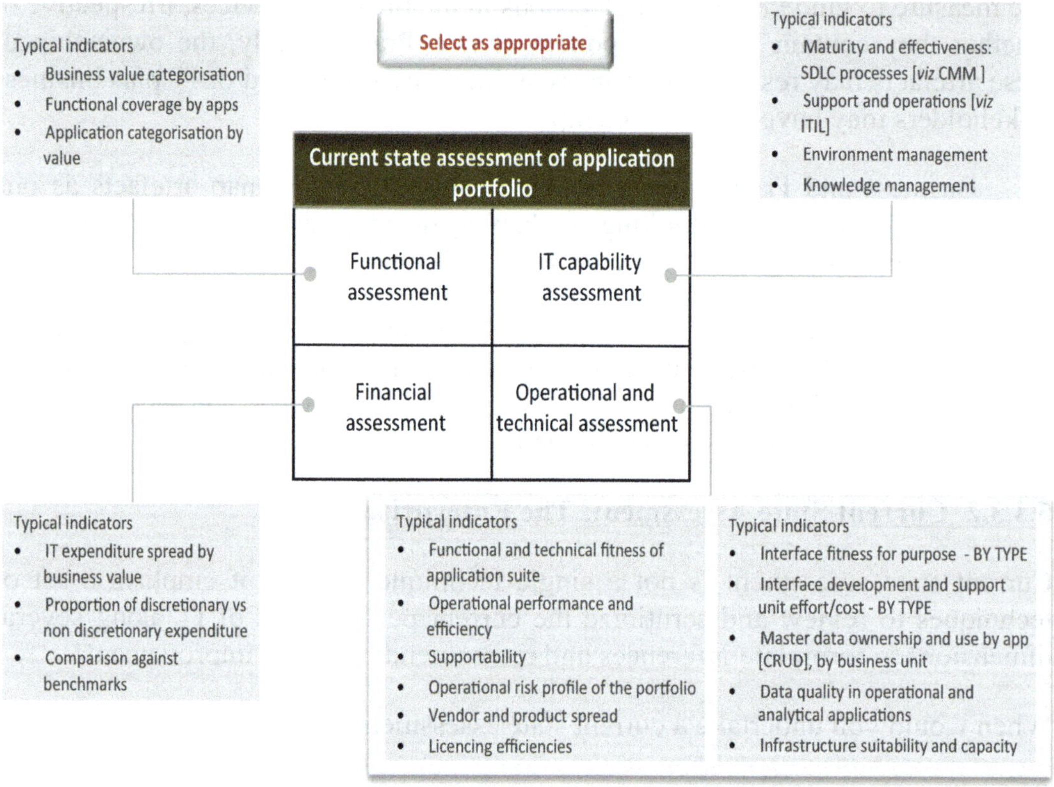

Fig. (5.10). Current state assessment.

As Fig. (**5.10**) attests, a current state assessment is not confined simply to a technical assessment. Functional, financial, and IT capability assessments can yield very significant insights into the operations of the IT division and its IT estate. The most appropriate techniques to fit the current circumstances in the "Align" stage must be chosen.

Functional Assessment

Business service maps and business value categorization are extremely valuable tools to guide the analysis here. Using business services heat-maps as a base, a few more artefacts can be constructed: one is explored below, and another under financial assessment:

- Application coverage of business services (Fig. **5.11**).

  The heat-mapped business services (columns in the figure below) are mapped against the applications of the IT estate (the rows in the figure). Application coverage is then depicted as shown below. Even if it is not possible to differentiate the quality of coverage, this type of analysis can be very insightful. For example;

  - Row => # of business services that each application serves

  - Column => # applications serving each business service

What inferences can we draw on application coverage?

- As a guide, we should expect a high quality of functional fit against high differentiating business services; high quality of non-functional fit (performance, scalability, availability) against high impact business services.

- Several applications supporting the same business function (cells down a single column) generally means duplication or fragmentation of application functionality.

- We can also infer the relative importance of applications (or application modules of large ERPs); if for example an application spans mostly HDI business services, then the application itself can be categorized as HDI.

- These types of inference can be employed as an input to determine opportunities for rationalization, consolidation, and possible shifts of IT focus (*i.e.* towards high differentiation and high impact business services).

Fig. (5.11). Application coverage of business services: quality.

Financial Assessment

Spread of IT Expenditure Against Business Services

An artefact very similar in form to functional coverage is the spread of IT expenditure across business services. Heat-mapped business services (columns) are mapped against the applications of the IT estate (rows). For each application, the IT expenditure against each business service it covers is shown.

If possible, two plots may be constructed:

- Operational expenditure (support and maintenance)
- Project expenditure

We need to have reasonable ways of defining high, medium, and low quanta of expenditure, and of apportioning costs against each business service (Fig. **5.12**).

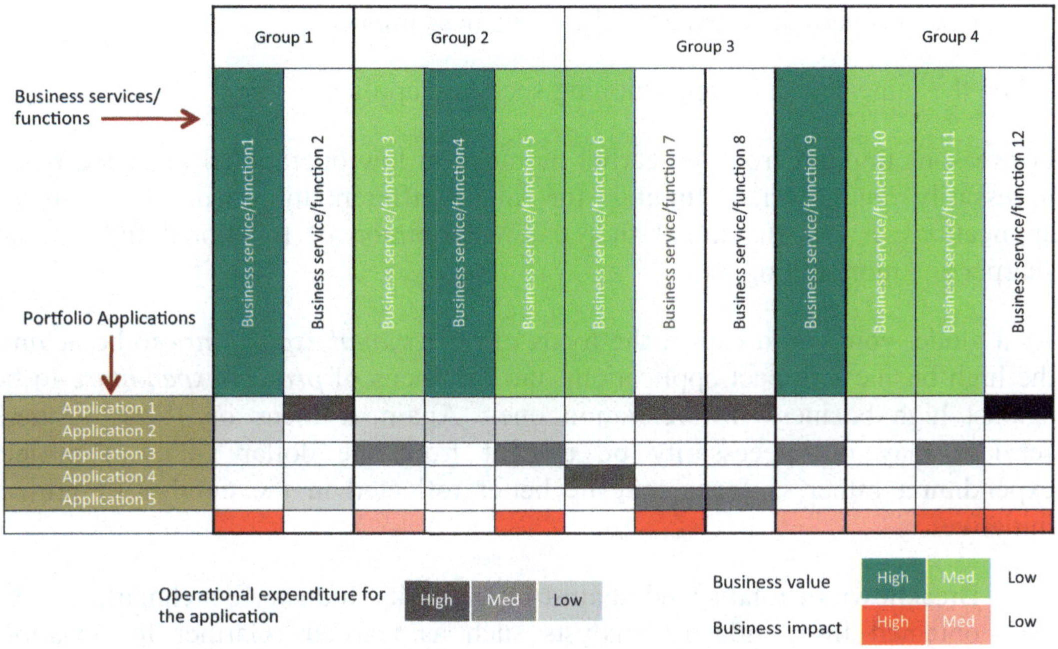

Fig. (5.12). Application coverage of business services: expenditure.

What inferences can we draw? Obviously, the relative magnitudes of application related IT expenditure against each business service can be inferred from this. But there are a couple of caveats: the first being, as indicated earlier, apportioning accuracy and reliability. The second is an interesting one; for example imagine a relatively small, custom developed application targeting one of your high differentiation business services, say product development. At a relatively small level of outlay, this application performs its job extremely well. There is a low differentiation business service, financial accounting, that uses a module of the organization's main ERP, that even when apportioned shows an order of magnitude higher expenditure than your product development application.

Spread of *aggregate* operational spending against the business service *categories* may also yield useful insights: What is the aggregate spending under each of these categories?

- High business differentiation/High business impact
- High business differentiation/Low business impact
- Low business differentiation/High business impact

- Low business differentiation/Low business impact

Again the same caveat on apportioning spending applies.

For reasons implicit from the earlier narrative, a low operational IT spend is not necessarily an adverse finding for high differentiation and low impact applications; a low functional fit (*i.e.* SME opinion of functional fit) is a far sharper and more telling one.

As a guide, you would expect the focus of *operational expenditure* to be against the high business impact applications and the focus of *project expenditure* to be against high business differentiation ones. Again, a focus on HBD business services may not necessarily be evident from the dollar value of project expenditure; rather, a focus may be better reflected in the number of project initiatives.

- Breakdown of total spend against benchmarks. Industry benchmarks can be obtained from industry analysts such as Gartner (Gartner for example benchmarks major industry verticals every year). Metrics such as:
    - IT spend as a proportion of total revenue
    - IT spend per employee
    - IT cost per customer (useful for banking, insurance, health insurance verticals)
    - IT spend proportion for competitiveness, business operations, compliance (financial services vertical)
    - Proportion of IT spend on discretionary (*i.e.* project) *vs* non-discretionary (operations, support and maintenance)

These are useful as objective illustrations of how your enterprise fares in terms of IT spending against the industry norm; properly used they can take the heat out of arguments and differences of opinion and help our focus return to the essentials.

Operational and Technical Assessment

The criteria of traditional IT assessments are found in this quadrant. For example:

- Operational risk profile of the portfolio (impact of an adverse event multiplied by the likelihood of occurrence)
- Non-functional attributes
    - Level of technical fitness: how the actual non-functionals (performance, scalability, availability, *etc.*) fit the requirement
    - Operational performance and efficiency
    - Infrastructure suitability and capacity (application NFRs *vs* infrastructure features)
- Maintenance and support
    - Supportability (The level of ease/ difficulty of supporting the application: cost of support, quality of support, available support skills)
    - Vendor and product spread across the IT estate ("Can we rationalise?")
    - Licensing efficiencies
- Integration
    - Fitness for purpose by type of interface
    - Development and support unit effort/cost by type of interface
- Data
    - Master data ownership and use by applications: are there issues of data ownership/conflict in creating, reading, updating, deleting (CRUD) data? By business unit; similarly, do multiple business units lay claim to the ownership of a particular data entity?
    - Data quality in operational and analytical applications

These indicators must be operationalized: for example, how do you measure the level of technical fitness? Where do you draw the line for high, medium and low levels of technical fitness?

Evidence is gathered by way of a questionnaire/data collection sheet where SMEs provide their opinion or factual data is collected. An example of the latter is where the data on problem tickets raised over a period is gathered for an application: an analysis can attest to the application's actual availability and stability.

Capability Assessment

Some may argue that an IT capability assessment does not fall within the traditional ambit of enterprise architecture. We have, however, defined the responsibilities of 'doing enterprise architecture' within the context of IT strategy and planning. An IT capability assessment is central to ensuring that the IT engine is capable of supporting the ship of the enterprise as it navigates its way through treacherous competitive waters.

You may assess capability along dimensions such as;

- Maturity and effectiveness of SDLC processes (*viz.* CMM)
- Maturity and effectiveness of support and operations (*viz.* ITIL/ITSM)
- IT management and governance (*viz.* COBIT)

Another angle you could consider is capabilities in the major 'business' services in an IT division, such as:

- Strategy and planning
- Architecture
- Program and portfolio management
- Development
- Testing
- Operations and support
- Information management (analytics)
- Integration

- Knowledge management

For the industry standard capability frameworks—CMM and ITSM, COBIT—there are standard assessments that can be used; else you can develop your own assessment. Depending on the time and resources available, you could carry out a detailed assessment, or a high-level one; if the latter, an assessment by a few SMEs should give you a reasonable picture. Typically though, in the Align stage, you want a broad picture, and undertaking the latter should be enough to provide you the main strengths and weaknesses of IT capability.

5.3.3.3. Scenarios: Involving the Business

This approach complements the more analytical techniques, such as current state assessments. The execution of scenarios in a workshop environment by groups of business and technology stakeholders helps understand the strengths, weaknesses and opportunities of the current enterprise (processes, capabilities, systems and technology) and help identify appropriate responses to the strategic imperatives.

We have earlier identified two stages where scenarios can usefully be employed. The actual scenarios must be constructed to suit the needs of each occasion, but the principles are the same:

- Think of scenarios as being very similar to test scripts in IT testing. Like test scripts coverage and mix is critical to obtain the right balance of outcomes

    - Ensure coverage. For our purposes, coverage is predicated upon the source strategy drivers; if for example our purpose is to move from level 1 to 2, construct each scenario so that it maps to one or more level 1 strategy drivers; ensure all drivers are adequately covered

    - Ensure right mix of business as usual (functional testing), stretch (performance/ stress testing) scenarios. In the latter, we deliberately stretch the organization's capabilities and processes to understand better how the business is placed to cope with unusual and stressful situations

Scenarios: Clarifying Business Strategy

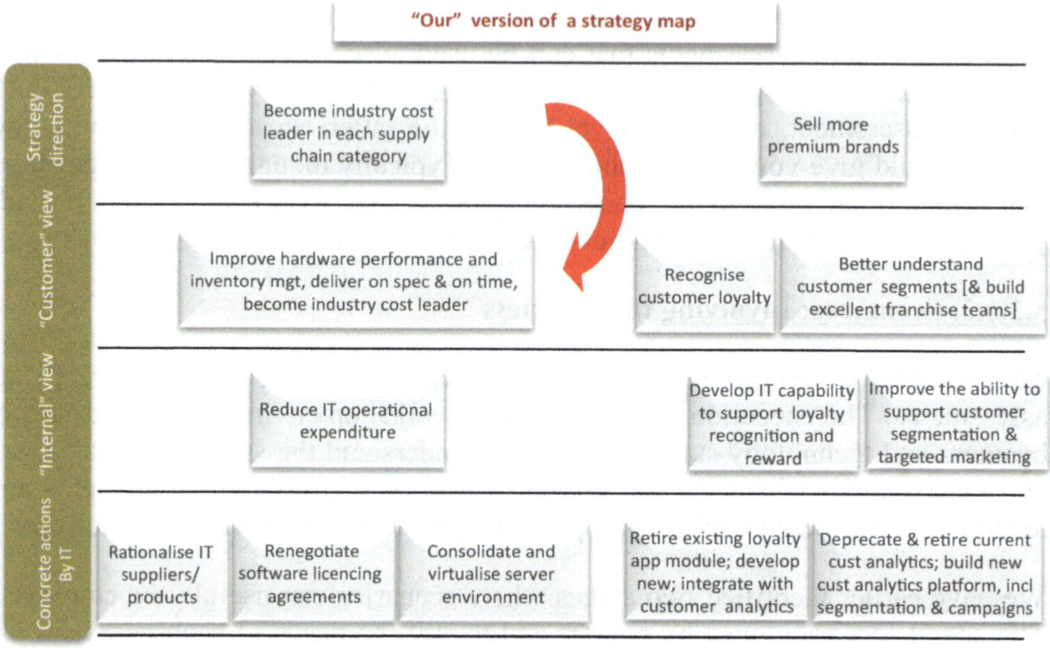

Image (5.8).

Here, exercising an appropriate set of scenarios can help in moving from the first row to the second row of our strategy map (Image **5.8**).

Some examples of business as usual (BAU) scenarios:

- Smith & Co receives an order for 1000 widgets. How long does it take to (a) deliver and (b) receive & process payment? Maps to top-level driver 'improve operational efficiency'.
- Mrs. Gray makes a complaint. How long to process and resolve? Maps to drivers 'achieve excellent customer service' and 'improve operational efficiency'.
- An acquisition results in transaction volumes growing by 30%. What are the effects on the IT estate? System service levels (performance, availability, throughput), IT skills, IT operational costs? Maps to driver 'improve operational efficiency' and 'grow revenue by 20%'.

- A knowledge worker develops an innovative new product. How does the company identify, capture and industrialize the idea? Maps to drivers 'improve operational efficiency', 'develop competitive products'.

More examples, stretch scenarios:

- Business needs to place a new product in the market within two months. How can this be done? Maps to driver 'improve operational efficiency', 'develop competitive products'.
- A new competitor emerges on the market with a product 30% cheaper than ours. How do we claw back our position? Maps to drivers 'develop competitive products', 'improve business agility'.

We would exercise these scenarios in a workshop environment, where small teams of business and IT stakeholders exercise the enterprise's business and, where appropriate, IT processes in the context of these scenarios.

Scenarios: Realizing Strategy Requirements (Image 5.9)

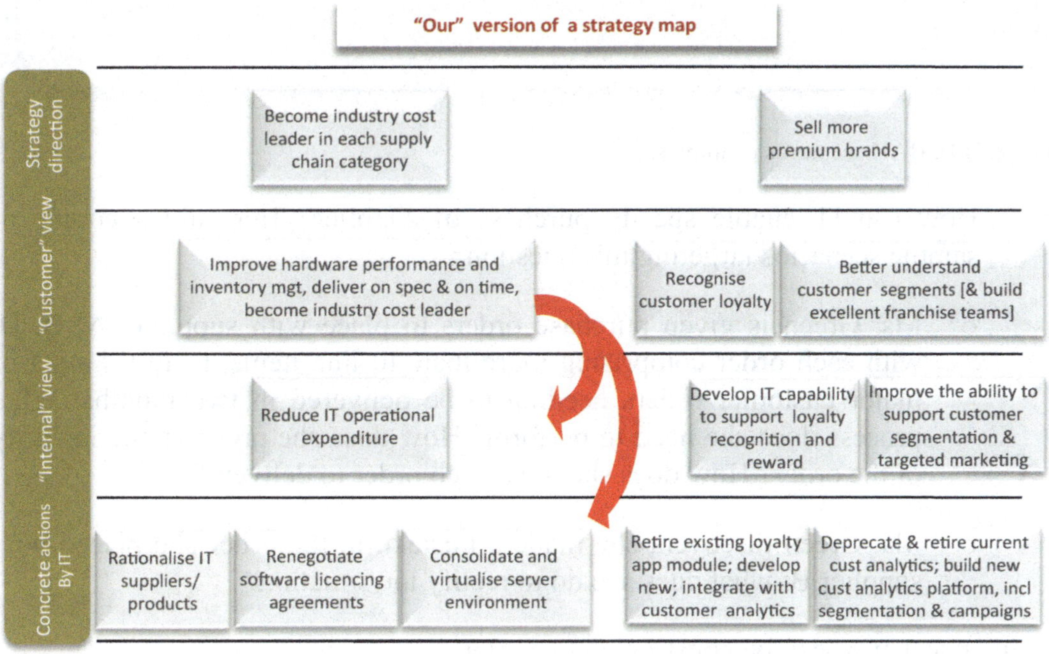

Image (5.9).

This is the same technique as discussed earlier, but is now used to assist in moving from IT's customer view to IT's internal view, moving from tiers 2 and/or 3 to tier 4 of a strategy map.

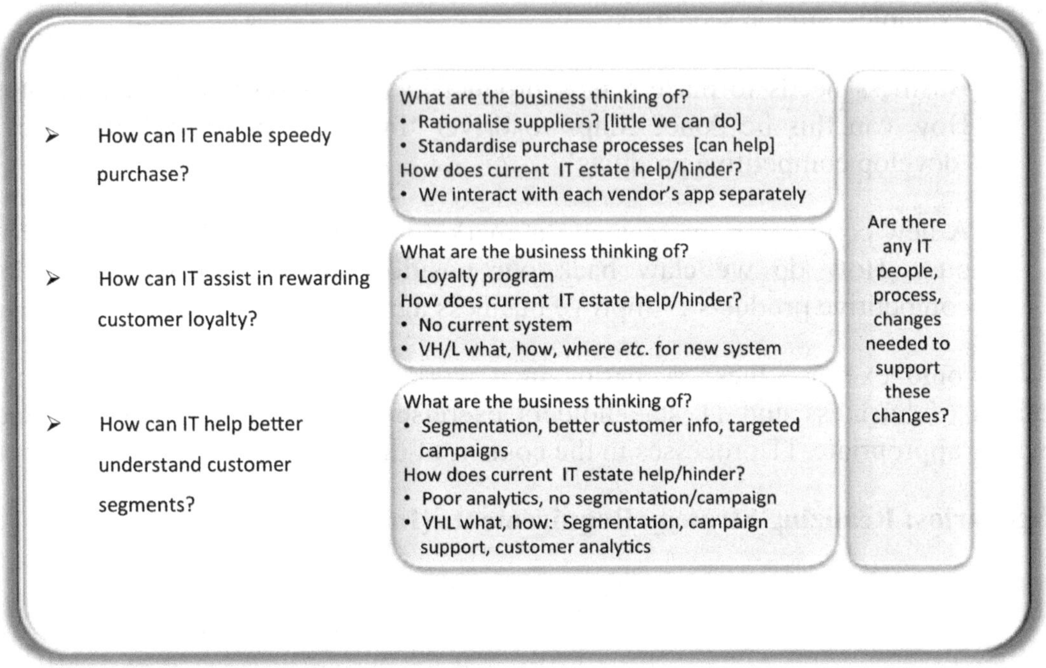

Fig. (5.13). BAU scenarios examples.

- How can IT enable speedy purchase of supplies? Here are a couple of sample scenarios targeting this question.
  - Ms. Green is given purchase orders to place with suppliers A, B, D, with each order comprising more than 40 line items, to fulfill a set of major customer orders needing to be delivered in two months. What process does she need to perform? How does she preserve the integrity of the order? How does she track each order to delivery?
  - Ms. Green discovers she made a mistake in the order she placed with supplier B; what does she do to rectify the situation?

Similar scenarios can be constructed to explore

- How can IT assist in rewarding customer loyalty?

- How can IT help better understand customer segments?

You will notice that the scenarios may now be, as compared to the previous set, more operationally focused. The key to success in the technique is to tailor the scenarios appropriately to the needs of the situation—focus, coverage, mix. As we've said before, the right mix of people exercising scenarios in an appropriate setting helps crystallize what needs to be done.

5.3.3.4. Using Business Services

A few instances of the use of business services in analysis were explored earlier. This section describes more analytical techniques that employ business services.

Systematic Rationalization

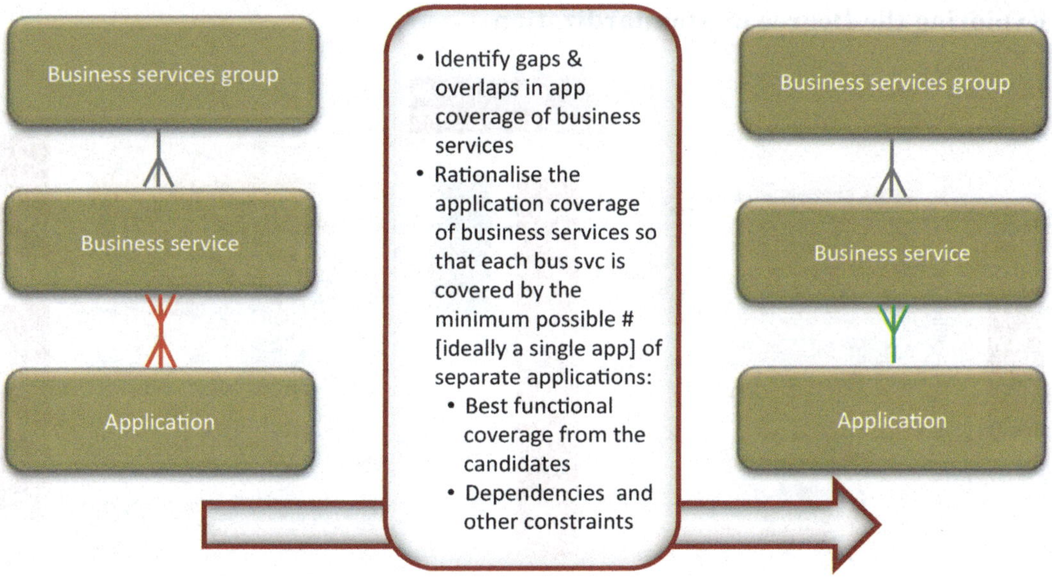

Image (5.10).

Once you have an application to business services mapping (see current state analysis), you may see opportunities for rationalization, *e.g.* the same business service is supported by many applications (Image **5.10**). The case for rationalization would in most cases be supported by the financial analysis: non-discretionary expenditure (support and maintenance) and potential savings through rationalization.

Questions to ask include:

- Which application/s is capable of best supporting the strategic direction as it applies to this group of business services?
- How can the best features of functional coverage be preserved in the post rationalization world?
- How quickly can you recover the rationalization project expenditure through gains in reduced operational expenditure and other business benefits?

Remember, these points need to be covered at a high level; typically, we do not look for exhaustive technical or financial analyses at this stage.

Exploring the Degree of Standardization

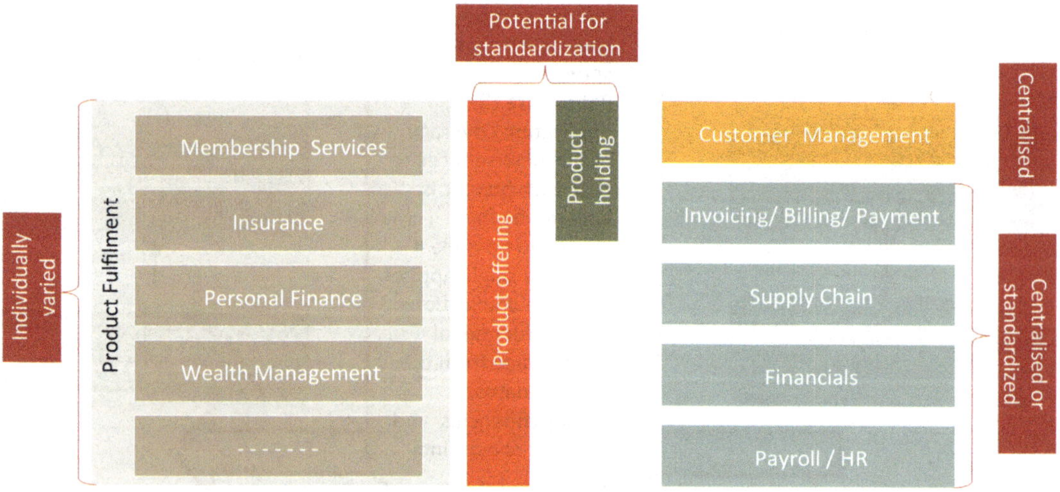

Image (5.11).

In this analysis (Image **5.11**), you first need to develop some insights around grouping business services. For example, we were able to develop this insight at a group of businesses operating in the financial services sector.

Across the various businesses of the group, there are:

- Product offerings encompassing business services in product design, deployment, retirement, product lifecycle management: banking products, insurance products, *etc.*

- Product holdings: that is, the intersection between the customer and the product, such as my insurance policy, my bank account, my superannuation account, *etc.*

- Product fulfillment, which is how the business fulfills its obligations associated with each product: claims, policy discounts, superannuation income streams, *etc.*

- Other: finally, groups of business services such as customer management, supply chain, *etc.*, shown on the right side of the figure are self-explanatory business functions.

This grouping presents a common framework into which the business services of each business unit can be mapped. Once this mapping is complete, we have the basis for a number of interesting cross-business discussions.

For instance, potential commonalities—lost under the business-unit specific representation of business services—may begin to emerge (Image **5.12**). There are obvious synergies and business benefits in all businesses centralizing their (hitherto) individual customer bases: upselling, cross-selling, loyalty, discounts, *etc.* There is potential to standardize certain ERP functions, such as common chart of accounts, single set of payroll/HR processes; and less obviously, potential to standardize supply chain as well as invoicing/payment business services, and so on. Potential may exist in the product space for some degree of commonality and standardization; worth exploring. There is however very little standardization possibilities in product fulfillment, since they necessarily are distinct (virtually none in our example). Another evidentiary factor to bring to this type of discussion is the business differentiation/impact classification of the business services: along with functional similarity, consider if the business service is a high differentiator. If this is the case, there is more of a business case to leave business-unit specific variations as they are, and *vice versa.*

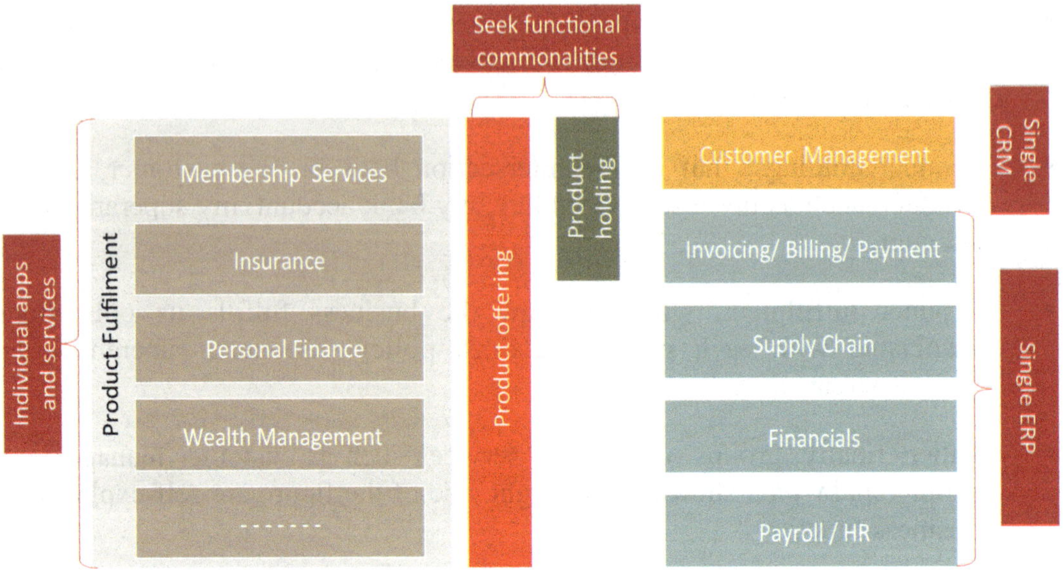

Image (5.12).

Once the business services discussion has reasonably progressed, you can bring application support options (and their relative cost profiles) to the table:

1. Single instance of the application and data supporting all consumers; for example, a single CRM engine for customer management.

2. Single application (or application product) that is replicated: application functions are the same in each replicated instance, but they serve distinct pools of data, for example for supply chain, invoicing/payment in the different business units.

3. Completely different applications servicing their distinct data pools (of course the 'space' between options 2 and 3 is a continuum).

Another interesting conversation here is one around metadata; not data types, but the business definitions of potentially common data. For example, a basic question such as "what is your definition of a 'customer'?" may yield different answers from the different business units: Each business unit may have a distinct definition for customer, and these definitions may not necessarily align.

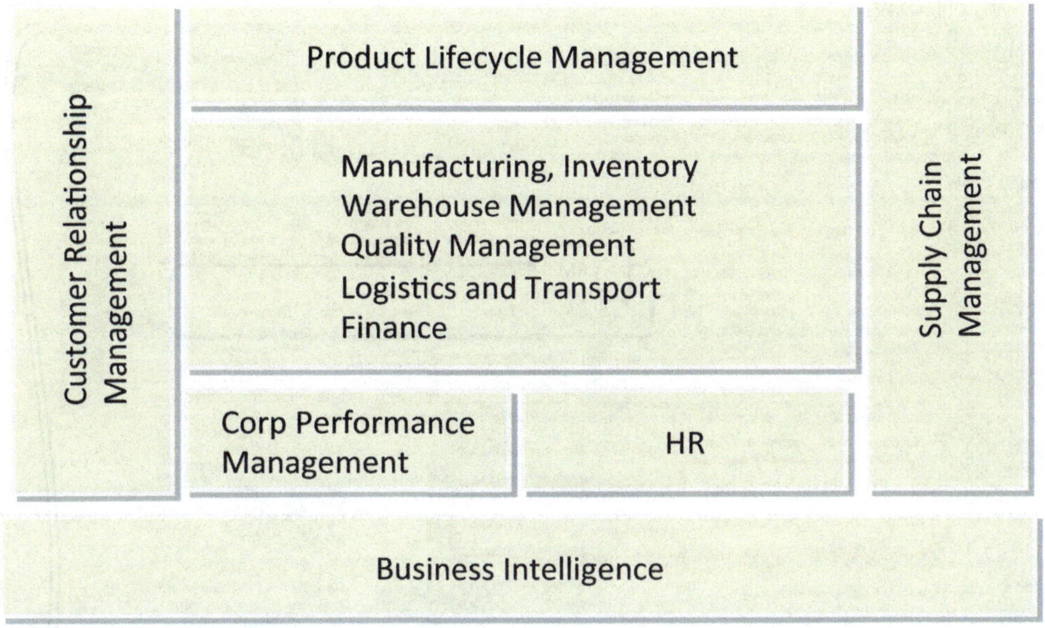

Fig. (5.14). Alternative business grouping.

Here is another way of grouping business services that is similar in concept to the one above but obviously suited to a different industry vertical (Fig. **5.14**).

Application Boundary Analysis

A related concept is application or service cluster boundary analysis: what clusters of business services form a boundary for provisioning *via* a single application or an application module? This is an essential technique in Greenfield situations, but can also be useful in existing IT estates, where any form of re-configuration of the estate is being considered. The figure below shows a logical cluster for provisioning *via* a CRM application, a Product Management cluster, and a Policy Servicing cluster (Fig. **5.15**).

The technique is significant from a service oriented architecture (SOA) perspective too: the 'application' boundary is nothing more than boundaries between clusters of SOA services. Interaction between clusters is strictly by service invocation, *via* an Enterprise Service Bus (ESB). Within a cluster though, tighter coupling is permitted and service internals may communicate with each other. For example a customer is created within the CRM service cluster; the

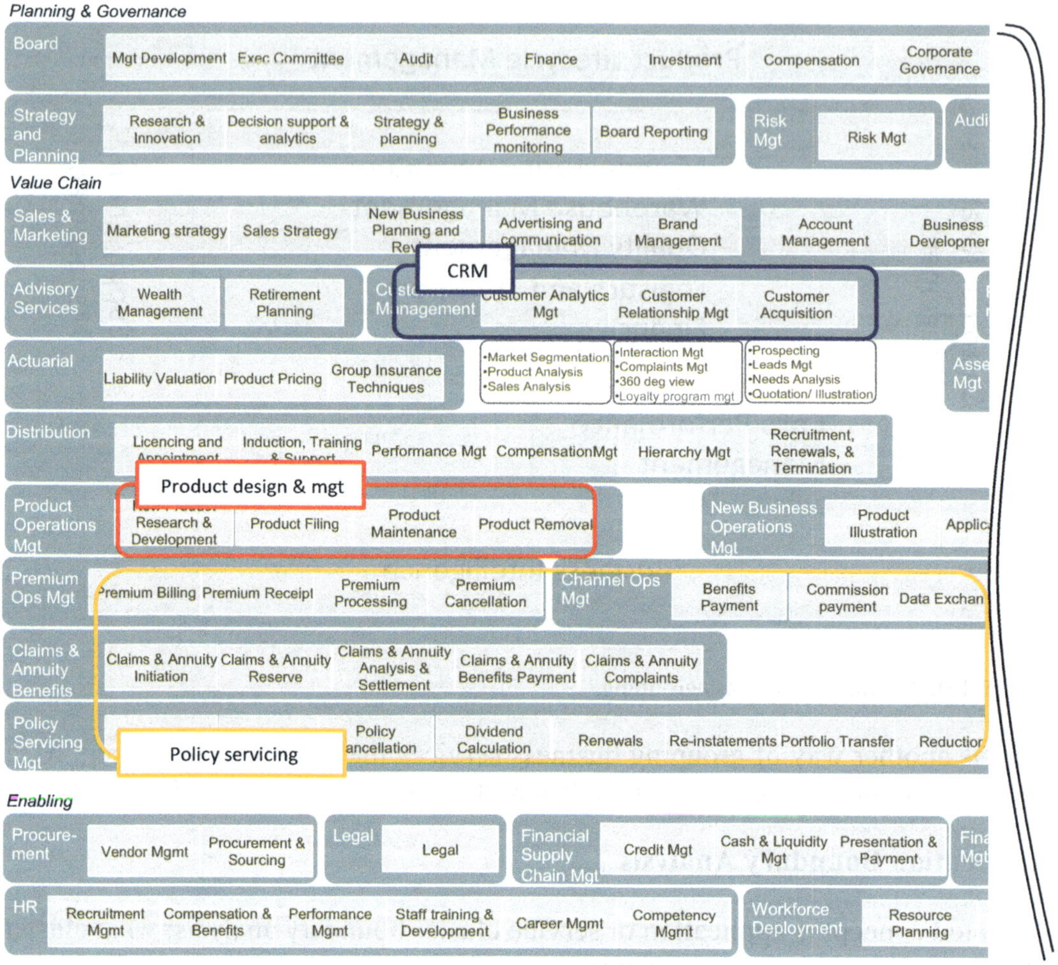

Fig. (5.15). Service cluster boundary analysis.

detail of this customer becomes available to the other services within the CRM service cluster. But services in the billing service cluster will need to make an explicit customer inquiry *via* the ESB.

5.3.3.5. Analysis of Enterprise-Level Architecture Artefacts

We have earlier discussed some enterprise-level artefacts such as business services maps and their significance in this context. The key in referring to enterprise-level architecture artefacts is their relevance and use at this stage of the process: you may have a wide and detailed variety of artefacts, but detail is not your friend in this stage of the game. Only use artefacts that can provide you insights to progress your analysis. Here are some more sample artefacts:

CRUD (Create, Read, Update, Delete) matrix: A matrix of corporate data entities *vs* applications, stating which applications Create, Read, Update, and Delete which data entities (Fig. **5.16**).

Applications

Data Subjects

	Customer	Accounts	Membershi p	Product	Credit Cards	Order	Package	Dispatch
Membershi p Main	CRUD	R	R	R				
ISSP	U	U	CRUD			CRUD		
Edanda Star		U	U	R	R	R		
PASAP		R	R	R				CRUD
Credit Master	U				U	CU	U	
LightFoot	CRUD	CRUD	R	R	R	R		
BigEndian	U	CU			U	CU	R	
Reconciliat ion module		R	R	R				
ODE Remote	U	CU	R	U	U	CU	CU	
SKINS			R	U				
EWEP		U	CU	R		R	R	R

Fig. (5.16). A partial CRUD matrix.

What does a CRUD matrix tell us that is significant for our purposes here?

- Is a corporate entity created by more than one application; updated by more than one application?

- What is the system of record for a corporate entity, or some attributes thereof?
- Is the data propagation between the master and others being managed to preserve consistency?

We can infer

- The integrity of managing master data: two or more applications responsible for the same operation on the same entity *can* point to data integrity issues, if there is no separation by range, type, *etc.*, or a master/slave relationship.
- Fragmentation of master data very likely indicates fragmentation of customer experience, as well as incurring additional maintenance costs.

What is this model below?

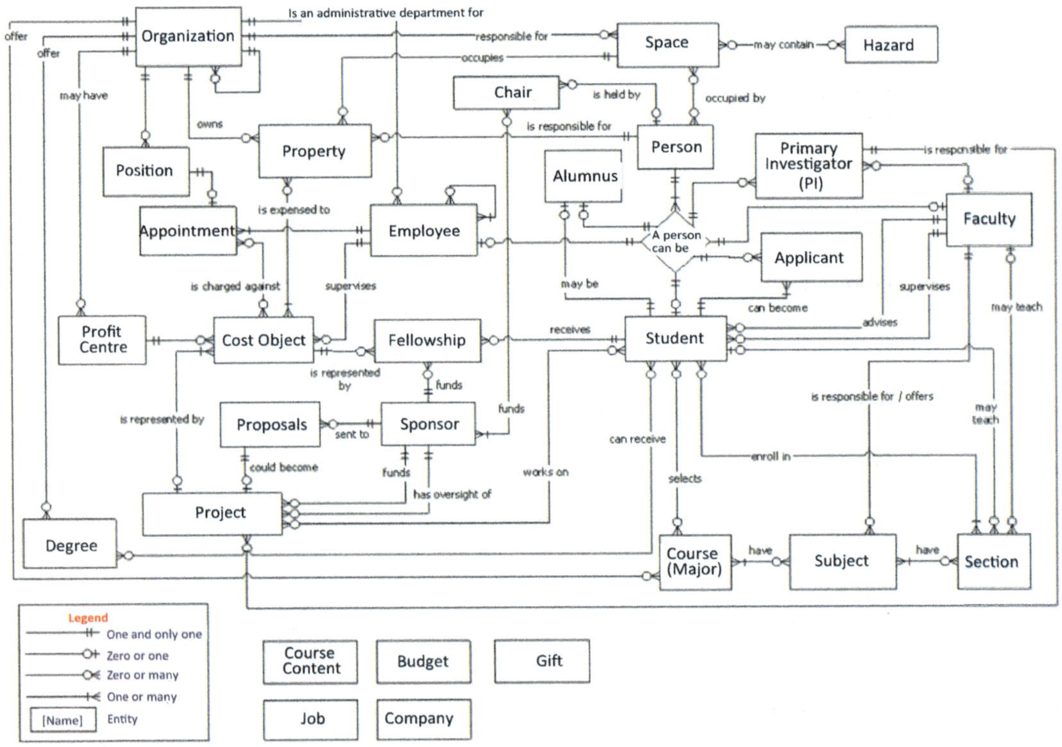

Image (5.13).

An entity-relationship model (Image **5.13**); encompasses many subject areas. It expresses the relationship between data entities of the enterprise. This in itself however, does not give us any information on which applications or business functions are associated with which data. What does it tell us that are useful for what we are currently doing? *Quite frankly, not much.*

Here is an infrastructure diagram (Image **5.14**). This type of artefact can be useful in determining the strengths and limitations of the existing infrastructure in attempting to realize strategic requirements. For instance, assist in analyses such as the determination of the limitations of integration with the supplier systems in exploring supply chain integration.

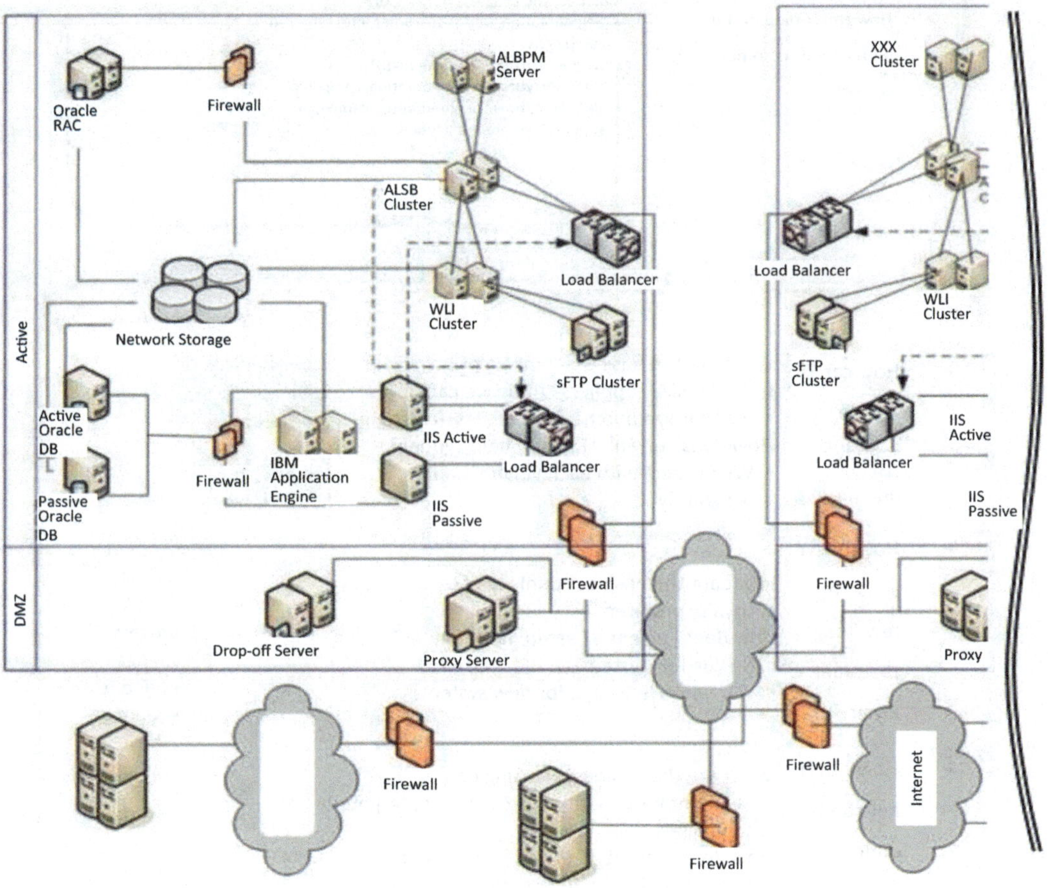

Image (5.14).

5.4. Realising the Strategy – Continued...

With this bag of techniques under our belt, let us revisit strategy realization.

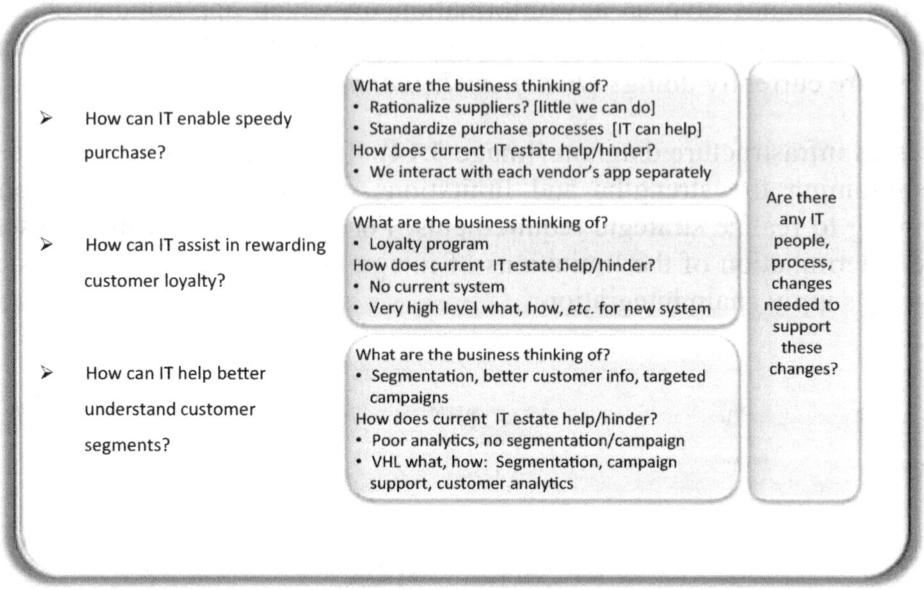
How can IT enable speedy purchase?
What are the business thinking of?
• Rationalize suppliers? [little we can do]
• Standardize purchase processes [IT can help]
How does current IT estate help/hinder?
• We interact with each vendor's app separately
How can IT assist in rewarding customer loyalty?
What are the business thinking of?
• Loyalty program
How does current IT estate help/hinder?
• No current system
• Very high level what, how, *etc.* for new system
How can IT help better understand customer segments?
What are the business thinking of?
• Segmentation, better customer info, targeted campaigns
How does current IT estate help/hinder?
• Poor analytics, no segmentation/campaign
• VHL what, how: Segmentation, campaign support, customer analytics
Are there any IT people, process, changes needed to support these changes?

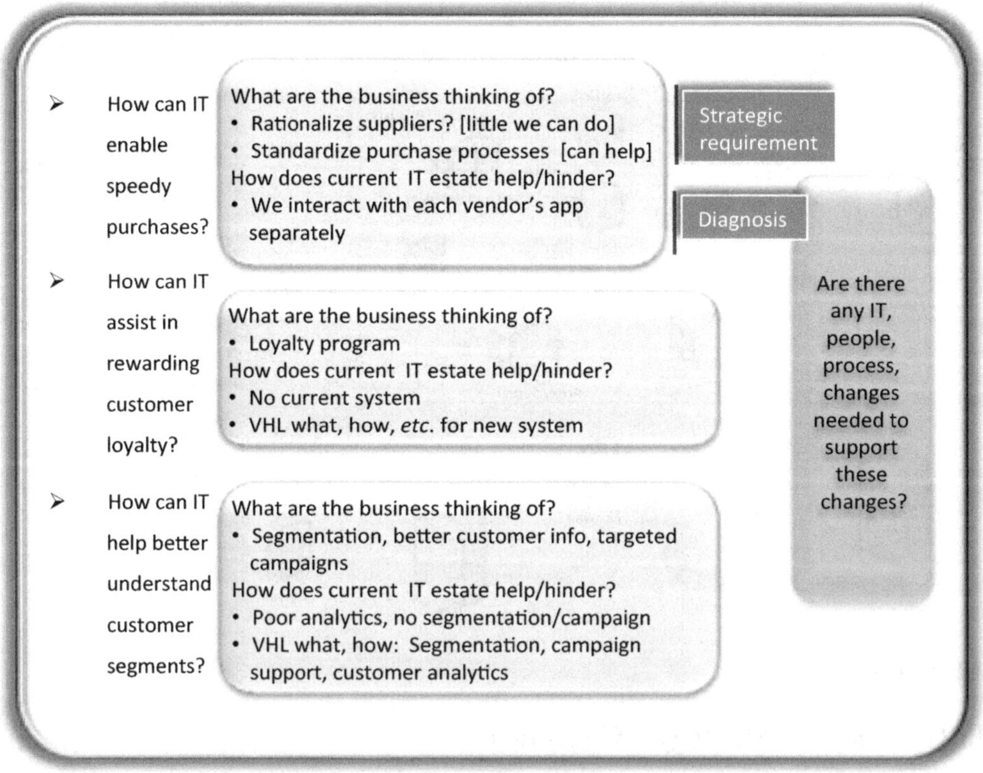
How can IT enable speedy purchases?
What are the business thinking of?
• Rationalize suppliers? [little we can do]
• Standardize purchase processes [can help]
How does current IT estate help/hinder?
• We interact with each vendor's app separately
Strategic requirement
Diagnosis
How can IT assist in rewarding customer loyalty?
What are the business thinking of?
• Loyalty program
How does current IT estate help/hinder?
• No current system
• VHL what, how, *etc.* for new system
How can IT help better understand customer segments?
What are the business thinking of?
• Segmentation, better customer info, targeted campaigns
How does current IT estate help/hinder?
• Poor analytics, no segmentation/campaign
• VHL what, how: Segmentation, campaign support, customer analytics
Are there any IT, people, process, changes needed to support these changes?

Image (5.15).

Suppose we have the following findings (uncovered through a workshop with business and IT SMEs) for the first bullet (enabling speedy purchases) of the figure above:

- We interact with each vendor application separately
- We then need to update our supply management systems with order and reference numbers; this may result in changes to expected cost and delivery information
- Vendor # 7 has system limitations on accepting orders larger than 10000 widgets; need to split orders artificially
- Vendor # 3 and 5 applications/ connections unreliable; problem not at our end; average of about 4 outages per month
- Impact assessment by business and IT: Current efficiency at 50% industry norm; significant loss of staff opportunity cost; average of 40% delays in deliveries directly attributed to purchasing problems
- Recommendations (joint business + IT): one Powerpoint slide
    - Implement a supplier gateway that interfaces to our current supply management application; all suppliers required to interface directly with it
    - Rationalize suppliers. Negotiate on price as well as ability to alleviate current problems (interfacing, order size, *etc.*)
    - Standardize and streamline ordering process
    - Expected benefit; expected cost

The above figure (Image **5.15**) and workings illustrate a path from strategic requirement to realization. In rationalizing suppliers and standardizing purchase processes as a means of enabling speedy purchases, we have identified some major bottlenecks stifling productivity. A supplier gateway (a business driven IT initiative) has been proposed; also proposed is to use this (supplier ability to integrate with a supplier gateway) as one lever in supplier rationalization negotiations. We observe here the synergy between IT and business in realizing this strategy requirement.

This is an illustration. In another setting a different path may be taken—see below for another example. A few pointers here:

- Be careful of preconceptions: IT's preconceptions of what is needed are often at variance with what the business actually need. Strangely enough, big ERPs, SOA, are not generally at front of mind for the business stakeholders; rather, they may very well be starved of reliable analytics.

- Relatively small solutions may be found that could have a highly beneficial impact. A search engine with an internal focus could well be an immediate answer, rather than a full-blown knowledge management strategy.

- Do not shirk from thinking through deconstruction scenarios: in this day and age, disaggregating a large and clumsy IT estate can offer great potential. Cloud vendors offer a variety of services, such as infrastructure, platform, application and business process as a service. So, outsourcing may be adroitly done, only targeting appropriate parts of your IT estate. Think ecosystems, rather than monoliths.

    - What parts of the business can someone else do better and cheaper than us?

    - What parts can we do better in collaboration with a partner?

    - What potential things have we not even attempted, that with the support of a partner we can now undertake?

    - What core competencies do we nurture ourselves in-house?

For example:

An insurance company with highest level strategic imperatives to improve operational efficiency, improve product profitability, and enhance brand value decides to

Partner with company A

- Completely outsource its premium processing, which it sees as parts of the business that simply needs to be managed to an SLA (SaaS + business process outsourcing)
- Co-source its claims processing plus supply chain management

process for replacement goods which it sees as conferring some competitive advantage (cloud-based internal systems and co-sourced processes)

Partner with company B

- Provide a mobile-phone based platform for claims assessors which the partner operates and runs

The company focuses internally on

- Product development, marketing, customer relationship management, and analytics

What business/IT initiatives will be needed to accomplish this intent?

This illustrates how relatively monolithic IT estates can fall prey to disaggregation pressures, and how ecosystems can gradually replace command and control structures.

5.5. Developing, Organizing, and Presenting the Findings (Image 5.16)

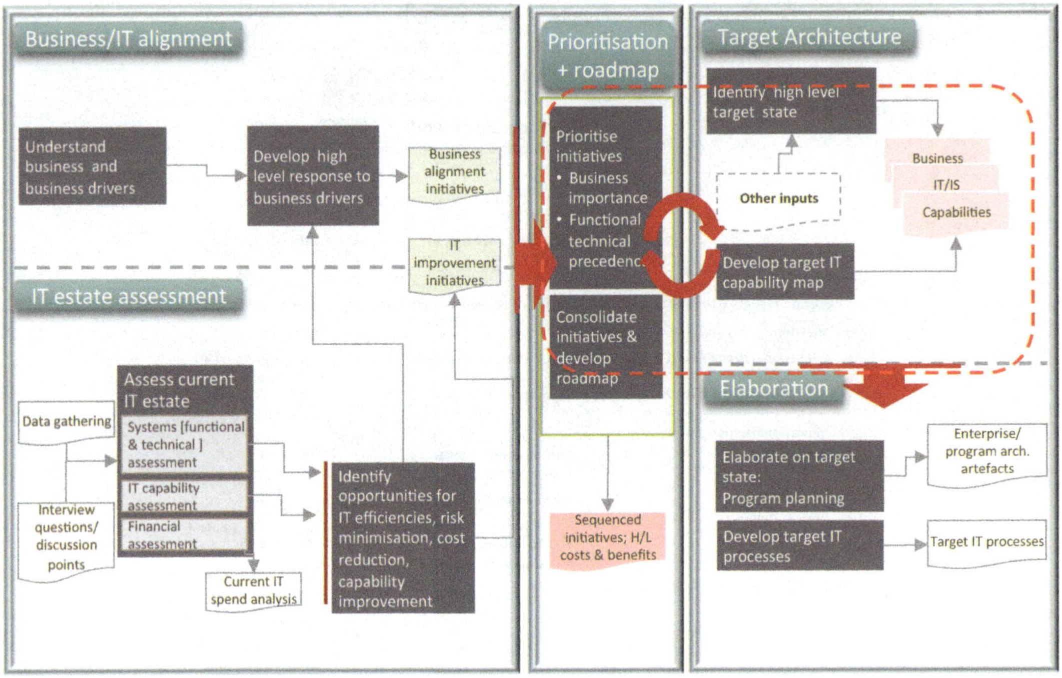

Image (5.16).

We have now done an initial identification of the initiatives that map back to the strategic objectives; *i.e.* we have a draft of 'our' version of the strategy map. Each initiative is scoped at a high level: an initial scoping containing some or all of the descriptive elements in the figure below (Fig. **5.17**).

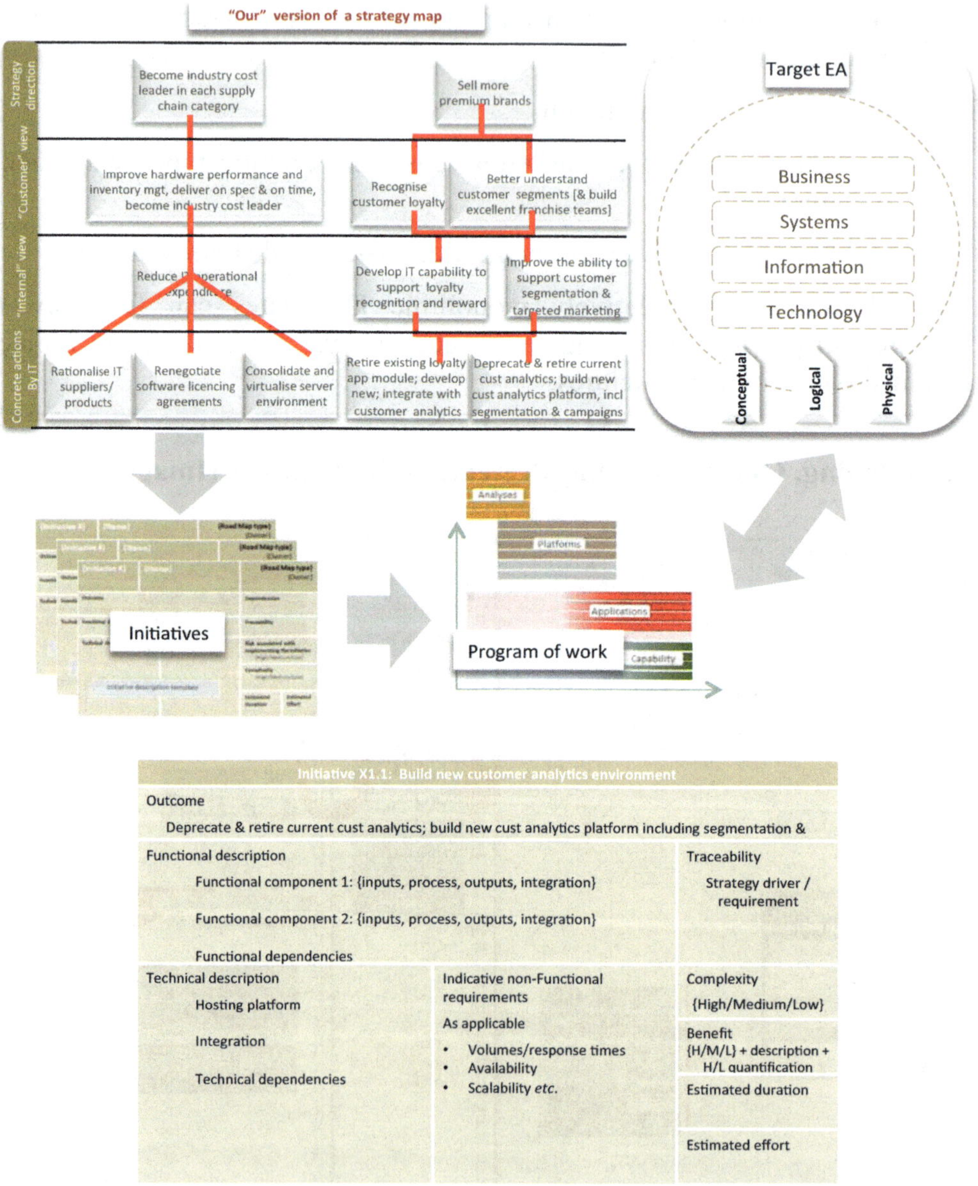

Fig. (5.17). Organising initiatives to form a roadmap plus target state; detail of an initiative template.

Now we need to shape and organize these initiatives to form a roadmap, and then to document the outcomes for stakeholders.

Consolidate and establish precedence relationships among the initiatives:

- The same or similar initiatives may have cropped up in multiple discussions
- There will be dependencies among different initiatives
- There may be precedence requirements that may not have been captured in the initial round

There is generally a precedence hierarchy among initiatives of the following form: say several business units regard provisioning of customer and channel-based analytics as a prime strategic requirement. At the same time, better customer focus and relations is also a strategic requirement. Since this is a group of relatively autonomous business units, they have multiple pools of customers; so we see that a key precedence requirement is to consolidate these pools of customer data into a single cohesive master pool, and then to maintain the integrity of the master as well as any residual individual pools that the business units may decide to maintain. That is, a customer Master Data Management system and process. So a precedence requirement is an MDM system and process, which will require an MDM product. Now if an MDM product is implemented, then once implemented, it can be used to Master other business relevant, but not as urgent, master data. But before the enterprise implements an MDM system it need to undertake an assessment (revisit the feasibility: costs and benefits, risks and constraints), then all going well evaluate and select one.

This thread of dependencies must involve aspects of capability, learning, organizational impediments too. For instance you also realize that the different business units define 'customer' slightly differently, differences that could be material to the lifecycle of a 'customer'. Hence the business data definition for a customer needs to be negotiated and sorted out among the businesses. Equally, master data management across business divisions involves a good deal of cooperation, taking down barriers erected to preserve divisional profitability. The idea that unfettered access to one another's customer bases is ultimately more profitable than maintaining protectionist barriers must be sold to and bought into by the business divisions: the perspective that 'customer' is probably a corporate business responsibility should dawn in the minds of the divisional stakeholders. Your role in facilitating this mind-set transformation may come to the fore when, say in the context of a master data management discussion, the operational implications of sharing customer bases become starkly clear to business stakeholders to whom a common pool of customers was hitherto an abstract concept.

The activities discussed above reveal a sequence: an initial stage of analyses combining proofs of concept where necessary; 'platform' implementation; application development using platform capabilities. It is important that both business and IT stakeholders are engaged in this process: firstly business stakeholders can provide insights that IT alone cannot. Secondly the cost and benefit equation, as well as the timeframe equation, evolve as this process evolves. To mix metaphors, the pot of gold at the end of the rainbow – customer and channel analytics; better customer relations – requires a chain of building blocks. Building and placing these blocks take time and money—it is critical that you carry your stakeholders through this, sometimes painful, exercise.

So the typical form of a roadmap takes the following shape (Image **5.17**):

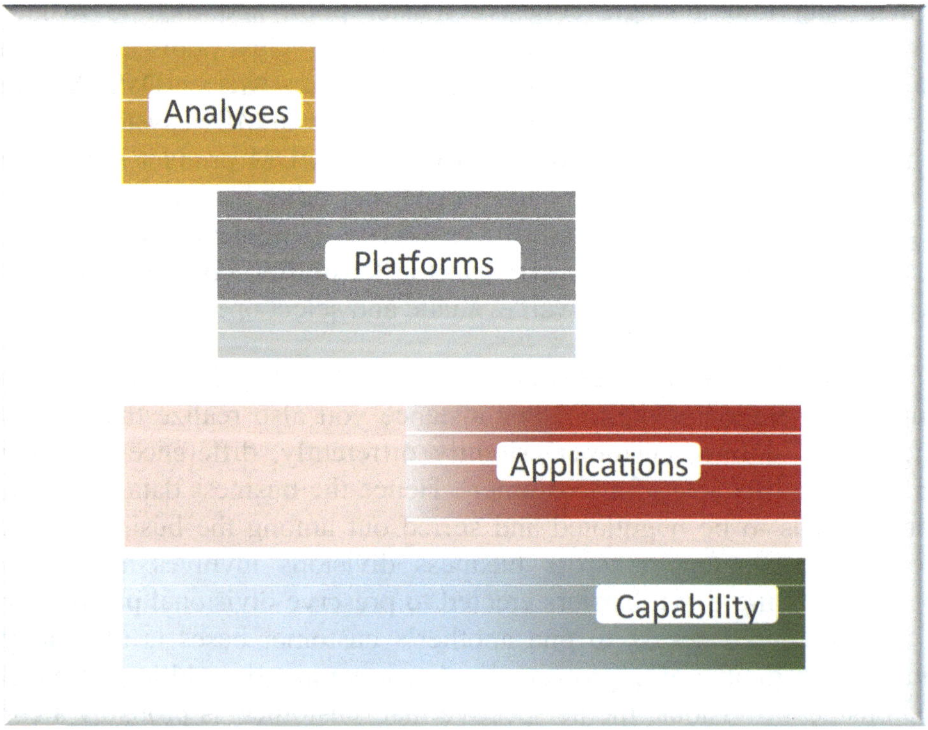

Image (5.17).

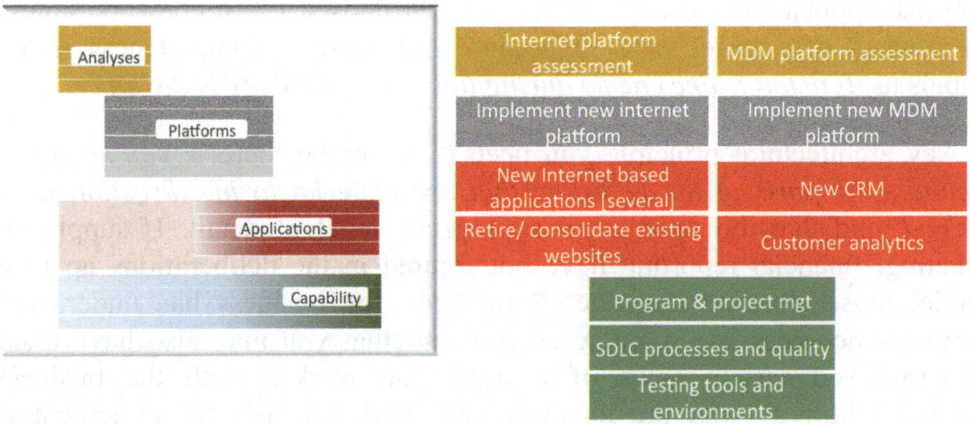

Fig. (5.18). A roadmap example.

Analyses of various types would typically signal the beginning of the roadmap; these analyses and proofs of concept would be followed by 'platform' implementations. What is a platform? A platform enables or supports the rapid generation of applications—for example a SOA platform—ESB, registry/repository, development environment, once implemented would support the design, deployment, and operation of services. A master data management platform enables management of not one, but successively to manage various types of master data of interest to the enterprise. Business-driven applications are developed utilizing platform capabilities. IT (and perhaps business) capability improvements are needed to support and sustain the program of change that we identify. The "roadmap example" shown in Fig. (**5.18**) illustrates this narrative.

You will also have noticed that this process of refining and organizing the initial roadmap involves enterprise architecture thinking in the traditional sense. While at the start of Align stage we relied heavily on artefacts of the 'business architecture' category—strategy maps, business services maps and various associated techniques, in consolidating the roadmap we stepped into the more familiar territory of high level application and technical architecture, in analyzing constraints, precedence requirements, and the like. When the need arose we also sketched some early and high-level platform architectures.

There is a vital point to note here: these architectural explorations and analyses took us to places identified to be material to strategic business objectives and imperatives. *That is all*. We have not ventured beyond that architectural terrain. We have not, for example, segued into an enterprise information model or enterprise application architecture because our chosen EA framework states that they are part of a target state, or because our sense of completeness as an EA compels us. *If detail is one enemy during this stage, ideology is the other.*

The key architectural principle you need to remember here is *you need only to illuminate the parts of the IT estate that are material to the direction that has emerged*; and that too only at an appropriate level of detail. If supply chain, marketing, financial reporting have not figured in the deliberations up to now, then let those sleeping dogs lie. Remember, the business has undertaken an enterprise-encompassing strategic assessment (that you may also have assisted) and earmarked certain areas of change; you worked with the business in identifying how IT and the business can work together to implement these changes. Some areas of the business and the IT estate remain undisturbed. There will be time enough later in your career to explore them; perhaps when they come into the business' radar in the next planning cycle. For now, you have limited time and limited resources to shape and present the outcomes of these deliberations; focus on them.

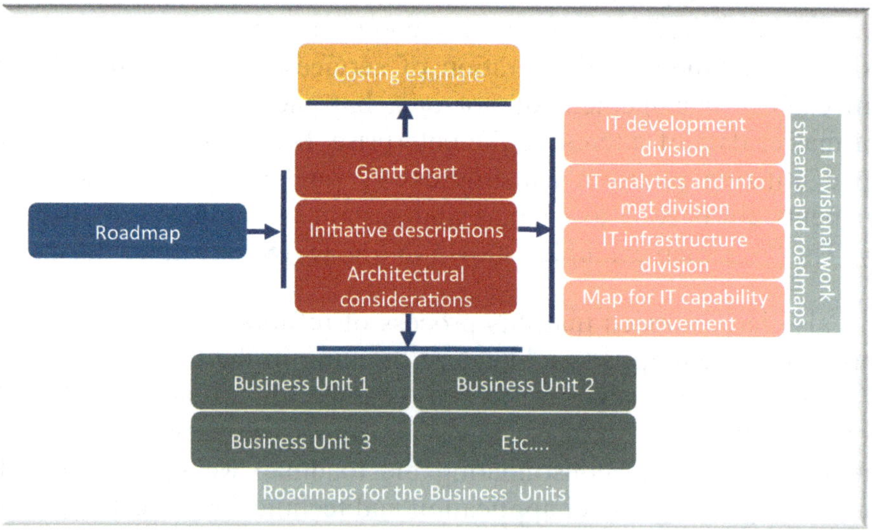

Image (5.18).

The complete roadmap deliverable contains the initiative descriptions and architectural considerations, a Gantt chart or equivalent capturing their precedence relationships and timeframes. A key presentation strategy here is to depict specific views of the complete roadmap relevant to each stakeholder community (Image **5.18**). Each view contains the scope of works relevant to the stakeholder, as well as high-level architectural aspects of the roadmap and target relevant to that stakeholder. There will obviously be overlaps – for example business unit one and two may share two platforms and three application initiatives. But it does not matter; presenting relevant views of the roadmap will cement ownership, especially if you had earlier carried the stakeholders along the roadmap formulation journey.

Typical contents for a Business Unit (BU) roadmap includes

Summary

- Strategy map for the business unit – traceability from corporate objectives through BU objectives to BU/IT initiatives
- High-level Gantt chart, tracing the specific BU initiatives to platforms and analyses
- Precedence relationships presented visually (*e.g.*, application X <= platform A, platform B <= analysis/assessment D)
- Key benefits (qualitative may do) and summary of high level cost estimates, pertaining to the business unit (Initiatives that the BU needs to fund: perhaps the IT initiatives for the BU – depending on enterprise's funding model), plus IT funded initiatives (perhaps the shared platforms – depending on the funding model)

Evidence

- Analysis and narrative describing the development of elements of the Business Unit view of the roadmap
- Evidence leading to roadmap development
    - Business services maps and heatmaps
    - Business service coverage by applications
    - Summary of current state assessment conclusions relevant to the business unit
    - New application boundary analysis/ centralization/decentralization analysis

- *etc.*

Detail

- Initiative descriptions – typically one PowerPoint slide per initiative

Typical contents for an IT divisional unit roadmap includes

Summary

- High-level Gantt chart, highlighting the specific initiatives relevant to the division – including dependent initiatives (*e.g.* infrastructure initiatives relevant to the Information Management division); also the appropriate capability improvement initiatives

Evidence and detail

- Platform architectural sketches and descriptions relevant to the IT division: *i.e.* EDW/Data mart platforms; ETL platform for the information management division
- Architectural considerations relevant to the division's set of initiatives
- Precedence relationships relevant to the IT division

5.6. Align Stage – Wrap Up

We have now developed and presented the Align stage outcomes to the stakeholders, and if we carry them through this process as we have explained in this Chapter, stakeholder approval should not pose a problem[1] – indeed, the pendulum may well have swung towards their enthusiastic engagement (their enthusiasm will of course be tempered by the delivery and business satisfaction track record of the IT division).

[1]The decision makers will have been across what was happening as the Align process progressed from identifying direction and focus [how IT can support what the business seeks] to the roadmap to the high level costs and benefits and there will have been no surprises at the end; under these circumstances stakeholder approval usually ceases to be a large hurdle and becomes more in the nature of a step in the process.

5.6.1. Revisiting the Artefacts

At the end of this 'Align' stage, what enterprise architecture artefacts have we produced?

Let us look to the Zachman framework to give us a frame of reference. The Zachman framework is regarded by many as providing the most comprehensive classification and coverage of enterprise architecture content. Let us map the outputs of this Alignment endeavor against the Zachman framework. The illustrations below display this mapping (Figs. **5.19-5.22**).

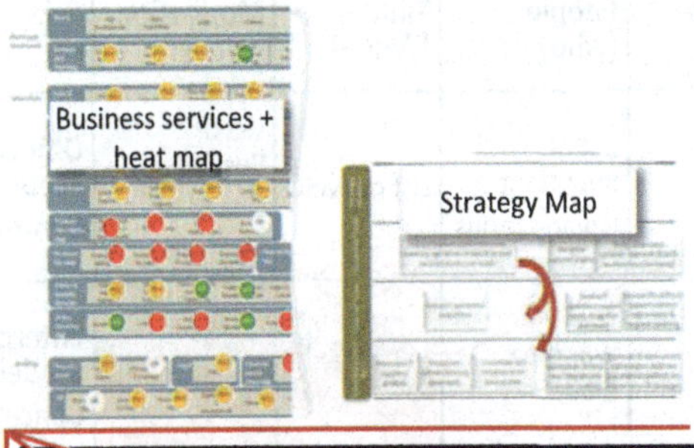

	Entities (What)	Activities (How)	Locations (Where)	People (who)	Time (When)	Motivation (Why)	
Planner	List of things important to the business	List of Core Business processes	List of Business Locations	List of important Organisations	List of events	List of Business Goals/ Strategies	**Objective/ Scope Contextual**
Owner	Conceptual Data/Object Model	Business process Model	Business Logistics System	Workflow Model	Master Schedule	Business Plan	**Enterprise Model Conceptual**
Designer	Logical Data Model	System Architecture Model	Distributed Systems Architecture	Human Interface Architecture	Processing Structure	Business Role Model	**System Model Logical**
Builder	Physical Data Model	Technology Design Model	Technology Architecture	Presentation Architecture	Control Structure	Rule Design	**Technical Model Physical**
Sub-contractor (Programmer)	Data Definitions	Program	Network Architecture	Security Architecture	Timing Definition	Rule Specification	**Components Out of context**
Functioning Enterprise	Usable Data	Working Function	Usable Network	Functioning Organisation	Implemented Schedule	Working Strategy	**Functioning Enterprise**

Zachman framework

Fig. (5.19). Strategy and business architecture artefacts.

	Entities (What)	Activities (How)	Locations (Where)	People (who)	Time (When)	Motivation (Why)	
Planner	List of things important to the business	List of Core Business processes	List of Business Locations	List of important Organisations	List of events	List of Business Goals/ Strategies	**Objective/ Scope Contextual**
Owner	Conceptual Data/Object Model	Business process Model	Business Logistics System	Workflow Model	Master Schedule	Business Plan	**Enterprise Model Conceptual**
Designer	Logical Data Model	System Architecture Model	Distributed Systems Architecture	Human Interface Architecture	Processing Structure	Business Role Model	**System Model Logical**
Builder	Physical Data Model	Technology Design Model	Technology Architecture	Presentation Architecture	Control Structure	Rule Design	**Technical Model Physical**
Sub-contractor (Programmer)	Data Definitions	Program	Network Architecture	Security Architecture	Timing Definition	Rule Specification	**Components Out of context**
Functioning Enterprise	Usable Data	Working Function	Usable Network	Functioning Organisation	Implemented Schedule	Working Strategy	**Functioning Enterprise**

Zachman framework

Fig. (5.20). Roadmap artefacts.

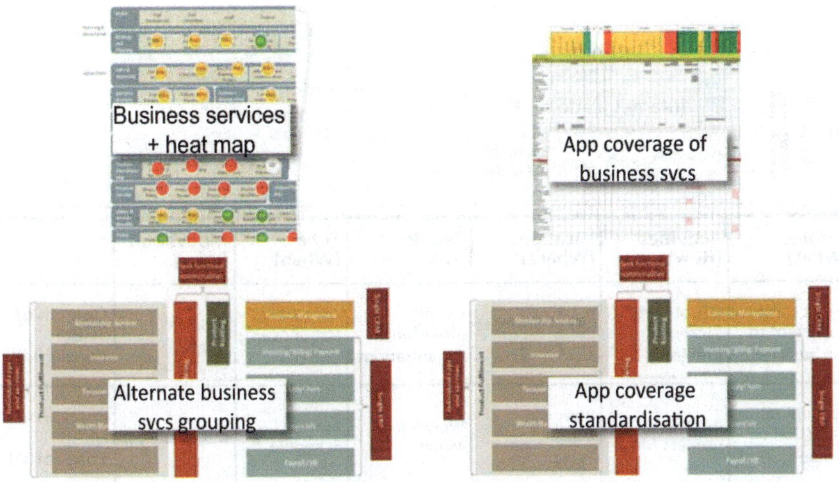

	Entities (What)	Activities (How)	Locations (Where)	People (who)	Time (When)	Motivation (Why)	
Planner	List of things important to the business	List of Core Business processes	List of Business Locations	List of important Organisations	List of events	List of Business Goals/ Strategies	**Objective/ Scope Contextual**
Owner	Conceptual Data/Object Model	Business Process Model	Business Logistics System	Workflow Model	Master Schedule	Business Plan	**Enterprise Model Conceptual**
Designer	Logical Data Model	System Architecture Model	Distributed Systems Architecture	Human Interface Architecture	Processing Structure	Business Role Model	**System Model Logical**
Builder	Physical Data Model	Technology Design Model	Technology Architecture	Presentation Architecture	Control Structure	Rule Design	**Technical Model Physical**
Sub-contractor (Programmer)	Data Definitions	Program	Network Architecture	Security Architecture	Timing Definition	Rule Specification	**Components Out of context**
Functioning Enterprise	Usable Data	Working Function	Usable Network	Functioning Organisation	Implemented Schedule	Working Strategy	**Functioning Enterprise**

Zachman framework

Fig. (5.21). Business and application architecture artefacts.

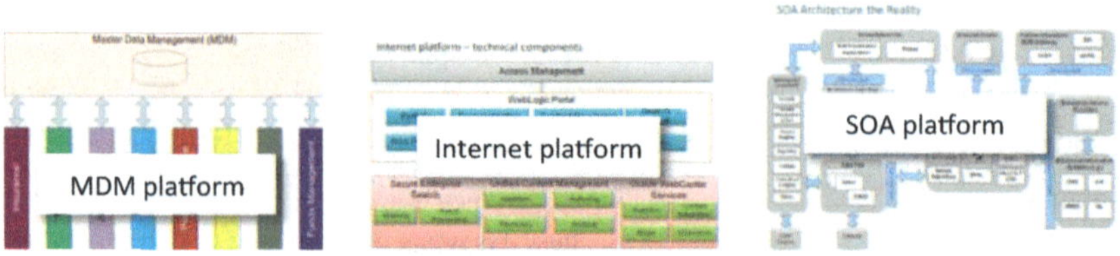

	Entities (What)	**Activities (How)**	**Locations (Where)**	**People (who)**	**Time (When)**	**Motivation (Why)**	
Planner	List of things important to the business	List of Core Business processes	List of Business Locations	List of important Organisations	List of events	List of Business Goals/ Strategies	**Objective/ Scope Contextual**
Owner	Conceptual Data/Object Model	Business process Model	Business Logistics System	Workflow Model	Master Schedule	Business Plan	**Enterprise Model Conceptual**
Designer	Logical Data Model	System Architecture Model	Distributed Systems Architecture	Human Interface Architecture	Processing Structure	Business Role Model	**System Model Logical**
Builder	Physical Data Model	Technology Design Model	Technology Architecture	Presentation Architecture	Control Structure	Rule Design	**Technical Model Physical**
Sub-contractor (Programmer)	Data Definitions	Program	Network Architecture	Security Architecture	Timing Definition	Rule Specification	**Components Out of context**
Functioning Enterprise	Usable Data	Working Function	Usable Network	Functioning Organisation	Implemented Schedule	Working Strategy	**Functioning Enterprise**

Zachman framework

Fig. (5.22). Application architecture artefacts.

So the main artefacts produced in this phase have found homes within the Zachman framework (Figs. **5.19-5.22**), in levels 1, 2, and 3. A somewhat surprising result is that the schedule aspects of the roadmap artefacts too have found a place in the framework. Moreover, current state assessment results can also be mapped to the motivation column of the framework, as part of the underpinning for the business goals and plan.

CHAPTER 6

Elaborate

Abstract: The align stage assists with the clarification of business objectives, to produce a set of high level initiatives which have in principle support by the stakeholders. This, "Elaborate" chapter now picks up the thread to provide the technical leadership for planning the transition represented by the identified initiatives. This advances the EA programme from alignment to elaboration: here is where we elaborate on the architecture to a level of detail that will support navigating the organisational journey that we have identified.

Keywords: Capability improvement, EA roadmap, EA stage deliverables, Elaborate stage, IT initiatives, mapping against frameworks, transformation program, transition plan.

6.1. Elaborate Stage Context: Preparing the Transition Plan

We have

- Assisted the business identify and clarify where the enterprise needs to go, and how IT can assist getting there.
- A set of business strategy-aligned initiatives, described at a high level with their costs and benefits; developed jointly by IT and the business, plus other useful artefacts.
- Obtained business and IT stakeholders' qualified approval and support. They have agreed in principle, and agreed to provide funding for a transition planning exercise.

Depending on the context, the scope of work identified in the Align stage may be large or small. It may contain a mix of:

- Business initiatives with a very small (if any) IT component
- Business plus IT initiatives
- IT initiatives with a very small (if any) business component. However, they all will have a business *impact* and a business *benefit*; hence their justification

Inji Wijegunaratne, George Fernandez & Peter Evans-Greenwood

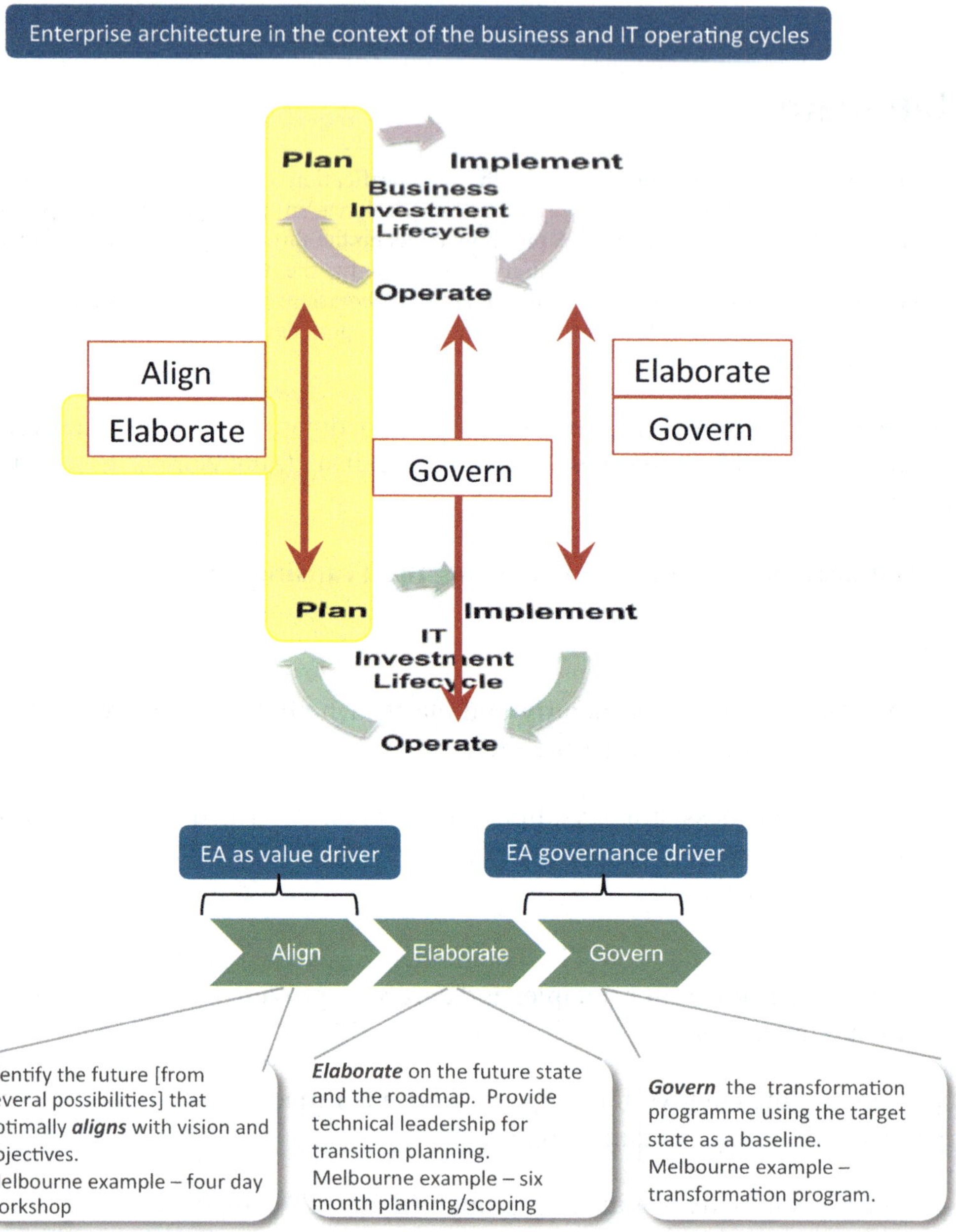

Image (6.1).

This stage is where you, as the enterprise architect, provide technical leadership in planning the program of work – the transition plan (Image **6.1**); this is the six month planning and scoping exercise that we discussed in Melbourne city planning.

This is where the Enterprise Architect passes the baton to the Program Architect as the focus shifts from enterprise-level artefacts to program-level artefacts.

In transition planning, we scope the initiatives identified in the Align stage in greater detail and estimate the most efficient implementation path. We need to configure the individual initiatives into work-streams; if already attempted in Align, we need to revisit and if necessary reconfigure them. Of course this detailed planning stage contains project planning activities that are not the architect's responsibility – but our ability to provide technical leadership is key: Indeed the architect's (enterprise and program architect) main responsibility during this stage *is* to provide technical leadership.

6.1.1. Structure and Responsibilities

The main setting has now moved from an assignment with strong links to business strategy development, to the confines of a project or program. That said, the planning effort and timeframe (and the organizational structures and relationships within which you undertake the planning effort) depend on the magnitude of the intended program – that is the magnitude of the changes scoped in the Align stage outcomes.

We focus in this Chapter on planning for a relatively large program of work, which is obviously the most complex scenario.

The organizational structure and relationships of an elaboration exercise is more structured than in Align, but again can be complex (Image. **6.2**).

In particular, see the dual reporting relationships of the two key architects.

- We have postulated Enterprise and Program Architect (EA and PA) roles—that could well be discharged by the same person—working closely and reporting to a Program Director. EA responsibilities are wider than the program, but intersect the program scope in certain key areas. PA's responsibilities are mainly confined to the program.

- As the program transitions into the execution stages, the EA role will move out of the program into EA governance. The PA role will continue with the program, providing program technical leadership and governance.

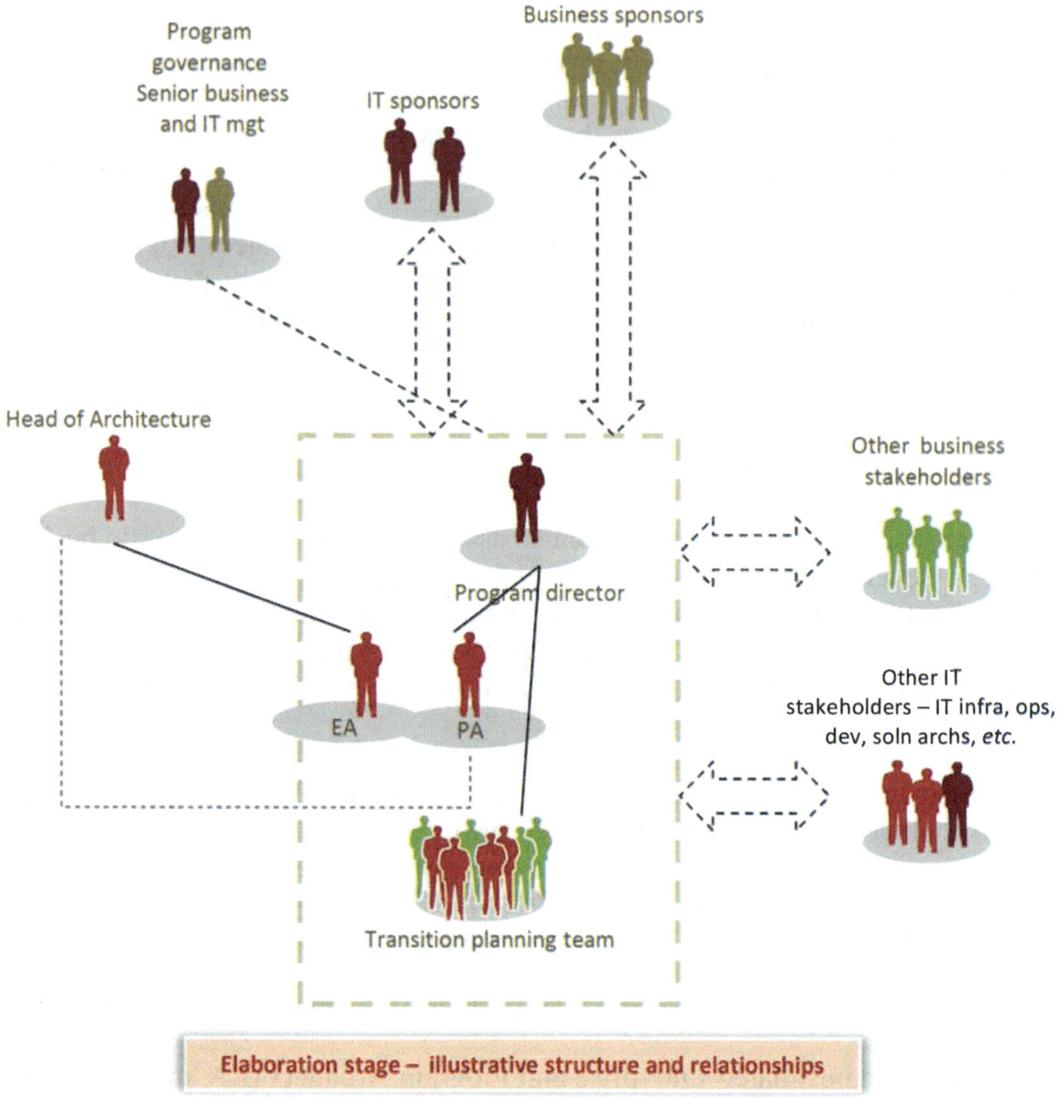

Image (6.2).

A simpler scope of work merits a simpler structure; for example for a smaller company the EA and PA roles may be undertaken by a single person, but it would still be useful to understand the distinction between the two types of responsibilities and the underlying roles associated with each set of responsibilities. A small scope of work may see a more lightweight structure with perhaps a project manager anchoring it, plus a planning team of one or two people including the EA/PA.

6.2. Process: From Alignment to Planning

- What do we have?
  - A set of business strategy-aligned initiatives, described at a high level with their costs and benefits; developed jointly by IT & business
  - An initial take on the dependencies between the initiatives and the nature of their result
  - Some of the following
    - Current state assessment outcomes
    - Business functions/services heat map; application coverage; application heat map
    - Current state architecture artifacts largely as we've found them – the artifacts, their detail, currency *etc.* varies

- What do we need to deliver by the end of this stage?
  - The scope of a set of work-streams [representing the scope of work identified in the initiatives, possibly reconfigured to support efficient implementation]
  - Their precedence relationships
  - Effort, cost, timelines, resourcing for the program of work [supporting the project/program management in deriving them]
  - Costs and benefits identified to a level of detail and rigour
  - A set of architectural artifacts for use in governing the technical aspects of the ensuing project or program of work
  - Key architectural decisions of enterprise significance
  - H/L platform architectures
  - A baselined representation of the overall solution

  The program's individual solutions must align to this
  - Residuals identified in Align but not in transition plan scope

Fig. (6.1). Transition from alignment to planning.

These figures (Figs. **6.1-6.3**) broadly depict the process: in this stage we elaborate on the areas of change that were agreed upon. The Elaborate stage activities can be grouped into two broad parts: Develop a first cut of the workstreams, and elaborate on the workstreams and program plan.

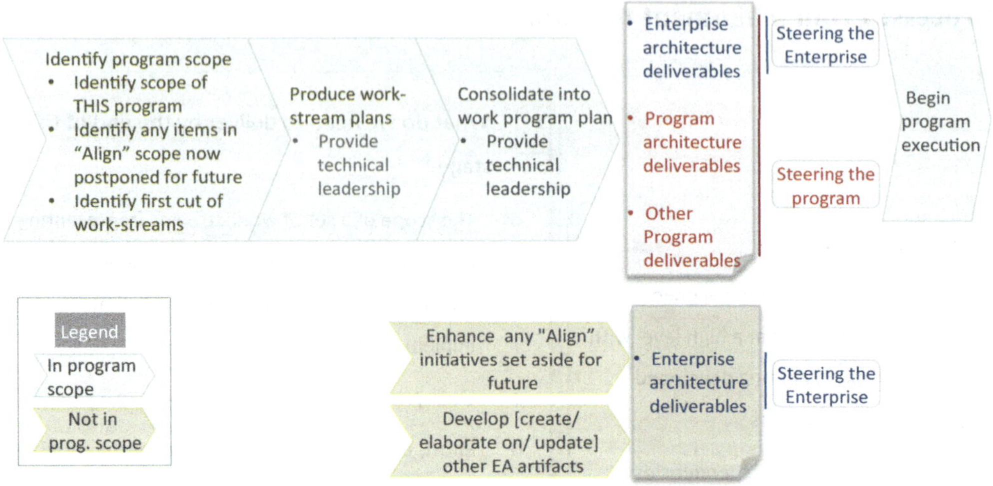

Fig. (6.2). Activities and deliverables.

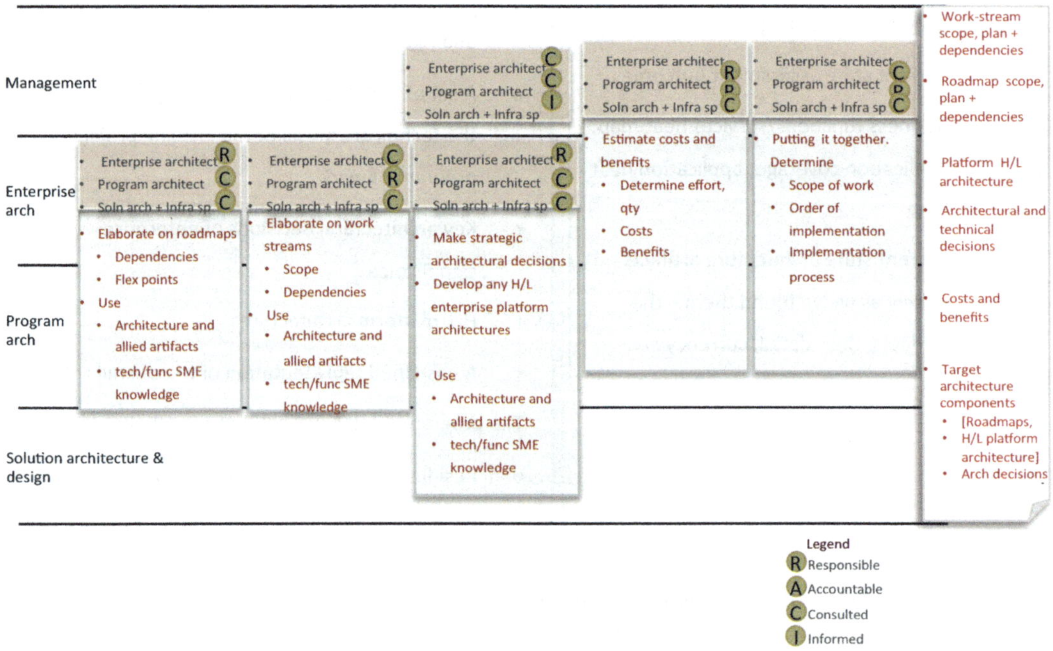

Fig. (6.3). RACI for planning.

There are many non-architecture activities that also happen in program planning stage that we do not discuss; only the activities of interest from an EA and related viewpoints are documented in this Chapter. The "Management" layer of the RACI charts for example will have many actors and responsibilities not addressed in this discussion.

Certain enterprise-level artefacts relevant to the program are developed in this "Elaborate" stage and the EA will take the lead for these activities: for example an integration platform, though initially deployed to service the program, will be rolled out to the enterprise; an enterprise analytical platform will see the initial light of day here. The PA will take the lead in developing program-specific architecture artefacts.

Another aspect to note is that the construction of solution specific artefacts has not yet begun. Creation of individual solution architectures and technical architectures will begin once the program planning stage completes successfully (with the – now much more detailed and rigorous – business case and program budget being approved) and the individual projects are kicked off.

We have also shown some EA activities not in program scope. These may be undertaken only if resource bandwidth permits; the main focus of attention and effort here is the planning for the impending change program.

As we stated earlier, these successively detailed sets of artefacts, compiled at different stages of the process, all fit into categories expressed in EA frameworks such as Zachman or TOGAF; the EA has responsibility personally to create only a small part of these artefacts. But the 'levels' of artefacts—Enterprise, Program, and Solution/Technical—have an overall relationship, with higher levels governing the detail of lower ones.

Where the overall business direction and priorities have been successfully captured, addressed, and bought into (*i.e.* a successfully completed Align stage), maintaining this governance relationship is feasible, although it can still be difficult due, for example, to project managers cutting architectural corners due to delivery/budget pressures. Where alignment has not happened, it is virtually impossible – many a time has EAs, after developing technology-driven enterprise architecture end states, watched in bemusement while the organization marches off in a completely different direction and their output is blithely disregarded.

6.3. Content: What we have and what we need

These artefacts depict how the initial identification of initiatives are grouped into work-streams, and the work-stream related planning and 'doing' activities that occur in this stage (Fig. **6.4**). Closely related initiatives are allocated into individual work-streams, for example all the infrastructure related activities are in Work-stream 1,

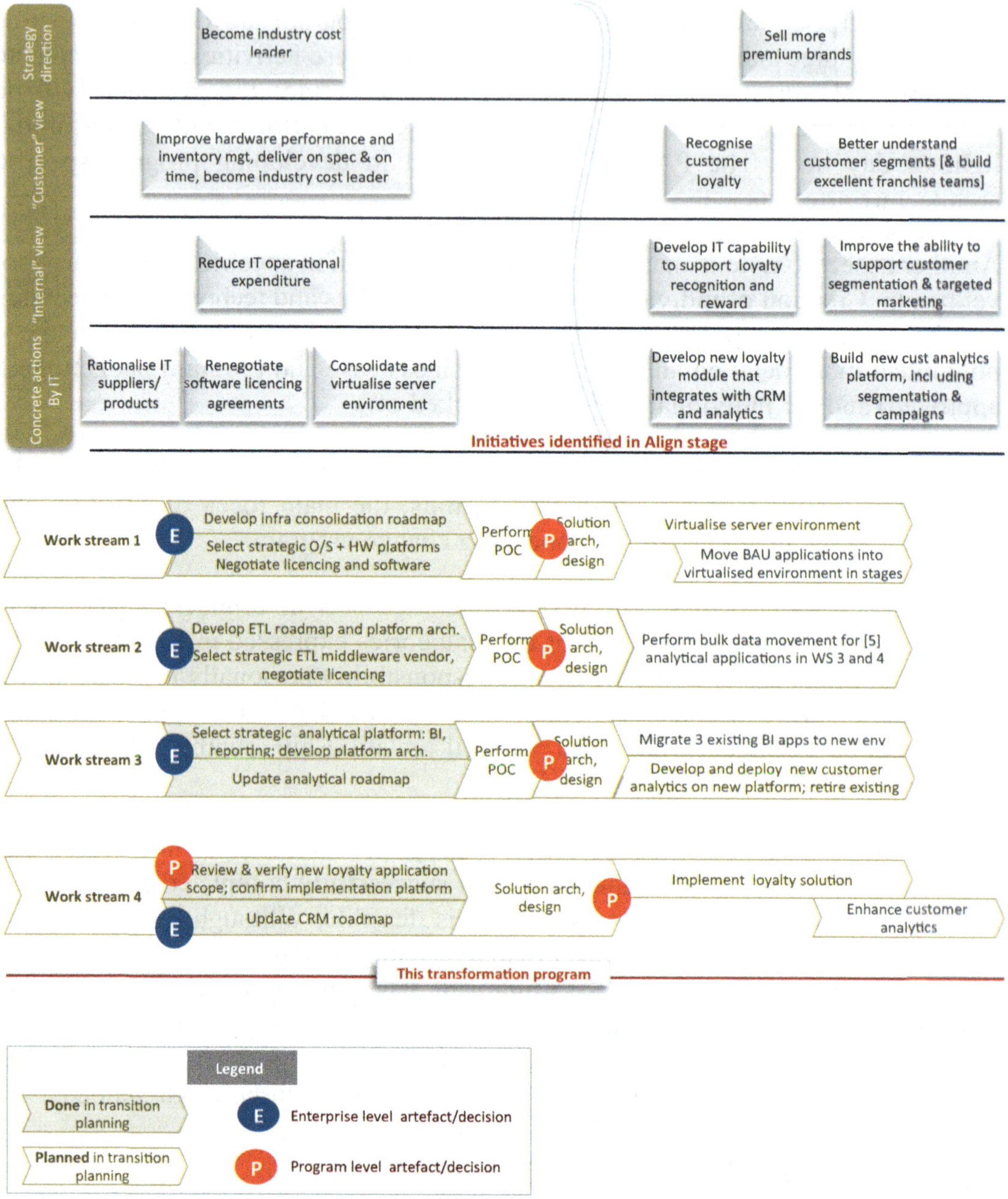

Fig. (6.4). Transformation program and related artefacts.

and so forth. For each work-stream, there are certain 'doing' tasks we need to undertake, such as developing platform architectures, developing or elaborating on roadmaps, and generally assisting the program manager in technical and architectural decisions that need to be taken now. There are also planning activities – where we plan the program execution stage. These planning activities include

- Specifying work-stream (and program) scope
- Developing work-stream and program plans including the order of implementation and dependencies
- Developing detailed cost benefit analyses and business case/s
- Developing a program architecture, containing the aspects of platform architectures and roadmaps (typically of enterprise scope) relevant to the program and how the individual solutions of the program hang together. The Program architecture is at a level higher than the individual solution architectures of the program, and is used to govern the latter as they begin to be developed later in program execution.

6.3.1. Deliverables

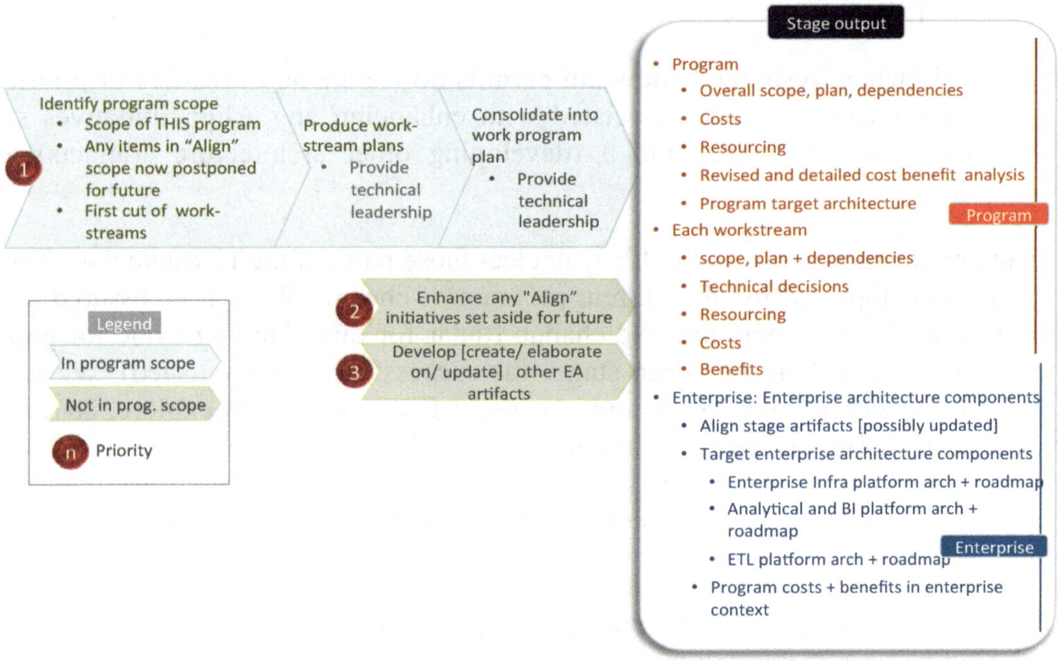

Fig. (6.5). Outcomes/deliverables of Elaborate.

The Stage outcomes are business case/s and detailed program plans. From an architecture perspective, all the architecture artefacts material to program planning will have been done. We have advocated a strategy of only focusing on the architecture that is relevant to the matter at hand – In Align, we counselled to confine our attention and focus on those parts of the IT estate of interest to the business in this cycle; here we take the same tack, but with a slight twist (Fig. **6.5**):

- We elaborate on artefacts relevant to the program as the primary priority
    - Elaborate on Program level artefacts.
    - Take the opportunity to elaborate on artefacts of enterprise scope pertinent to the program. That is, the constructs that will be part of the program but whose scope will exceed that of the program; for example the ETL platform, Analytical platform, SOA platform architectures, and associated roadmaps.
    - Included in the above artefacts are not only the architectures themselves but also the key architecture decisions (why X was decided as the approach and not Y or Z), architectural standards, patterns (and anti-patterns).
- Only where resource bandwidth permits do we attend to matters of priority 2 (architectural work associated with enhancing any Align initiatives set aside for the future) and 3 (developing other architecture artefacts) as shown.

In an architectural sense, we wilfully neglect those parts of the IT estate that is not part of, nor impacted by, the current program of change. We can be assured that these areas did not come into the change Radar for this planning cycle for good reason (assuming that the Align stage was successfully accomplished). We turn the full attention of our scarce and expensive EA resources to explore, analyse, and architecturally prepare those parts of the IT estate that is the focus of the impending changes; we do this within the timeframe that the enterprise requires. Time enough to attend to the other parts later – some of them may well come into focus at the next planning cycle.

We have viewed the time period in which the Align and Elaborate activities occurred through the particular lens of enterprise and IT planning. This was done for the sake of clarity – for presenting a clear thread of reasoning. In a real life situation, though these activities will still command most of the enterprise architect's attention, part of the EA's time and effort will be occupied by events that occur outside of this trajectory. For example an unexpected issue in the Production environment may percolate up through the Service Management staff to the solution architects, who may escalate matters to the EA's domain for a decision, input, or advice.

6.3.2. Capability Improvement

We have left capability improvement to the last, since it could well be the most contentious. In Align we identified certain capability improvements for the IT division. These capability improvement activities, where they have a material impact on program delivery, should become part of the program plan. For example, a new performance testing capability has been identified for the IT division, and two of the identified projects develop performance sensitive systems. There is now a dependency on this capability being established by the time these two projects are ready for testing. An improved integration capability would be another example. If for example a SOA solution is proposed, it is extremely important that the stakeholders recognise that a range of capabilities – from both business and technical perspectives – are required and the level of sophistication of the SOA deliverables matches the capability levels available in the enterprise.

This discussion signals our foray into contentious waters.

Think: How many large IT projects (say in excess of US$ 100M) do you know have succeeded in delivering its original objectives in time and on budget? Most large projects in our experience have failed to deliver on original targets; not marginally, but generally tending towards the abysmal end of the scale. Projects that are not terminated usually manage to save public face only through generous doses of management spin.

The callout below substantiates our view. It references two reports: the first is an article published in an Australian newspaper in the State of Victoria in 2011. The story it tells though is not unique to Australia but is a very common one in the Western world, as we see by the second, which is an analysis of over 5000 IT projects undertaken in 2012 (Image **6.3**).

Delivering large-scale IT projects

Public Sector IT project blowouts – Victoria, Australia

In November 2011 the State Ombudsman (for the State of Victoria in Australia) tabled a report delivering a deeply critical assessment of 10 large public sector information technology projects. The report found:

- The estimated cost of delivering the 10 projects that he examined was a combined $1.44 billion more than originally budgeted
- At the time of tabling the report, the two largest projects, myki (the transport ticketing system) and the Health Department's patient management and finance application, HealthSMART, had been delayed for years and required $600 million more than originally budgeted.
- The Department of Human Services' new Client Relationship Information System and Victoria Police Link database (since abandoned), both tripled in estimated cost
- Other projects cited in the report included the VicRoads Vehicle Registration and Licensing project, Housing Department's management system, the Ultranet online education network for school students and the Justice Department's system to integrate court and tribunal IT.

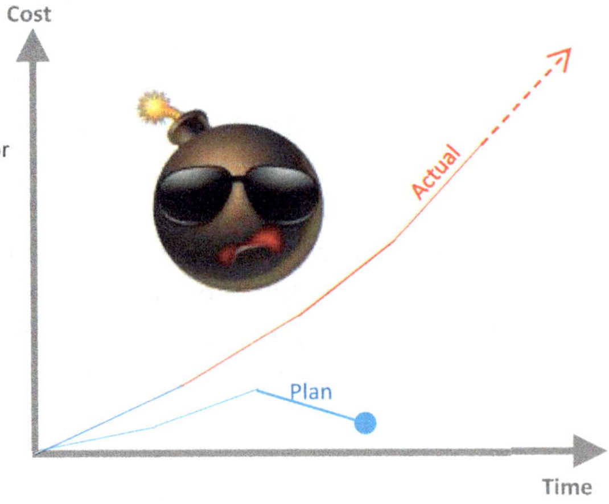

The report identified the following broad categories of problems

- Leadership
- Accountability and governance
- Planning
- Funding
- Probity and procurement
- Project management

Source: "Bungling in state public sector blamed for IT blowouts", Reid Sexton, The AGE newspaper, Victoria, Australia, 24th November 2014

Overruns in large IT projects

A research study conducted in 2012 on more than 5,400 IT projects by the consulting firm McKinsey and the BT Centre for Major Programme Management at the University of Oxford found the following:

- Half of all large IT projects—defined as those with initial price tags exceeding $15 million—massively blew their budgets
- On average, large IT projects ran 45 percent over budget and 7 percent over time, while delivering 56 percent less value than predicted. Software projects carried the highest risk of cost and schedule overruns
- These IT projects, in total, had a cost overrun of a staggering $(US) 66 billion
- 17 percent of large IT projects perform so badly that they can threaten the very existence of the company. These overruns ("Black Swans" - budget overruns of more than 200 percent) occur significantly more often than would be expected under a normal distribution

Source: "Delivering large-scale IT projects on time, on budget, and on value" Michael Bloch, Sven Blumberg, and Jürgen Laartz, McKinsey Insights, October 2012.

Image (6.3).

Why do so many large projects fail to deliver? The exact causes vary from case to case; in any event this is not a eBook on project and program management and this is not the place for a detailed treatment on the subject. It is however crucial to our endeavours that we, as architects, assist in creating a framework for the impending program that has the best possible chance of success. We will therefore discuss a few rules of thumb that and EA will do well to remember and, although not part of an EA's natural patch, must strive to influence.

The obvious answer to the above question is that organisation capability has been found wanting in one or more areas. The actual area or combination of areas may vary – poor selection of product/SI partner; poorly organised contracts with SI partners; governance; poor estimating and unrealistic time/budgets; poor requirements management; poor organisational change management; and so on. However, in the final analysis, these all boil down to some aspect of capability. How can we use this heuristic to better our implementation prospects?

> Here is a cardinal rule on capability: A project, or a program of closely related projects, whose size lies clearly outside the enterprise's zone of familiarity/ comfort has a high risk of failure; larger the disparity, higher the risk.

Enterprises, largely based on their size and corporate history, generally settle into a size range for their IT projects. They are generally comfortable within this range, having developed experience to handle/ manage them through repeated delivery: the run of the mill maintenance, enhancement, and "new" projects. Let us say that, for a particular firm, these projects lie in a size range up to \$ 12M, with a \$12M project being considered a "large" project. However, our Align exercise has uncovered, and obtained in-principle management blessing for, a \$120M organisational transformation programme. *There is a very high risk that this program will fail.*

Faced with this situation, enterprises often resort to a strategy of bringing in external assistance by contracting the delivery to a systems integration partner, or partners – multiple vendor scenarios, with each responsible for a part of the program, are also common.

> Outsourcing program delivery may reduce delivery risk, but by very little.

The vendors may possess requisite capability levels in the core capabilities (*i.e.* design, build, test) to handle a project of $120M. However, they will need to interface with your enterprise on many fronts – organisational change management, requirements management, dependency management, testing, release management, procurement; the list goes on – and the enterprise's level of capability on these fronts still remains the same; at levels suitable for projects under $12M. Moreover, unless they are incumbent service providers, the vendors are new to your organisational context and idiosyncrasies. We must also acknowledge that each vendor adds complexity to the mix, and also that the vendor represents a party whose objectives are not entirely aligned with that of the client. At a high level then, these are some of the reasons that militate against SI partners reducing large chunks of delivery risk.

So what can be done?

Use the organisational heuristic as the main yardstick in organising the program of work:

> The program of work will have the best chance of success if it can be divided into independent pieces of work, with each being well within the enterprise's delivery comfort zone.

Accordingly, guide the shaping of the program of work by the answers to these questions.

- Historically, what is the typical size of a large project within the enterprise's comfort zone?

- Historically, how many projects is the enterprise comfortable with digesting in parallel?

Here is an example. The output of the Align phase is shown first, and then the elaborated program structure is illustrated (Figs. **6.6**, **6.7**).

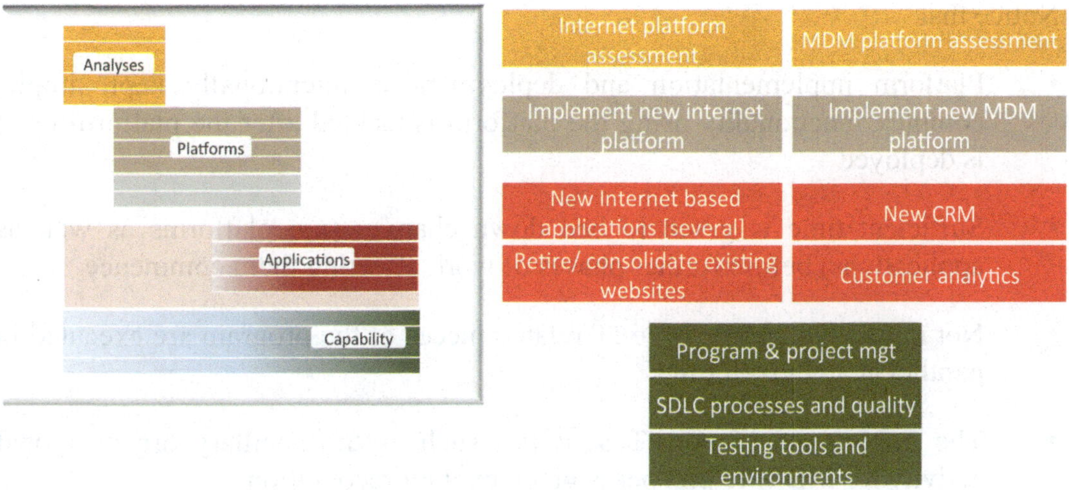

Fig. (6.6). Output of Align phase.

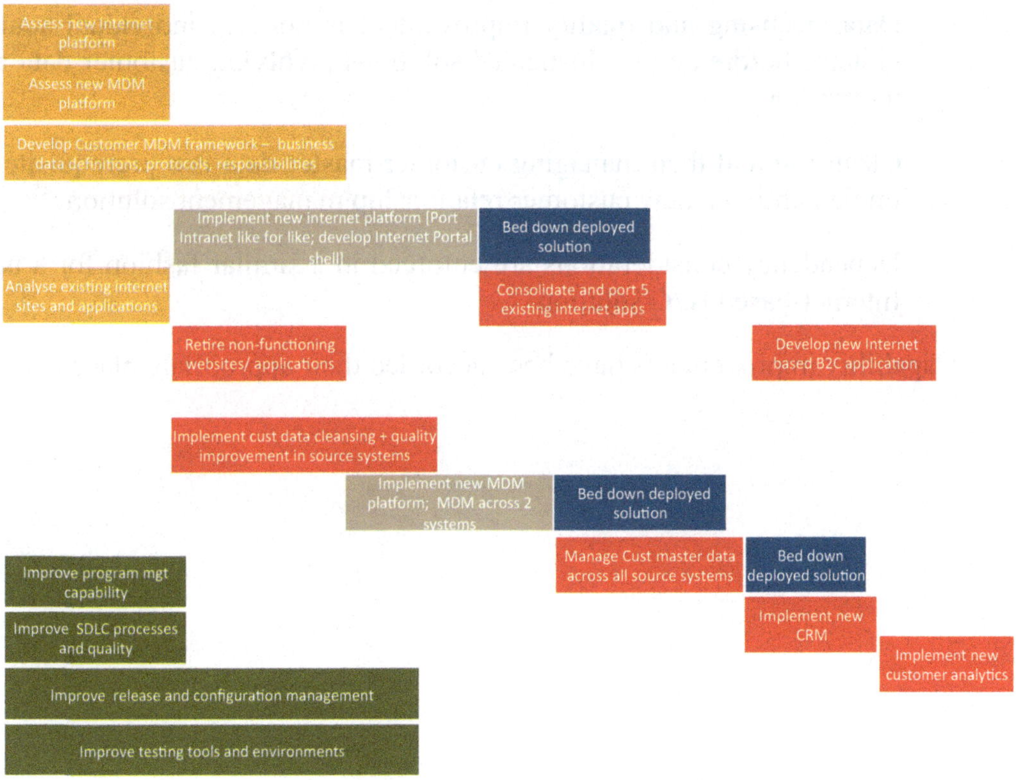

Fig. (6.7). Elaborated program structure.

Notice that

- Platform implementation and deployment is intentionally kept simple; complex functionality using the platform is tackled after the platform itself is deployed

- Sufficient time is given to bed down changes (*i.e.* platforms as well as applications) before further phases of work affecting them commence

- Not more than two to three IT related pieces of the program are executed in parallel at any given time

- The importance of non-IT activities such as the ancillary organisational activity for MDM to prosper is given explicit recognition

- Dependencies have been thought out; for example

    - Data cleansing and quality improvement is done in individual source systems before any sophisticated solutions involving customer data are undertaken

    - Cleansing and then managing customer master data is a prerequisite to implementing a new customer relationship management solution

    - Dependency considerations are enforced in a similar fashion for a new Internet-based B2C solution

- Capability improvements have been accorded their appropriate place

6.4. Organising and Presenting the Findings

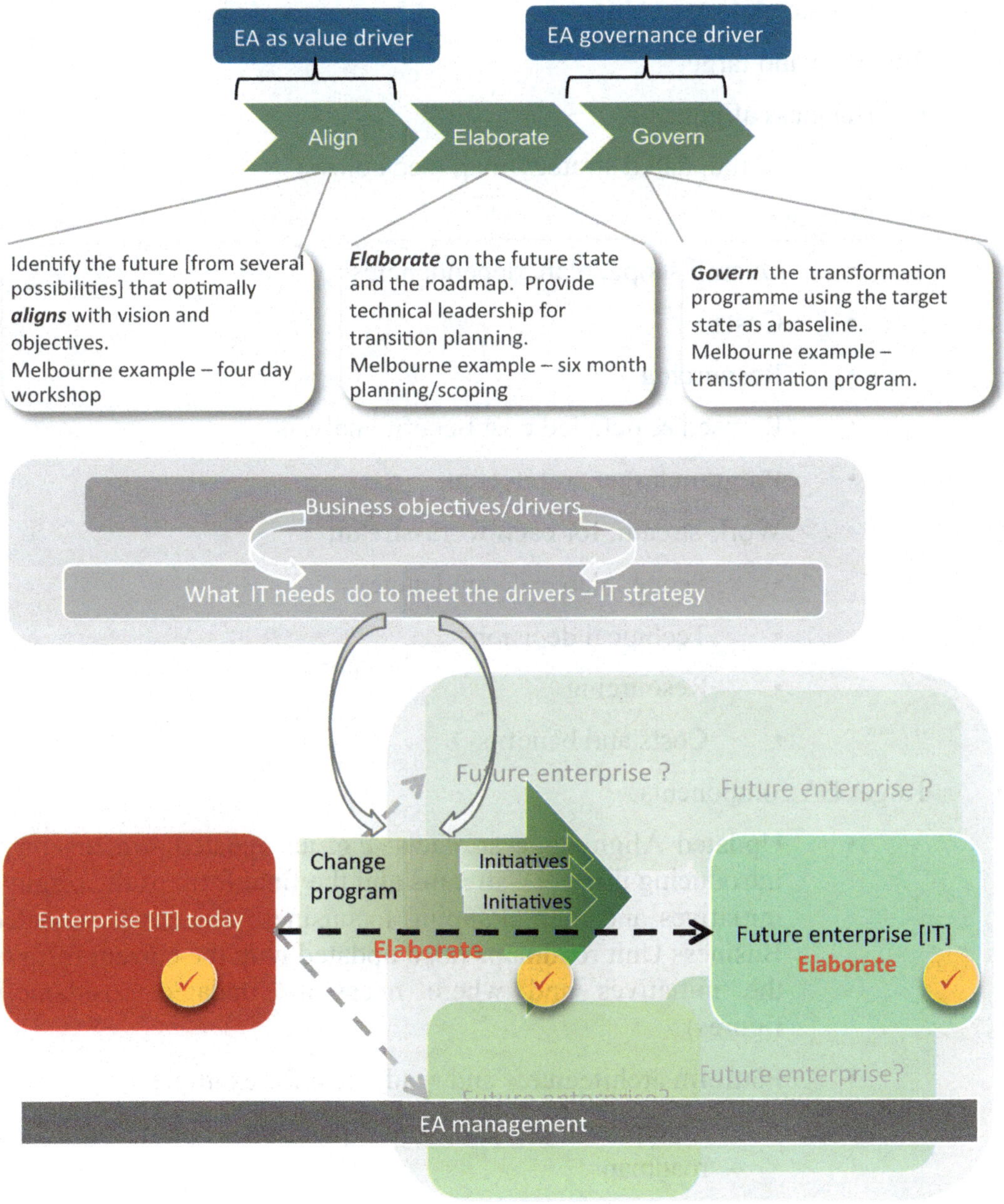

Image (6.4).

We have now come to the end of the Elaborate stage proceedings (Image. **6.4**). At the end of this stage, we would expect the following output.

- Current IT estate assessment
  - Unchanged from Align
- Roadmap and target
  - Business alignment
    - An updated strategy map (see below)
  - Program
    - Overall scope, plan, dependencies
    - Costs
    - Resourcing
    - Revised & detailed cost benefit analysis
    - Program target architecture
    - Work-stream; for each work-stream
      - Scope, plan + dependencies
      - Technical decisions
      - Resourcing
      - Costs and benefits
- Target EA components
    - Updated Align stage artefacts; *e.g.* an updated strategy map, introducing the work-streams and the final form of the original initiatives and their mapping to business objectives; updated Business Unit roadmaps (also updated with the current form of the initiatives and where necessary updated cost/benefit figures)
    - Platform architectures and roadmaps; for example
      - Enterprise infrastructure platform architecture and roadmap
      - Analytical and business intelligence platform and roadmap
    - Program costs and benefits in enterprise context; for example
    - Projected assessment on how the program target state will perform

- Financial – spend spread, focus, benchmark comparison; improvements as against today
- Technical – tech assessment of target; improvements as against today
- Capability – capability assessment of target; improvements as against today
- Business – target application coverage across heat mapped functions/services; improvements as against today

Our overall objective here is no different from Align; that is to help business steer the ship: assist the business now in mapping out the path to where the enterprise needs to go. As before, we conducted this planning exercise at the speed that business wanted: we enjoyed business and IT stakeholders' qualified approval and support; they funded the transition planning exercise, which was expected to expend the time and effort to plan the work in detail.

In this Stage we focused on the transition plan, but also opportunistically developed EA artefacts whose focus is wider and longer than that of the program: for example the platform architectures and roadmaps, whose scope and horizon would be longer than that of the program. The odds that we can develop enterprise-level artefacts in areas connected with the program will be quite good if the Align stage was a success; we can argue with a good deal of justification that an enterprise view with a scope and horizon wider than that of the immediate program of work needs to be developed for key product suites, platforms and the like, to best leverage the enterprise's investment in them. Nevertheless, the attention was firmly on the parts of the IT estate subject to change in the current cycle. As we reasoned earlier in this Chapter, there is time enough for the others.

Now we need to obtain acceptance and approval of the detailed program plan by IT and business stakeholders before commencing the change program.

6.5. Elaborate Stage Wrap Up

6.5.1. Mapping Against Architecture Frameworks

In Align, the discussion was structured around a few key artefacts. In this stage though, the elaboration could have proceeded along many paths, using artefacts specific to that path. We used the Zachman framework at the end of the Align stage discussion; we reproduce below (Image **6.5**) the TOGAF classification of architecture content (TOGAF 9). The reader will see that by this stage, we would have utilised business, data, application, and technology architecture artefacts. In making architectural decisions, we may also have developed or referred to architecture principles.

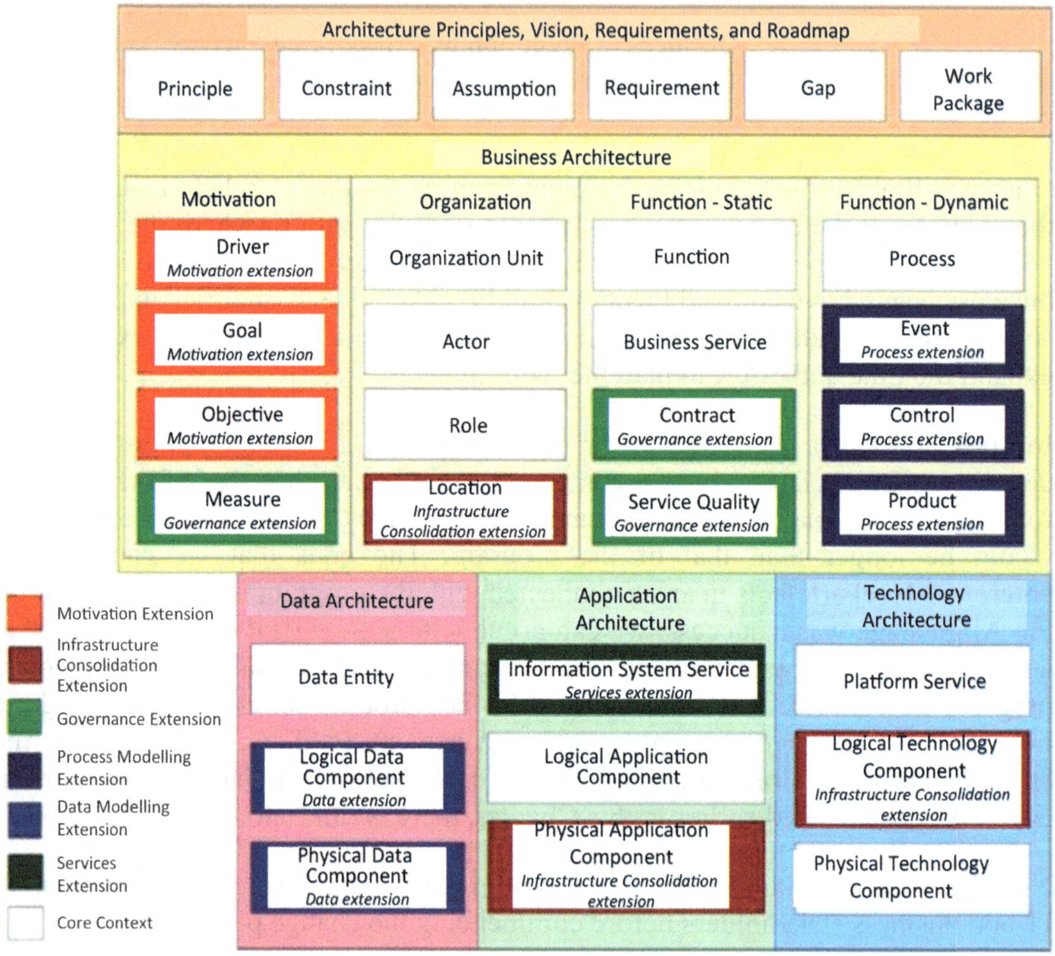

Image (6.5).

6.5.2. Supporting Business Cycles

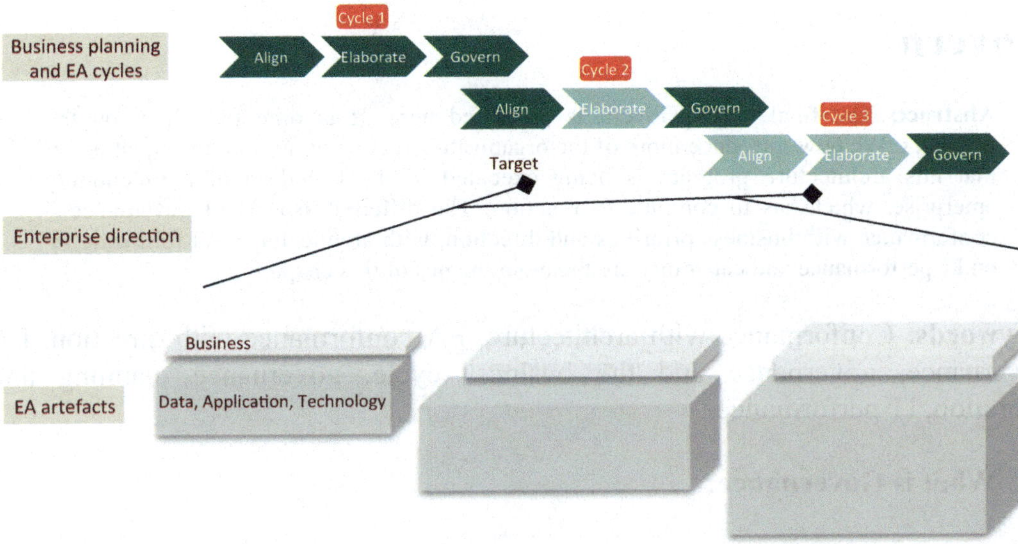

Image (6.6).

Remember that we do not stop to accumulate EA artefacts. Rather, we create them in step with the main evolutionary process of the enterprise. The extent and quality of artefacts will improve with time. In Align, we are as lightweight as needed. In Elaborate, the first priority is to the program; the second to "spillovers" (roadmaps, platform architectures *etc.* for product suites and platforms used in the program); other artefacts get third priority.

Finally, notice that the target state is always aspirational, but distant. Each planning cycle will modify the target based on the change of circumstances since the previous cycle (Image **6.6**).

CHAPTER 7

Govern

Abstract: The final stage, Govern is presented here. It is time to deliver on the promises. We now introduce more of the organisational complexity into the equation, in that this architecture program is being executed in the backdrop of a functioning enterprise, which has to continue to function. The different aspects of governance – conformance with business priorities and direction, with architecture, and following up on IT performance and capability are the main themes of this chapter.

Keywords: Conformance with architecture, EA conformance with direction, EA governance, governance and the business cycle, governance planning and operation, IT performance.

7.1. What is Governance?

Before delving into governance, let us first explore what it actually means.

Some definitions of governance from the literature:

- Weill & Ross: "Specifying the decision rights and accountability framework to encourage desirable behavior in the use of IT" [17].
- IT Governance Institute: "Leadership and organizational structures and processes that ensure that the organization's IT sustains and extends the organization's strategies and objectives".
- Karen D. Schwartz: "Putting structure around how organizations align IT strategy with business strategy, ensuring that companies stay on track to achieve their strategies and goals, and implementing good ways to measure IT's performance".
- Governance is not the decisions themselves, but the framework of structure, process, and accountability put in place to make good decisions.

Where does governance sit in relation to management? Several classifications of management functions exist; all variations of the original by Henri Fayol:

- planning

Inji Wijegunaratne, George Fernandez & Peter Evans-Greenwood

- organizing
- leading
- coordinating
- controlling
- staffing
- motivating

Accordingly, governance can be claimed to be within the remit of management functions: *i.e.* governance has a narrower scope than management, and is contained within the organizing and controlling dimension of management.

7.2. Context: Where are we?

7.2.1. Governance: to Deliver on the Promises

In collaboration with the business, we identified a set of business aligned initiatives that enable/support the business in achieving its strategic objectives. Thereafter we engaged in developing a transition plan for the change program. The business and IT have now accepted the recommendations and the program is set to commence.

We need to ensure that the change program actually delivers on what it set out to achieve.

But is this all? We have thus far focused on aligning business and IT at a particular point in time and then following through. But take a step back: our world is a little more complex than we have let on…..

We are the IT Architecture group, part of the IT division of the company. What structures and mechanisms need to be in place to make us optimally effective?

- How do we ensure that business and IT continue to be aligned?
- In "Elaborate" we discussed carrying the EA decisions and artefacts of the Align stage through to program planning. How do we ensure that this actually happens?

- We need also to ensure that project/program planning artefacts are followed through into implementation, completing the chain that began in the Align stage.
- Moreover, we need to ensure that where relevant, the same thing happens in ALL IT activity – in BAU operations and small enhancements, and in other projects and supporting competencies.
- Finally, it is all very well to say that the BI project will result in an overall benefit of $12 M over two years. Once the change is implemented, how do we track the realization of this benefit and others like this?

Let us therefore explore the context in some detail.

7.2.2. Governance in the Business Cycle

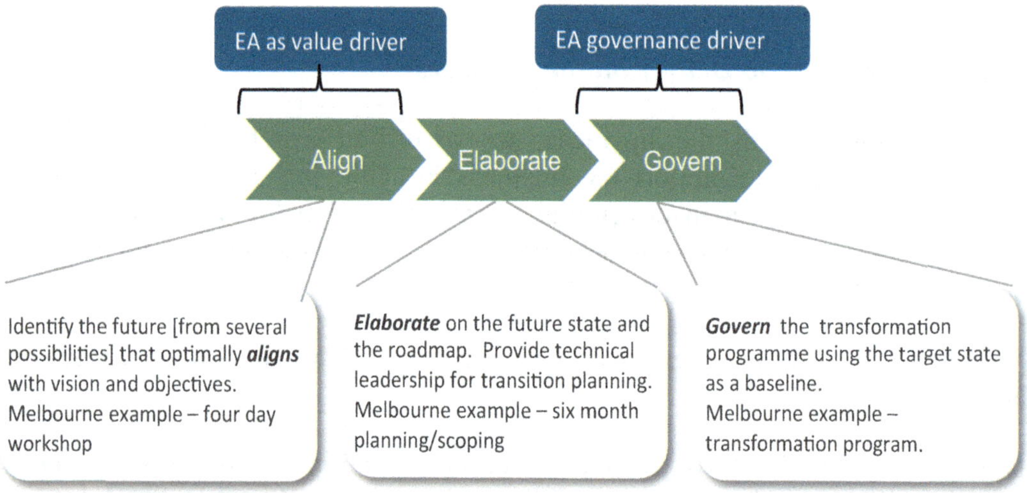

Image (7.1).

We have used a linear representation for the Align, Elaborate, and Govern stages – the one reproduced above (Image **7.1**). We also pointed out that these map to the natural cycle – of plan, implement, and operate – of the business. In practice though, the enterprise continues its day to day activities while it plans and implements. A more accurate representation of governance must therefore span the entire business cycle. And so the linear representation of align, elaborate, and govern is a simplification; Fig. (**7.1**) is a better representation of governance in context.

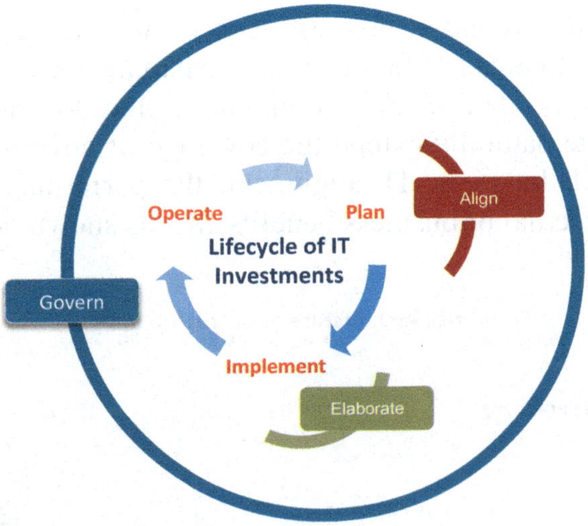

Fig. (7.1). Governance spanning the business cycle.

7.2.3. What do we Govern?

Traditionally, an EA's burden is focused on the custodianship and policing aspects of enterprise architecture, as shown below (Image **7.2**).

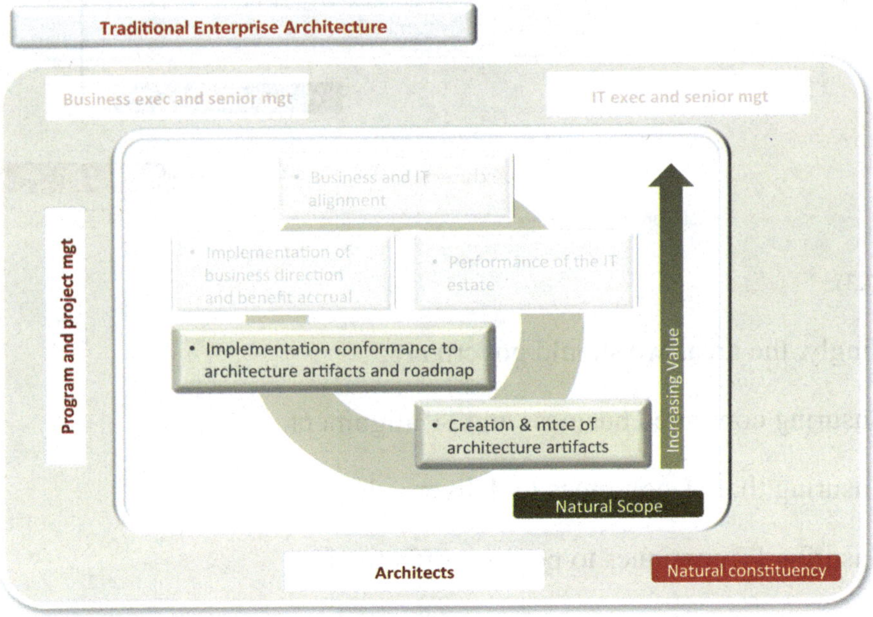

Image (7.2).

We have consistently argued in this eBook that this must change; that the EA's domain must extent to areas of higher value – shaping the enterprise architecture, shaping it in a way that confers optimum value to the enterprise. These responsibilities quite naturally extend the coverage of governance to these higher value areas as well: business/ IT alignment, the performance of the IT estate, identification and accrual of business benefits *etc.*, as shown below (Image **7.3**).

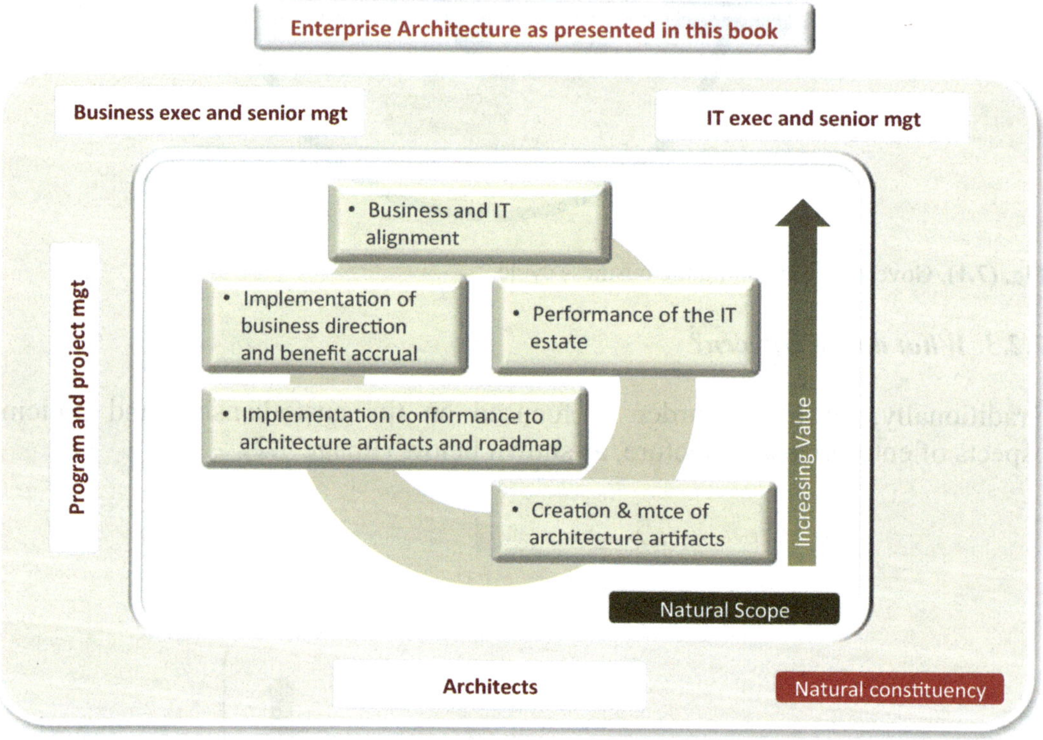

Image (7.3).

Accordingly, the areas we should govern are;

- Ensuring continued business and IT alignment
- Ensuring that IT continues to deliver value
- Ensuring IT continues to perform effectively
- Ensuring IT Architecture structures and processes continue to be effective

To express the problem from another angle, the artefacts we have produced may be categorized as follows (Image **7.4**):

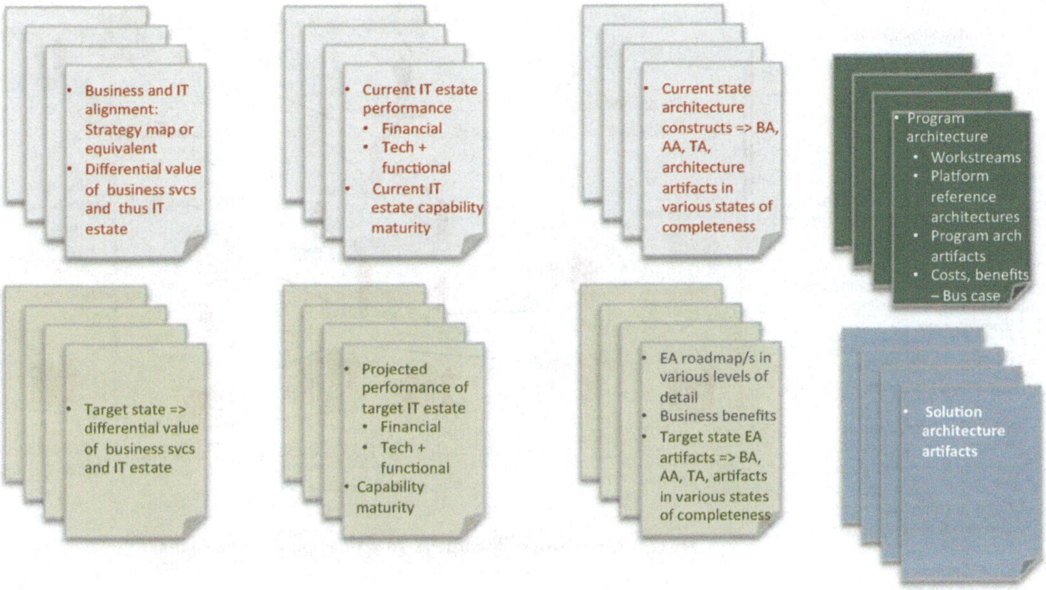

Image (7.4).

We need structures and processes in place to ensure their continued effectiveness. That is:

- Changes of high-level organizational intent and direction are understood, agreed, captured in the relevant artefacts, and guide the navigation of the organizational journey

- The artefacts indicating direction (temporal – roadmaps; technical – hierarchy of architecture artefacts) actually guide what happens on the ground

- Planned/ estimated outcomes – benefits, IT performance and capability outcomes – are realized; if not, the variance ascertained

- The representations we have created – the various artefacts (high level to detail) – evolve by capturing changes that happen on the ground

7.2.4. Structure and Relationships of the IT Architecture Function

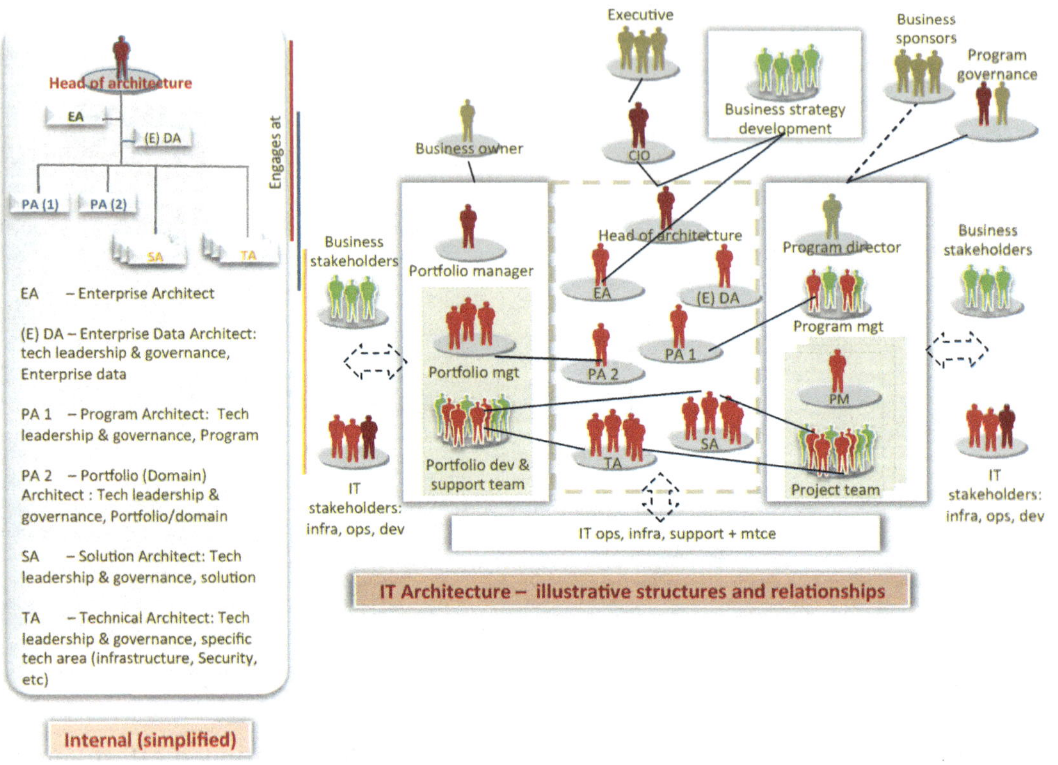

Image (7.5).

Image (**7.5**) is illustrative of the structures and relationships that exist in relation to an IT Architecture group within an enterprise. Though it appears complex, it is in fact a simplified picture; large enterprises often carry structures and relationships that are far more complex than that shown. Governance needs to take place within this convoluted organizational context.

7.3. Governance Process: Conformance

7.3.1. Governance Process Implement Stage

Let us start the discussion on governance processes in the implement stage (Fig. **7.2**). That is, we are currently implementing a program of work that has been agreed between business and IT.

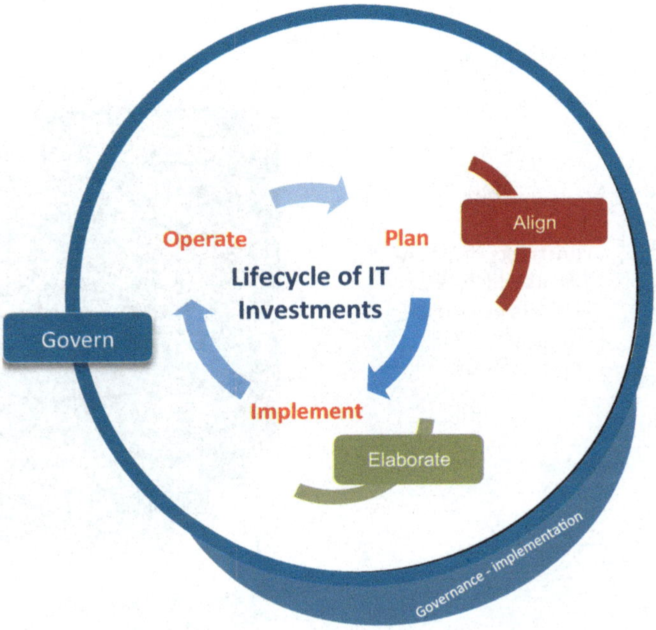

Fig. (7.2). Governance implementation.

The governance objectives for this stage are relatively clear and straightforward: the priorities, direction, and roadmap agreed and accepted in the planning stage must fuel and anchor this program of work. That is (See Image **7.6** for the respective artefacts);

- Conformance with direction: Align stage outcomes, which express and represent the business (and IT) direction must be maintained in implementation.
- Conformance with architecture: Lower levels of architecture must evolve in conformity with higher level artefacts.
- Artefacts and reality in step: Any changes made at the coalface of implementation must be reflected back into the relevant architecture and design artefacts: typically the solution, program, and EA level artefacts below.

Image (7.6).

7.3.1.1. Conformance with Direction

This is not part of traditional EA governance, but is encompassed within the span of EA responsibilities as advocated in this eBook.

The appropriate forum to assess this is the Business/IT Planning Council, introduced and described in the section below on governance of planning and operation. The head of each program or major project plus relevant senior officers (*i.e.* program architect) must present to this forum on their continued conformance with direction; the enterprise architect would be a key IT stakeholder in the review process, perhaps preparing an independent review brief for the consumption of the other reviewers.

The agenda of this forum should include the review all programs and major projects for conformance with direction.

7.3.1.2. Conformance with Architecture

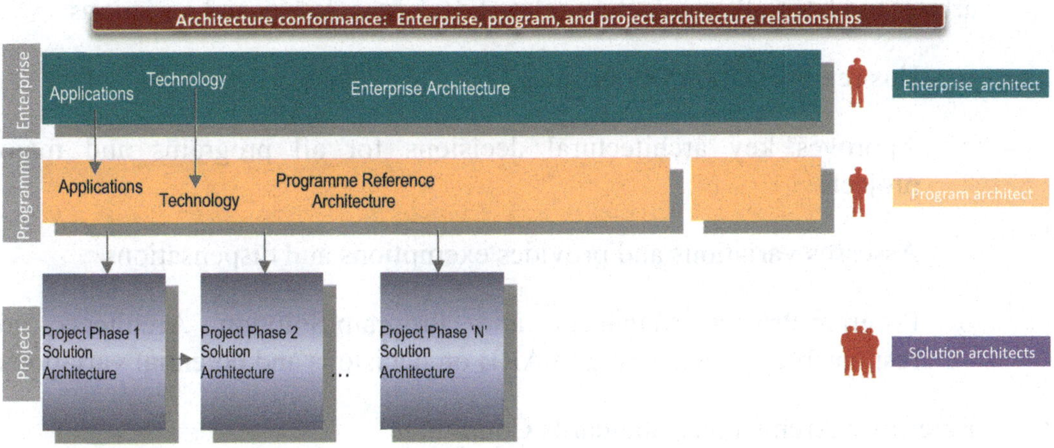

Image (7.7).

This policing activity is part of traditional architecture governance. As illustrated in Image (**7.7**), enterprise level architecture artefacts set the parameters for program level artefacts, which in turn drive the solution level architectures. Governance of proper conformance is typically undertaken in the first instance by the architects in the hierarchy:

The enterprise architect reviews the program architecture artefacts; the program architect oversees the development of the solution architecture artefacts, and the solution architect the design/development constructs.

The escalation path is the inverse; typically the solution architect escalates any issues to the program architect and the portfolio/domain architect, if it cannot be resolved there (or if the latter uncovers an issue), it is escalated to the EA and to the Program Design Authority, and finally to the Architecture Review Board.

Governance structures for conformance typically are:

- Program Design Authority

  The highest technical authority for the program, and is the highest arbiter within the program of all architecture and design issues and variations

- Architecture Review Board

  The highest IT technical authority for the enterprise, and is the highest arbiter in IT for all architecture related decisions, issues and variations

  - Has representation from across IT
  - Approves key architectural decisions for all programs and major projects
  - Assesses variations and provides exemptions and dispensations
  - Program/Project Managers and Program/Solution Architects are responsible for presenting to ARB on decisions and potential variations

- Enterprise Architecture Standards Committee

  For reasons of bureaucratic simplicity, it is desirable to constitute this forum as a committee of the ARB rather than an entirely separate entity

  - Has representation from across IT
  - This forum signoff technical standards and mandates
  - Technical groups develop and present architecture, design, and technology standards for approval

7.3.2. Governance Process: Plan and Operate Stages

Underlining the cyclic and interrelated nature of business processes, of planning, implementing, operating, planning, implementing, *etc.*, we next discuss the planning stage. The context here is that we as IT continue to operate production systems; we have delivered into production some of the outcomes of a previously agreed program of work and are about to enter another planning cycle (Fig. **7.3**).

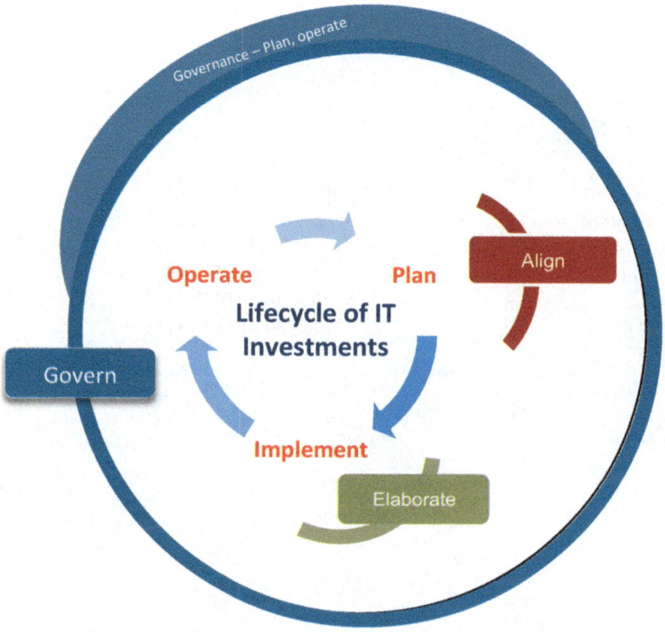

Fig. (7.3). Governance-plan and operate.

Governance objectives for this stage focus primarily on alignment: Does IT continue to be aligned with business priorities and direction?

We must of course understand that in the background IT development activity – programs, major projects, enhancements, *etc.* – are happening and the associated governance mechanisms described previously in "implement" are in operation. As the business cycle turns though, it is now time to take stock prior to entering another planning cycle and it is appropriate to turn our attention to the associated governance structures and processes.

The overall alignment objective can be classified under the following (See Image **7.8** for the respective artefacts):

- Business and IT alignment
- IT performance and capability

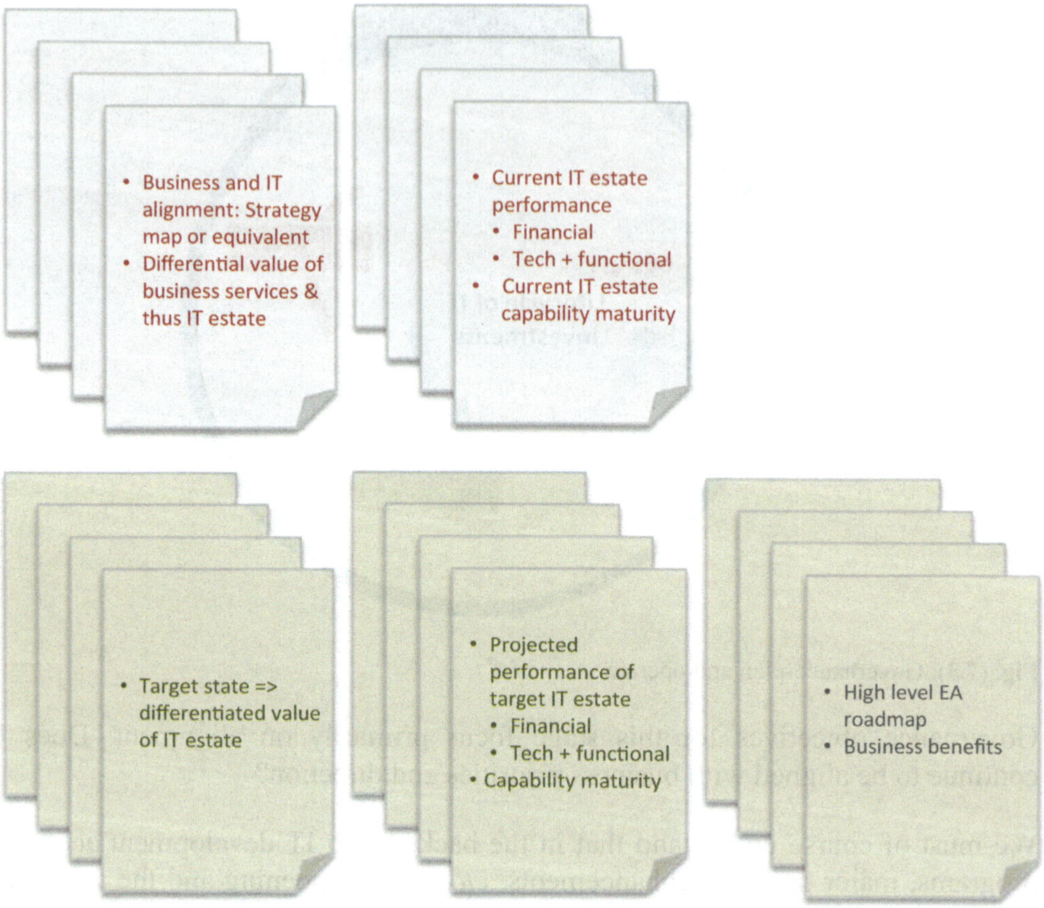

Image (7.8).

7.3.2.1. Business and IT Alignment

- Has business priorities changed since last review, do we need to correct the alignment tack?
- Do major program/project activities continue to align with business priorities?
- Are we realizing the planned business benefits from completed projects and programs?

As we have indicated earlier, these aspects do not form part of traditional EA governance, but is certainly encompassed within the expanded span of EA responsibilities that we have advocated. In our view business alignment is pivotal to an IT division within an enterprise; the EA has led the capture and recording of alignment artefacts in "Align" activity, and accordingly the EA must play a central role in review and governance.

The forum to assess these areas is not the Architecture Review Board, the highest governing body for an architect's traditional responsibilities. ARB and equivalent bodies, typically constituted from representatives within IT and having little if any representation from the business, in our view should continue with their usual responsibilities.

Matters of alignment and benefit realization should be taken up by the forum/structures created for business and IT alignment – let us call it the Business/IT Planning Council. Business/IT alignment must be undertaken periodically as part of the business planning cycle, and this monitoring/ governance activity is the first task of that process.

The forum should include executive management from the business and IT, any designated business/IT liaison managers, plus the EA. For large or federated organizations, it may make sense to have a separate forum for each business division, and also to include the relevant domain/ portfolio architect. Where programs or major projects are undertaken, each project or program must present to this body on their continued alignment to business priorities.

The forum should convene two to three times a year, and its agenda should cover the three bullet points raised at the beginning of this section.

7.3.2.2. IT Performance and Capability

- Are the identified changes in the performance of the IT estate occurring as projected?
- Is the capability IT of identified areas improving as projected?

These criteria relate to the current state assessments we advocated be undertaken as part of the Align stage activity. These assessments are likely to have identified IT performance and capability uplift targets for the period. As part of the review we need to assess how the IT division has performed with respect to achieving these targets.

This again is not a traditional EA responsibility. Neither is a forum that consolidates the governance of IT performance as a whole a traditional structure within IT. Usually this function is fragmented and siloed. Development and Operations (Service Management) functions possess their separate performance governance mechanisms, whilst not much focus is given to assessment and monitoring of capability.

We require a forum to assess and act on evidence; both on performance and capability across the entirety of IT; let us call this the IT Performance Assessment Council. The forum should include the CIO, the heads of IT development, operations, and service management; the enterprise architect (plus portfolio/domain architects for large or federated enterprises), as well as the manager responsible for accounting and finance within the IT division. The enterprise architect may prepare a brief for the council that gathers and presents the evidence for the assessment period.

7.3.3. Summary

Here is a summary of the responsibilities of each of the forums that have appeared thus far in the governance discussions

Forum	Objective	How measured and by whom?	EA responsibility
Business/IT Planning Council **The forum for business/IT alignment.** **The forum encompasses both planning and review activity.** **Only the review activity is illustrated here**	Has business priorities changed since last review?	Business executives present to the forum on any changes since the last planning sessions to the business priorities	Participant With the relevant business liaison managers, determine the impact of these changes on the relevant business architecture artefacts (strategy maps, business services heat maps, operating models) and prepare a brief for the planning sessions
	Do major program/project activities continue to align with business	Typically Program director/ Senior project manager for each major program or project will	Participant and reviewer In the reviewer role, may be required to

Forum	Objective	How measured and by whom?	EA responsibility
	priorities?	report on these: • Realisation of key functional components contributing to the strategic business objectives. • Realisation of similar key non-functional attributes • Timing – any major issues hindering progress (note that since this is not a program management/ delivery meeting, these issues should have been escalated separately)	produce an independent alignment report on some or all of the major initiatives. Else in the reviewer role, make an independent critical assessment of the project/program presentations and prepare a brief for the planning session.
	Any IT-related performance objectives that need to be reported upon?	There may be IT related performance improvements that may have been agreed with the business at the previous reporting cycle; *e.g.*, • Cost reductions • Improvements against industry benchmarks • SLA improvements CIO and the relevant IT officers will report on these matters.	Assist in preparation; participant at the forum The EA may collate the necessary information, and in cooperation with the relevant IT officers (development, operations managers and service management), and prepare a brief for the planning session.
	Is the organization reaping the planned business benefits from completed projects and programs?	Business benefit assessment The relevant business executive or senior business manager reports on the business benefit	Assist in preparation; participant at the forum The EA may help prepare the benefit assessments in collaboration with the relevant business/IT liaison officer and business managers; and

Forum	Objective	How measured and by whom?	EA responsibility
			prepare a brief for the planning session.

Forum	Objective	How measured and by whom?	EA responsibility
IT Performance Assessment Council **Internal to IT. Convened to assess IT performance and capability improvements agreed at the previous planning cycle (*e.g. via* the outcomes of the current state assessment)** **Some performance improvement targets may be visible to the Business (*e.g.* where cost reduction is a corporate imperative); some may be internal to IT, & not need 'external' reporting**	Are the identified changes in the performance of the IT estate occurring as projected?	The relevant IT management – operations, development, service management *etc.* – are responsible for reporting on identified metrics relevant to them.	Participant and reviewer. May also support the relevant managers in gathering and preparing the data Prepare a brief for the IT element of the business/IT planning session.
	Is the capability of identified areas in IT improving as projected?	The relevant IT management – operations, development, service management *etc.* – are responsible for reporting on identified capability improvements relevant to their responsibilities.	Participant and reviewer. Prepare a brief for the IT element of the business/IT planning session.

Forum	Objective	How measured and by whom?	EA responsibility
Architecture Review Board **Headed by the head of Architecture** **Main IT Architecture policing and**	Approves key architectural decisions for all programs and major projects.	Relevant Project managers; Program/ Solution architects will submit key architectural decisions.	Participant and key reviewer and decision maker. Plays a key role in acceptance/approval of architecture decisions.

Forum	Objective	How measured and by whom?	EA responsibility
compliance forum.			
	Assesses variations against an agreed higher level and provides exemptions and dispensations.	Program/Project managers; Program/ Solution architects submit variations from agreed architecture positions and standards: *i.e.* variations between enterprise and program architecture; program and solution architecture.	Plays a key role in providing exemptions/ dispensations for variations.

7.4. Governance Content

We have described the processes and the structures for EA governance; we have also mentioned, albeit briefly, what we should govern. In this Section, we will turn our attention in more detail to the latter.

7.4.1. Business Priority

Changes in business priority may well result in major changes to the company's current tack. Be that as it may, these changes will be relatively easy to capture as changes to our high level artefacts that represent business priority, which are:

- Strategy map: the strategic business objectives/ drivers may change.
- Business services heat map: some of the business services may move into different business value/impact quadrants.

At this level, the changes can be captured relatively easily. But their flow on impact can be major depending on the changes to business priorities.

The EA's role is to understand the new priorities (which typically will be articulated by business executives or senior business managers), and in collaboration with the relevant business representatives, to assess the impact. A briefing paper, assessing impact may be prepared for next business planning session.

The impact flows through to the roadmap of change initiatives. Typically though, major and unexpected change is rare, especially where these cyclic planning and assessment processes are institutionalised. When it occurs, it is fuelled by changes in external conditions such as rapid changes in economic/competitive climate, or internal circumstances such as the arrival of a new CEO with a new vision, M&A activity, *etc.* A major change in business priorities can impact delivery timelines, priority, functionality, or indeed the very existence of projects and programs of the roadmap. More typically though, the impact will be far less severe, confined to "course corrections".

There is another, perhaps a more common, reason impacting the roadmap – the failure of large projects/programs to deliver. Business stakeholders, in the face of schedule and cost overruns and functionality constriction, may radically revise or indeed pull the plug on large programs. Rather than a change to business drivers or priority, this represents a "Plan B" scenario – "Plan A did not work; how do we now cut our losses, lower the level of ambition, but still try to respond to our business drivers?"

But we are getting ahead of ourselves here. Whether it is minor or major change, the actual form of the new or amended roadmap will take shape during the business/IT planning sessions that would follow this review and governance activity. Where major business upheavals occur, we would still expect this process to occur in this order – articulation of changes by business executives at the review/governance forum, impact assessment, and re-planning at the planning forum – but of course with a sense of great urgency.

7.4.2. Business Benefits

Benefits should initially have been identified at the align stage and elaborated upon in creating the business cases in program/project planning. Hence the business benefits to track should be identified and well-articulated in business cases for the program/ projects.

In Align stage discussions, we talked about initial identification and capture of business benefits at a high-level. Image (**7.9**) illustrates this initial identification of business benefits. The reader is urged to think about the last two bullet points in the middle and right columns of the table above. In the business case either quantitative (numeric) or financial (dollar figure) targets will have been specified for these business benefit areas.

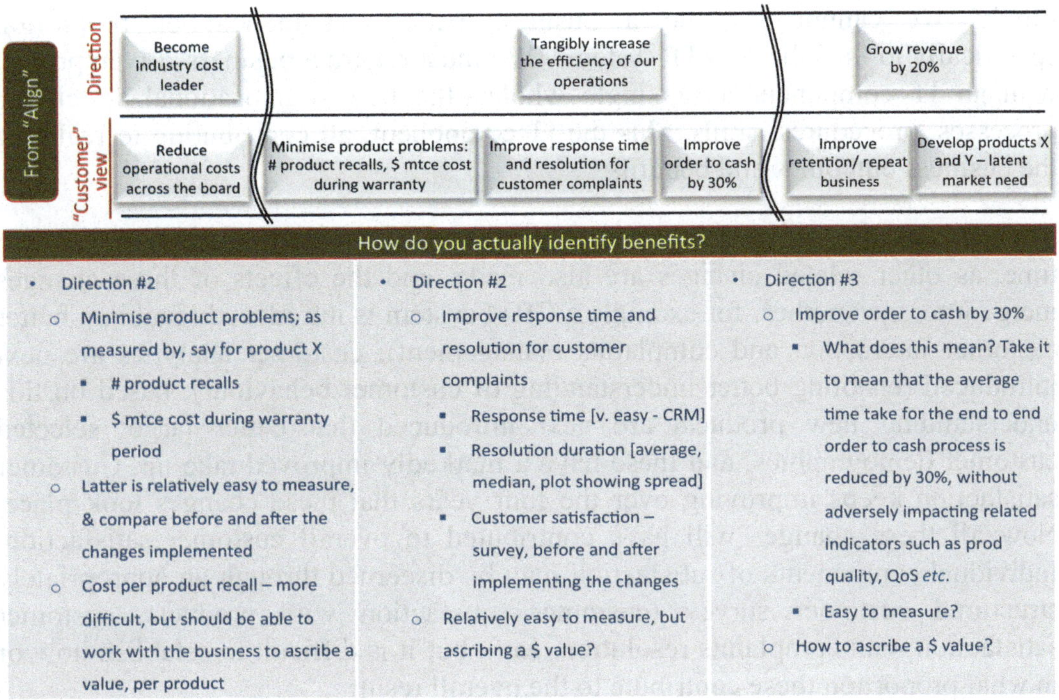

Image (7.9).

The burden now is to "chase them up"; that is, to collect evidence to show to what extent these targets have been achieved.

- How does the actual number of product recalls in the period compare with the target?
- How does the actual dollar maintenance costs for the product during warranty compare with the target?
- What is the actual average response time – how does it vary between peak and non-peak; how does this compare with the target?
- How does the actual customer satisfaction – measured *via* a survey – stack up against the projected improvement?

And so on.

There are a couple of things to note:

Firstly, we cannot attribute a business benefit component or proportion specifically to the "the new IT system". We must regard a business-driven project with an IT component as a single whole –the new organisational structures, processes, procedures, skills, plus the IT component, all contributing to realising the business outcomes and benefits.

Secondly, the benefit attributed to a particular change sometimes gets diluted with time, as other related changes are also made, and the effects of these changes merge into one another: for example a CRM system is introduced (enabling better customer interaction and complaints management); customer analytics are next introduced (enabling better understanding of customer behaviour); based on this understanding new products are next introduced that better target selected customer demographics, and these have a markedly improved take up. Customer satisfaction keeps improving over the four years that these changes took place. Now all these changes will have contributed to overall customer satisfaction. Individual components of satisfaction may be discerned through an appropriately structured customer survey (customer satisfaction with products, customer satisfaction with complaints resolution, *etc.*), but it is difficult to establish how or in what proportion these contribute to the overall result.

7.4.3. IT Performance

In the Align stage, we discussed assessing IT performance along the following dimensions.

- Financial
- Capability
- Operational and technical
- Functional

These assessments would normally have indicated improvement or uplift targets, either qualitatively, or by establishing quantitative or financial goals. The task now is to establish the degree to which these targets have been achieved in this review period.

Let us take some examples. Suppose we identified the following areas for IT performance improvement in the previous cycle

- Targeted capability improvement; *e.g.*
    - Supporting high business impact applications X and Y
    - Middleware/integration
    - Testing
    - Operations processes (configuration, release, incident, problem *etc.* management)
- Focused rationalization of IT estate
    - Applications
    - Infrastructure
    - Targeted outsourcing;

And

- Targeted improvement of applications
    - Functional improvement
    - Technical improvement
    - Support improvement;

<u>*Contributing to*</u>

- IT spend alignment
    - Alignment with business priority
    - Improvement against benchmarks

How do we measure the outcomes of such an exercise?

The table below illustrates metrics for measuring some of the assessment outcomes. The reader is encouraged to complete the list.

Assessment objective	Metric for outcome assessment
IT spend alignment: Alignment with business priority	• Spread of IT spend against (heat mapped) business services • IT spend against a business value/impact application classification • What is the (before and after) CAPEX and OPEX spend spread? What is the change? If a target was specified comparison of actual *vs* target.
IT spend alignment: comparison against benchmarks	Benchmarks: CAPEX *vs* OPEX (Industry benchmark say 35% *vs* 65%) Spend spread: staff/ hardware/ software/ external services (Industry benchmark say 36% / 21%/ 24%/ 19%) IT spend as a percentage of business revenue (industry benchmark say 5.7%) What is the IT division's performance against these benchmarks for the assessment period? If a target was specified comparison of actual *vs* target.
Targeted capability improvement: Supporting high business impact applications X and Y	• Support cost per annum for each of X and Y • Support quality o Incident/problem response time, resolution time o # of incidents, problems per period – and associated statistics What is the improvement along each of these indicators? If a target was specified comparison of actual *vs* target.
Targeted capability improvement: Middleware/integration	• Development cost, support cost per interface • Implementation lead time per interface What is the improvement along each of these indicators? If a target was specified comparison of actual *vs* target.
Focused rationalisation	• Reduction in application support costs • Reduction in infrastructure (and licensing) costs If a target was specified comparison of actual *vs* target.
Operations/ service management	• Creation of appropriate SLA definitions • SLA performance • IT customer (is business user) satisfaction

7.4.4. Policing and Compliance

This is the traditional area of architecture governance (Image **7.10**).

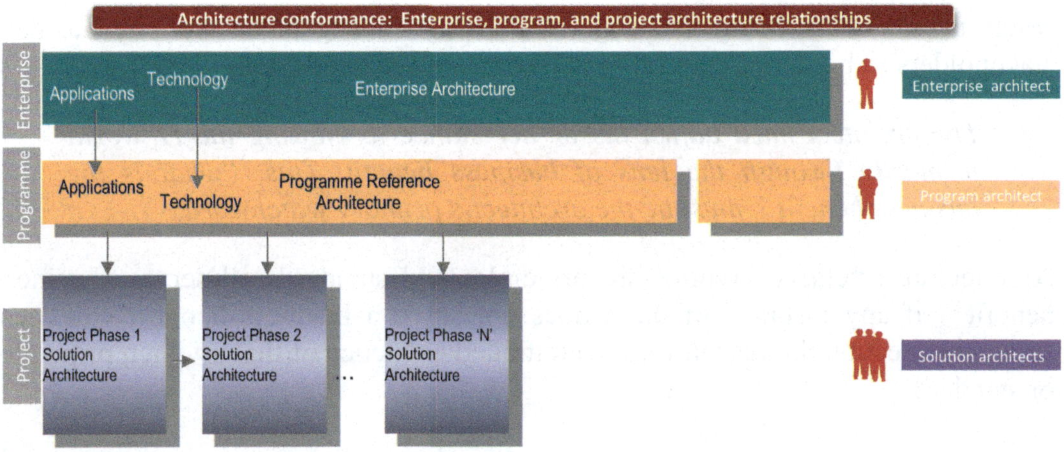

Image (7.10).

As we described earlier in this chapter enterprise level architecture artefacts set the parameters for program level artefacts, which in turn drive the solution level architectures.

The artefacts include

- Architecture principles
- Architecture standards
- Enterprise, Program, Solution level artefacts

Compliance of existing artefacts are policed (using the mechanisms and forums described earlier), deviations corrected or exemptions provided, or indeed variations that prove to be useful incorporated. This process updates and evolves the existing architecture framework.

The areas of violation are too numerous to mention here – any practising architect will have personal experience of policing as well as being policed.

A word of caution: the architect must be aware of the problems associated with zealotry and architecture purity at one extreme, and architectural lawlessness at the other. Often architects are acutely sensitive to the lawless side of the spectrum, but blind to the inimical effects of the other side. This skewed perception often result in architects being seen by IT delivery managers as well as business stakeholders as bottlenecks to rapid delivery.

> *The architect must adjust his or her stance to viewing the IT world primarily through the lens of business benefit. This, "what is the business benefit", must be the architect's primary watchword.*

Architecture artefacts, architecture principles and standards all serve a business benefit – if any instance of them does not serve a business benefit, you must seriously question the reason for the continued existence of that artefact, principle, or standard.

A couple of scenarios – though not directly about enterprise architecture – will serve to underline the point:

A project hastily convened to retrieve a rapidly deteriorating competitive position for the business proposes two point to point interfaces rather than employing the (as yet fledgling) corporate integration platform designated for all future integration. You know that at this stage of maturity, using the corporate platform will add cost and time to the schedule. *What would you do?*

At the same time, there is the perennial tension between architects and project managers. Some project managers care only about delivery – quality of the delivered system for them is a distant second priority. In the above example, the project manager proposes cutting down on system testing in the interests of speed to production. You know as the architect that this particular system needs to get into production quickly; you also know that this is a front line system and customers will directly experience any production glitches the system may exhibit. In a situation where your voice would count, *what would you do?*

One useful practice in cases where exemptions are accorded is to scope the effort and set aside budget for later remediation. Especially if you are successful in the latter endeavour, then you can rest relatively easy that remediation is likely to occur.

CHAPTER 8

How Our Approach Adds Value

Abstract: This eBook predicates the EA must add, and demonstrate that it does, add value to the enterprise. This chapter explores our concept of value, value indicators, and how to quantify and provide evidence that EA is adding and optimizing value.

Keywords: EA value, evidence of IT contribution, IT contribution, optimising IT spending.

8.1. "Value"

In this eBook we have spoken incessantly of "value" and EA being able to add "value". We have further asserted that value is positively associated with business and IT alignment.

Let us now explore this concept of value in more detail.

- What do we mean by the value of IT?
- How do we improve or optimize the value of IT?
- How can EA help in this process – does the approach we presented actually help?

"What is the value of IT" is a question that is difficult to answer when presented in that form since the concept is amorphous and very difficult to grasp. "Value" must be described so that the concept can be better expressed and scoped. Thus, we must first define "IT value" in a manner that has some hope of being assessed – *i.e.* construct an operational definition.

Let us define "IT value" as the contribution IT makes to the profitability of the business[1].

Our questions now can be rephrased as follows:

- How do we assess the contribution that IT makes to corporate profitability?

[1]We have not considered entities that are not for profit – Government institutions, charities, NGOs *etc.* – IT value for them would require a way to operationalize the entity's overall effectiveness.

Inji Wijegunaratne, George Fernandez & Peter Evans-Greenwood

- What then are the ways in which we can optimize this contribution?
- How can EA help in this process – does the approach we presented actually help?

8.1.1. Value Indicators

An indicator represents some "thing" in a way that enables its performance, or health and well-being to be revealed, moreover presented in a way that enables comparison and assessment. For example "return on equity" represents the profit of a company in a way that enables comparison with its own previous performance, and with those of other companies. "IT spending as a proportion of total expenditure", enables a company's IT spending to be similarly compared. Raw figures for profit or IT spending are relatively weaker in terms of their capacity for comparison.

Generally, we can use indicators in a few ways

- How does our company compare against other companies – *i.e.* the average performance in our industry vertical?
- How do our actuals compare against our projections?
- How does our year on year trend stack up?

8.1.2. Macro Level Indicators of IT Contribution to Business

At the macro level, interplay of many contributory causes gives rise to a particular result. For example a company's profit (expressed say as return on equity) may have been brought about by a combination of favorable economic factors, cost efficiencies the company instituted, better products, marketing, and customer service. Therefore macro level indicators must be used with care in drawing inferences about a particular contributory factor (such as IT) and its contribution to a given result.

Nevertheless, we do recognize that macro-level indicators, when used appropriately, can be capable of providing valuable insights.

What then are macro-level indicators that indicate IT's contribution to business health?

There are metrics that indicate IT investment, such as:

- IT spending per employee
- IT spend as a proportion of revenue or business operating expenses

Metrics, such as those below, are indicators of business profitability/productivity:

- Percentage return on equity
- Operating income or revenue per employee

These may be used in combination, as follows.

- Percentage return on equity against IT spend per employee
- Percentage return on equity against IT spend as a proportion of revenue
- Operating income per employee against IT spend per employee; *etc.*

The resulting data points can be used to draw some useful inferences. As we described previously, we can ascertain;

- How our company compares against our industry vertical by comparing our result against a benchmark value for our industry vertical that, for example, Gartner Group produces periodically: is our result favorable; if so why? Is it that our profit is high and masks our IT spending, which is very much higher than industry average? Is it unfavorable; if so why? Is it that we have invested a great deal in IT this year, which would bear fruit in two years? *etc.*
- How our actuals compare against our projections by computing our actuals and comparing it against the projected value (if the projections have been made during the planning cycle)
- How our year on year trend stacks up may be ascertained by computing actuals year on year and establishing the trend

However, as we reasoned earlier, these indicators cannot generally be used to draw cause and effect inferences: X amount of dollars was spent this year on IT, and the company returned a good profitability result – *i.e.* the one followed the other; the most optimistic inference we can draw is our IT spending is *associated* with good profitability; to say our IT spending was a *causal factor* in good profitability is an inference too far.

8.1.2.1. Quantum of the IT Contribution

Peter Strassman, a key figure in IT economics has carried out pioneering work in this area. He has developed a metric that he terms "Information Productivity", which aims to show the amount of IT's contribution to corporate productivity.

He subtracts the expected return (the return the company *should be* earning) on capital assets from the actual profit the company has made. The difference (that he terms "Information Management Value Added") he attributes to good information management.

That is; "Information Management Value Added" (the value added to a company's performance by good information management) equals actual profit minus the cost of capital invested by shareholders.

Information Productivity (a metric that can be used to compare performance of different companies) is the Information Management Added divided by the company's transaction costs.

Interested readers should refer to his website (http://www.strassmann.com/) for further information.

8.1.3. IT Value – The Evidence

Strassmann's work also underlines a very important point: he has shown that there is no correlation between IT spending and profitability [18]. A plot of return on equity against IT spending per employee for a large number of enterprises indicates absolutely no correlation between IT spending and profitability: organisations that spend heavily on IT are not assured of higher profitability. This is an obvious statement, but many CIOs and senior managers in IT appear deluded into thinking that organisational benefit from IT is proportional to IT spending: here is the evidence that it is not!

Strassmann also establishes a corollary [19]: better performing companies do not necessarily spend lavishly on IT. Certain companies in an industry sector in the US have invested modestly in IT over several years and have performed consistently well during that time; other companies in the same US industry sector have spent lavishly on IT over the same period of time but shown a lower return on shareholder equity.

8.1.4. Value – Where Do We Stand?

We have now answered the first of the questions asked at the outset: What do we mean by the value of IT?

By the value of IT, we mean the contribution that IT makes to a company's profitability

This is easy to say, but rather more difficult to ascertain. To summarise the preceding discussion:

- By combining IT investment metrics and corporate profitability metrics, we can draw inferences such as
    - Is our result favorable or unfavorable in comparison with the industry as a whole?
    - How well does the projected result compare with actuals?
    - Is the year on year trend favorable?

A favorable metric is obviously a good result, but does not in itself indicate how IT contributed to corporate profitability – *i.e.* to what extend IT was a causal factor in corporate profitability

- However, by conducting further analyses, we may take a cautious step or two along inferring IT's contribution: for example
    - % return on equity against IT spend per employee is favorable against the industry benchmark; IT spend as a proportion of revenue is also favorable against the industry benchmark; an internal survey of business users reveals a favorable level of satisfaction with IT. In combination, these factors would enable a cautious inference that IT has contributed positively to corporate profitability.
    - IT spend indicators are high, but we recognize that we are investing a large amount in readiness for new business capability scheduled to come on stream next year. If this quantum is taken away, then the indicators turn positive, and an analysis similar to above indicates a favorable contribution.

- % return on equity against IT spend per employee is favorable against the industry benchmark; however, IT spend as a proportion of revenue is very high against the industry benchmark; an internal survey of business users reveals a low level of satisfaction with IT. Here, it would appear that IT has spent heavily but not to good effect, and the favorable IT spend/profitability metric is sustained only by high corporate profit, achieved in spite of relatively poor IT service.

In this way, we can make a reasonable assessment of IT's contribution to corporate profitability using multiple indicators at hand, which in combination would yield a qualitative (*i.e.* non-numeric) overall inference.

- Paul Strassman's metric of Information Productivity aims to show the quantum of IT's contribution to corporate productivity; this may provide useful for those who desire a quantitative indication

So we come to the second question that was posed at the outset: How do we improve or optimize the value of IT?

8.2. Optimising IT Spend for Better Value

8.2.1 Affordability

First, we must attend to what seems to be an obvious point. Sadly though, it often tends to get lost in the scramble for the corporate IT dollar. It is this: enterprises spend a limited amount on IT, typically a small proportion of their overall expenditure. Accordingly, how much the enterprise can afford to spend on IT is the overarching parameter that predicates all that follows.

How much do enterprises actually spend on IT? In 2009 companies in Banking and Finance spent an average of 7.4% of operational expenditure on IT; in 2010, companies in the Media and Entertainment industry spent an average of 6.0% of operational expenditure on IT; in 2011, Health Care Providers spent an average of 3.5% of operational expenditure on IT [20].

An insurance company known to the authors, circa 2000, was spending on average around $20M per annum on IT, out of an operational expenditure of around $200M per annum. During one year in early 2000s though, the IT expenditure blew out to over $40M, and the resulting fallout caused a major upheaval in the senior IT management ranks.

All this this underlines the fact that effective IT spending is less about going cap in hand to the holders of corporate purse strings, like Oliver Twist, "to ask for more". Rather, it is about understanding the realities of what a company can spend on IT, and targeting the limited IT dollar to be most effective.

8.2.2. Targeting the IT Dollar

There are two basic calls on the IT dollar:

- New projects/investments: The spending on the provision of new or changed capabilities. These are typically justified *via* business cases; typically capitalized

- Business as usual (BAU): The spend on IT operations and support; typically not capitalized

In 2009 companies in Banking and Finance spent an average of 35% of total IT spend on capital expenditure and 65% BAU. In 2011, Health Care Providers spent an average of 29% of total IT spend on capital expenditure and 71% BAU [20]. It is common practice to justify project expenditure, but these figures show that it is a relatively small percentage of total spending. It becomes evident that we need to tackle the entire spend spectrum in order effectively to optimise IT expenditure.

IT divisions can optimize the IT dollar in two ways: aligning with business priorities, and efficiently managing IT's performance. In other words:

- Business alignment: Is IT spending aligned with business objectives and priorities?

- IT performance: Is the IT expenditure prudently and efficiently managed?

How does aligning with business objectives help optimize IT's contribution to corporate profitability? The bottom line responsibility for the enterprise lies with the Business; as opposed to IT[2]. Although we as IT may assist – see the Chapter on "Align" – the Business is responsible for identifying their objectives and priorities. As IT people, we make the entirely reasonable assumption that the Business is competent enough to be able to identify their objectives and priorities in a manner that enhances the company's bottom line. In aligning with these objectives, IT supports the

---

[2]Except in one respect – see below.

Business in achieving their aims, which then would contribute positively to corporate profitability. IT's primary burden therefore is not the *identification* of business objectives and priority but *aligning* with them.

Controlling IT cost is the other, rather more straightforward, aspect to optimizing the IT dollar: other things being equal, cost efficiencies will also flow through to the bottom line.

As discussed previously in "Align" and illustrated in strategy maps, a company may improve its position by exercising one or more of four fundamental levers [21] (Image **8.1**): Of these, cost efficiency and improving asset utilization may directly engender IT initiated action. In other words, IT instigated initiatives to improve its operational performance can ultimately be traced directly through to the corporate business objective of operational excellence and thence to one or both of the top-level aims of cost efficiency and improving asset utilization.

IT alignment on the other hand obviously needs intervening business/IT initiatives that ultimately trace through to one or more of the four top level business imperatives.

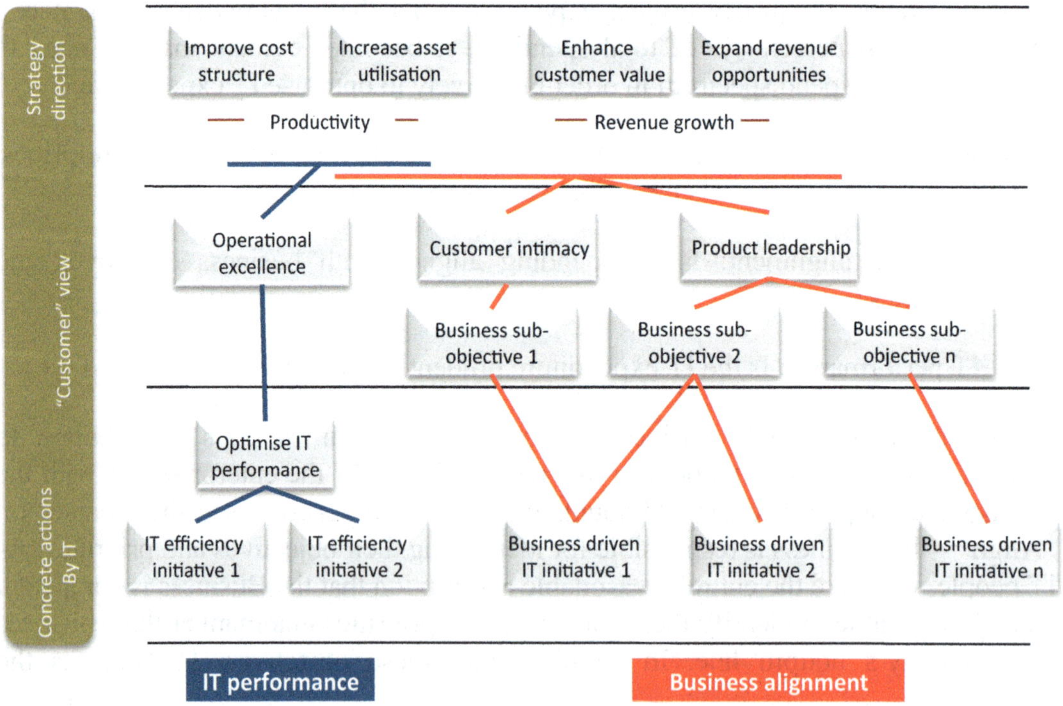

Image (8.1).

We now turn our attention back to the four dimensions, two on demands on the IT dollar and two on optimizing the IT dollar spend, discussed earlier. These four facets can be displayed in a four-quadrant grid, as follows (Image **8.2**):

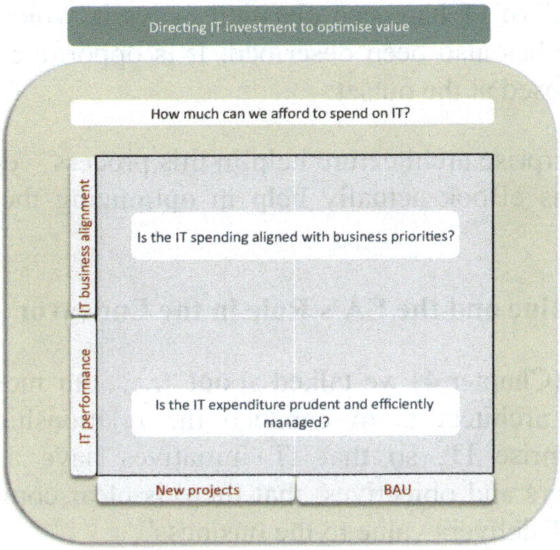

Image (8.2).

Let us explore this further. What are the key features to consider for each quadrant (Image **8.3**)?

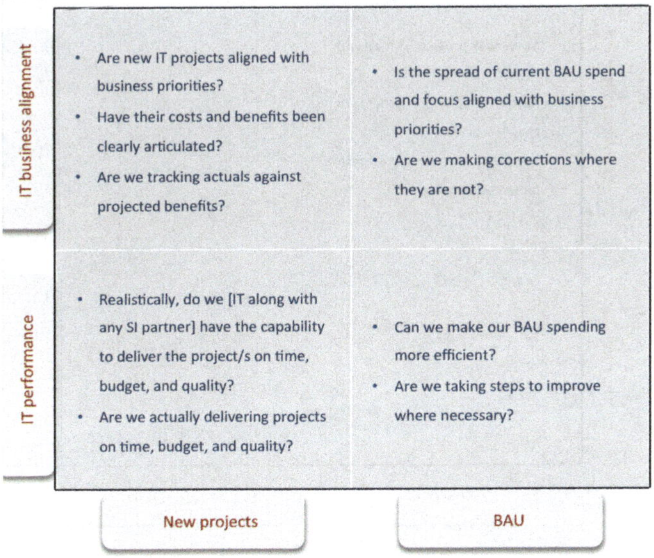

Image (8.3).

As shown, each of the four quadrants has particular elements that need to be considered in directing IT investment to optimize the value of IT to the business.

To recap, we have now sufficiently operationalized the concept of "value": What we mean by "value" of IT has been clarified; ways in which we can improve or optimize this value has also been described. It is opportune now to move to the third question we posed at the outset:

- How can enterprise architecture help in this process – does the approach we present in this eBook actually help in optimizing the value of IT to the business?

8.3. Optimizing Value and the EA's Role in the Endeavor

At the very outset (Chapter 4) we talked about "......our more realistic objective for the enterprise architect is to enhance the relationship between business strategy and enterprise IT, so that IT initiatives have a direct mapping to organisational drivers and objectives, that there is clear communication between the two areas and IT delivers value to the business".

So we now take each quadrant, its particular "value" questions, and see how enterprise architects and enterprise architecture as presented in this eBook address these questions (Images **8.4-8.7**).

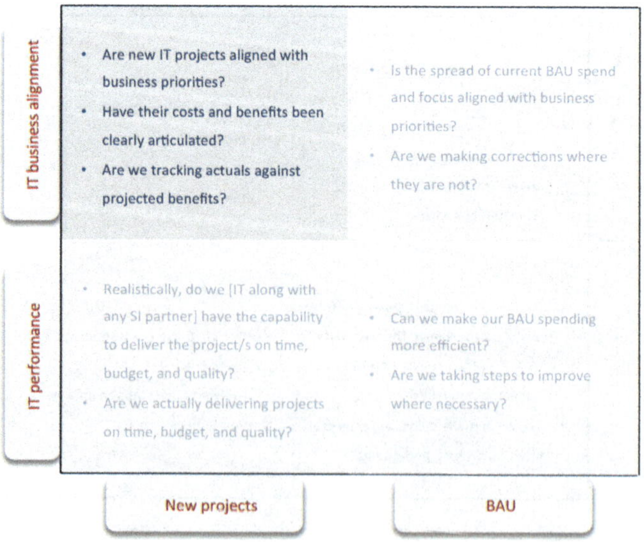

Image (8.4).

IT alignment with Business, and the EA's pivotal role in that alignment, was the subject of the Chapter on Alignment. In collaboration with Business stakeholders, identifying the business drivers and developing a set of initiatives that address and fulfill these objectives, was the key concern of the Enterprise Architect in planning.

Obviously these initiatives need to be justified – justification is worked into the very beginning, an essential ingredient in the initial identification of the business/IT initiatives. Subsequently, candidate initiatives are justified more rigorously in project/program planning (described in the Chapter "Elaborate"), by developing and assessing business cases.

The third value ingredient was discussed in the Chapter "Govern", where we underlined the importance of actually tracking the business benefits identified in planning and business case development.

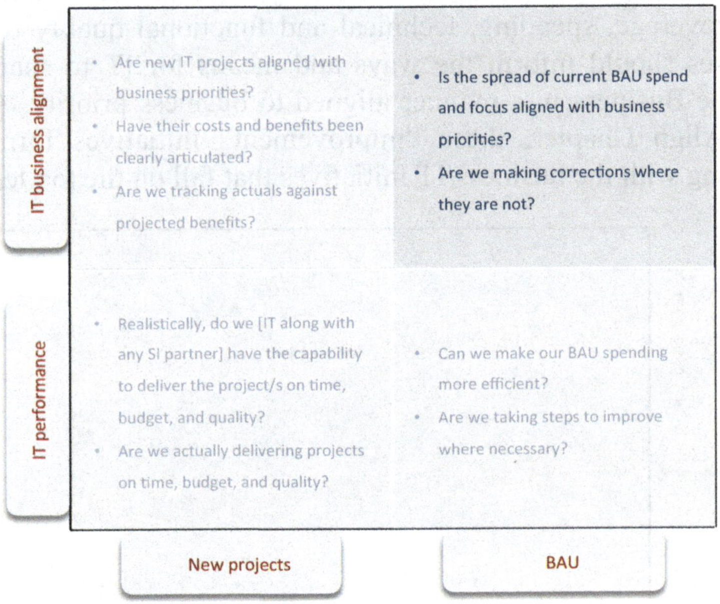

Image (8.5).

We have earlier reasoned that the needs of different parts of the business are not uniformly similar. Hence rather than supporting all parts of the business in the same fashion, a far better way to allocate the scarce IT support dollar is to tailor IT support to the nature of the needs of different parts of the business. We also described the manner in which this may be achieved:

- The business value/business impact assessment of the enterprise's business services is a good indicator of the particular needs, in terms of the type of need as well as the relative significance, *i.e.* priority, of the needs

- IT support to the business must be shaped by these criteria

In other words, "business alignment and business priority" in this quadrant is indicated by the business value/business impact measures of the enterprise's business services, and hence IT must tailor the support it provides to a specific business service to align with the latter's business value/impact positioning.

We discussed current state assessment as an important task for the planning stage (in the "Align" Chapter). A number of techniques were presented – functional, IT capability, financial, and operational + technical. Fundamental amongst these are methods of assessing the level of current IT focus and support against the enterprise's business services characterized by their business value and impact: application coverage, spending, technical and functional quality of the systems. These analyses should inform the ways and means for IT to shape its existing services to the Business in a manner aligned to business priority. As we pointed out in the Align Chapter, these "improvement" initiatives form part of the roadmap, along with the business/IT initiatives that fall on the top left quadrant.

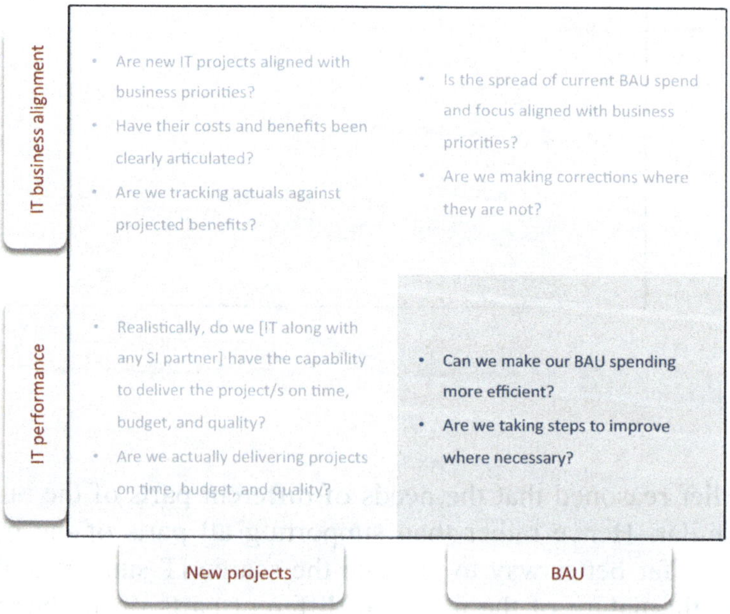

Image (8.6).

Having tailored the BAU spending to be more business aligned, how do we make it more efficient? Again, the current state assessment we presented in the "Align" Chapter has the tools and techniques to asses these matters. Along with spending alignment, the techniques we presented therein can be employed to assess the efficiency of IT spending in BAU. The financial assessment, coupled with the operational and technical assessment and capability maturity assessment (especially ITIL/ITSM) have the wherewithal to address the concerns of this quadrant.

There will be areas here that are within the EA's domain of responsibility (for example creating infrastructure efficiencies *via* virtualization of hardware, cloud services, *etc*.), and some that are not (for example service management capability improvement). Although the EA was part of the assessment and the initial identification of initiatives during the planning stage, his/her subsequent involvement with the latter will diminish.

In the "Align" Chapter we discussed the desirability of IT planning being aligned with the planning processes of the enterprise, and how, in this activity, business and IT alignment is facilitated by the EA. We proposed that in this exercise, the EA employs several techniques, some to assess alignment and some to assess IT performance. It is quite possible that especially assessments of IT performance may be undertaken by the IT division outside of this planning period. The EA may not have visibility of these events, especially in operational or service management assessments undertaken from time to time by the operational divisions of the IT organization.

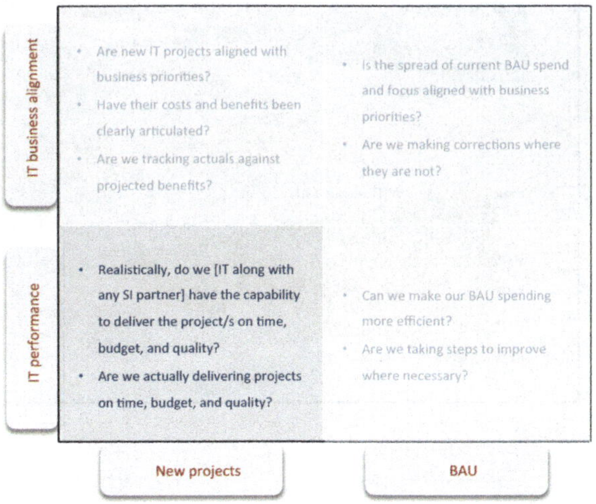

Image (8.7).

This quadrant is about the performance of IT in delivering new projects: we made the point earlier (in "Elaborate") that misconceived optimism or confidence in this quadrant is perhaps the single biggest reason that large IT initiatives generally do not deliver satisfactory outcomes.

An honest assessment of capability during the planning stages of the business lifecycle, as described in "Align" (current state assessment), can serve to uncover and hopefully address capability gaps in IT in areas impacting development and delivery of new systems.

As described in "Align", the enterprise architect's responsibilities in the current state assessment, (of course working with relevant stakeholders) should encompass the initial identification of areas for capability uplift; but the EA typically will have little responsibility in the actual capability uplift programs in these areas.

To conclude, the astute reader may have noticed that frameworks such as CMMI address capabilities and maturity in project-related disciplines, and ITIL/ITSM does the equivalent for operations and support activities. Properly used, enterprise architecture artefacts, especially those that we have illustrated in "Align", play a significant role in the top two, alignment, quadrants (Image **8.8**).

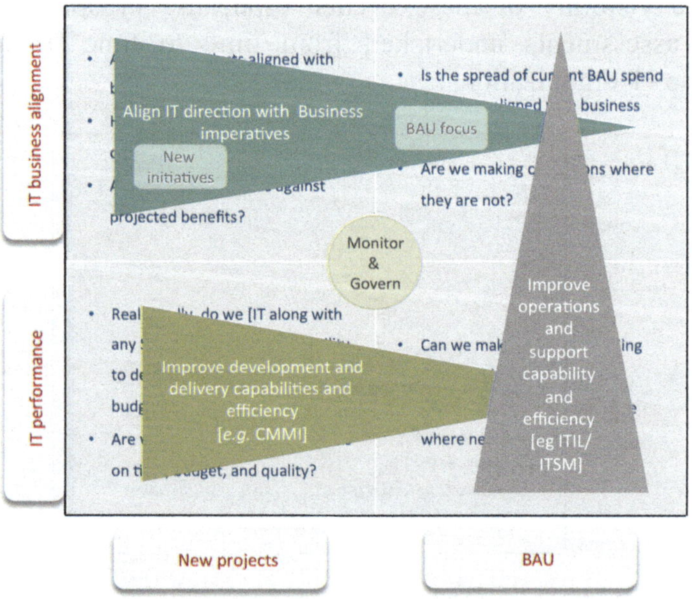

Image (8.8).

8.4. The Enterprise Architect's Domain

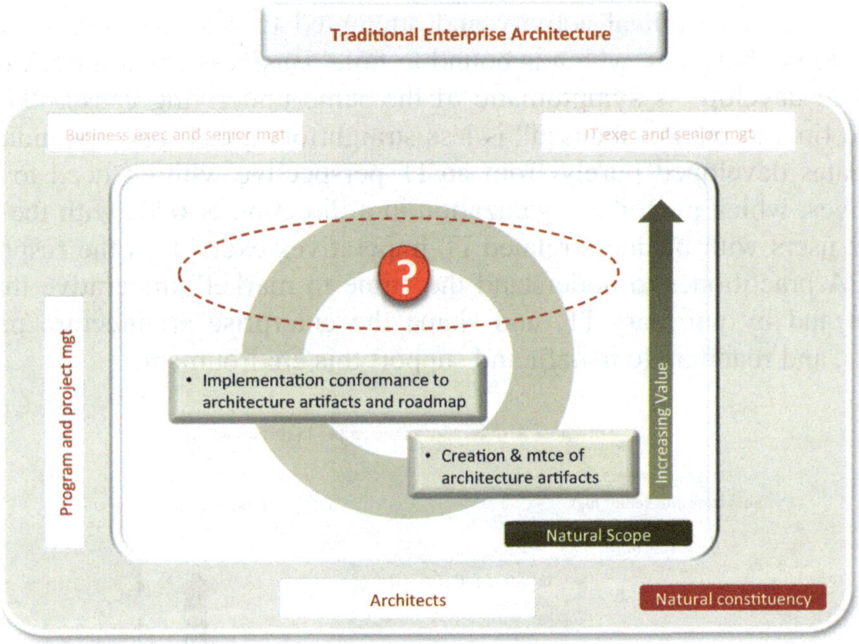

Image (8.9).

Traditionally, the ambit of the EA has focused on custodianship and policing aspects of enterprise architecture, often conceived in a zone of scarce business requirements (Image **8.9**). We have consistently argued that, without the crucial link to strategic business intent, EA activity can easily become meaningless and wasteful.

In an Infosys EA Survey undertaken in 2007, 32% of organizations surveyed were unable to justify investment in EA. The main reasons for this were[3]:

- Business does not understand the value of EA – it's too technical (57%)
- IT is short term and time to market focused (53%)
- Business case too difficult to develop (24%)

[3]A respondent was obviously able to give multiple reasons.

These responses in itself tell the story: if "EA is too technical" and "Business does not understand the value of EA" then the enterprise architects have very likely defined EA as a technical activity and attempted to send a primarily technical message to the business, which is bound to fail. "Business cases for EA being too difficult to develop" is symptomatic of the same underlying cause. "IT is short term and time to market focused" is less straightforward. It perhaps indicates EA target states developed purely from an IT perspective without heed to business imperatives, which push the organization in a direction at odds with the pull that business users with business-related IT imperatives exert. It is the responsibility of the EA practitioner to understand the "time to market" imperative that drives business and by corollary IT, and shape the enterprise architecture principles, practices, and roadmap to benefit and support this environment.

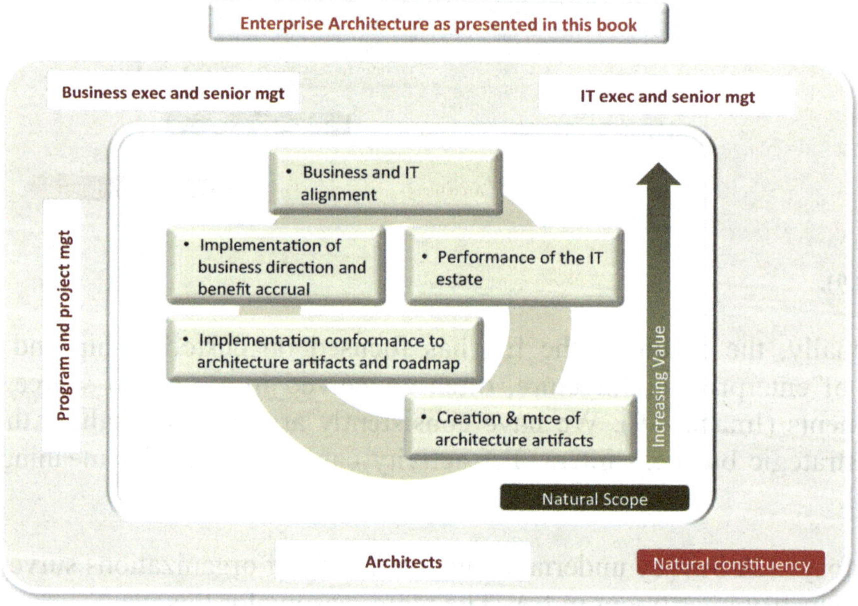

Image (8.10).

In this eBook we have consistently advocated an expanded role for the EA (Image **8.10**), asserting that the non-traditional concerns that we propose represent higher value to the enterprise. In this Chapter, we have shown the veracity of this assertion using a relatively rigorous analysis of IT value and how that value may be optimized. In other words, we have shown the worth of areas such as those below in creating value to the business, and the EA's role in these activities.

- Business and IT alignment

- IT's close association with implementing the desired business direction
- Aligning the performance of the IT estate with business value
- Improving efficiency of IT's performance

This expanded scope of an enterprise architect extends over some of the existing role and responsibility boundaries that usually exist in an IT division. For example, IT capability improvement spans all areas of the IT division – development, support, operations; the financial analysis activity intrudes into territory that IT management may regard as their domain; the CIO and business and IT management may regard business alignment as their patch. We do not for a moment suggest that the EA usurps and appropriates to him/herself the responsibilities of these various roles. Rather we propose that the EA acts as a consultant within IT and the IT/Business interface, working in collaboration and cooperation with incumbent staff, to carve a niche as a trusted advisor to senior Business and IT management.

Ironically, this expanded role is now more congruent with realizing the traditional aspirations of enterprise architects – in terms of the influence and the effectiveness of enterprise architecture.

These expanded responsibilities will not materialize overnight: first and foremost, EAs must develop skills to undertake these tasks successfully – softer skills of managing senior stakeholders, skills in business strategy, planning and business architecture, appropriate financial and analytical skills and the ability to rise above detail, to operate comfortably in the big picture landscape. Selling the broader scope of the EA's role to IT management and the Business is the next challenge. Above all though, EAs must deliver in their expanded role.

CHAPTER 9

Case Studies

Abstract: In previous chapters we observed how enterprise architecture programs are often unsuccessful, with many not progressing past the initial stages losing support and momentum, or running to a conclusion only for their output to be reduced to shelfware.

This chapter presents case studies of three quite different projects from our experience that in their own ways avoided these relevance problems plaguing EA.

Keywords: Business drivers, EA case studies, mapping to EA frameworks, methodology and process, Process Classification Framework (APQC), stakeholder management.

We have argued in this eBook that traditional enterprise architecture is often ineffective. And throughout this eBook we have suggested remedies to address the problem and redress the situation. We believe that these case studies demonstrate these virtues. All three case studies focus on the planning stage of the business cycle, mapping mainly to the key "align" stage of the EA cycle.

In these examples we have applied the techniques we discuss in the eBook; we have also abstracted artefacts from these and other EA assignments to show them elsewhere in this eBook. As such, you may find some material from previous chapters repeated here.

9.1. Case Study 1: Organisational Context

This organisation provides insurance, travel and financial services to a large customer base. It comprises several autonomous business units both customer-facing and internal divisions. The IT Division is shared, providing services to the business units within the organisation.

9.1.1. Business Challenges/Drivers

The new CIO, appointed some months prior to the engagement, inherited several issues:

- Underinvestment in IT for some years

Inji Wijegunaratne, George Fernandez & Peter Evans-Greenwood

- Historically, disengagement by IT from the businesses and their needs
- Historically, perceived failures of IT to deliver

Business units were becoming increasingly concerned with the need for rapid response in a progressively tighter competitive environment, and saw elements of the existing IT estate as hindering this imperative; moreover they were not comforted by IT's poor history of delivery on significant initiatives.

In parallel, technology-centric opinions were being expressed within IT (and with business stakeholders) on IT's direction—such as a push for a Service Oriented Architecture—based largely on individual technical preferences rather than evidence.

The CIO was of the view that an evidence-based strategic direction was needed for the IT Division. The central questions were:

- What were the issues with the IT legacy that the CIO inherited—on systems, technology, and capability fronts—and how to improve them?
- What did the business want to do—what business plans were they developing—and how could IT assist?
- Importantly, can this exercise be accomplished within the span of the annual business planning cycle?

The intended output was to be a roadmap which would carve out a business-aligned path for IT, refined *via*:

- Negotiating with business stakeholders on priorities, and setting expectations on how quickly business solutions can be delivered.
- Understanding the key technical and architectural decision points and decisions along the roadmap.

The assignment was an outstanding success, with business and IT ownership and buy-in flowing naturally, each business unit assuming ownership of their Business Information Systems Plan, and the executive and the Board endorsing the roadmap and granting in-principle approval for the IT funded elements of the plan. At the time of writing, the program of work had commenced and was well under way.

9.2. Approach

9.2.1. Methodology/Process (Image 9.1)

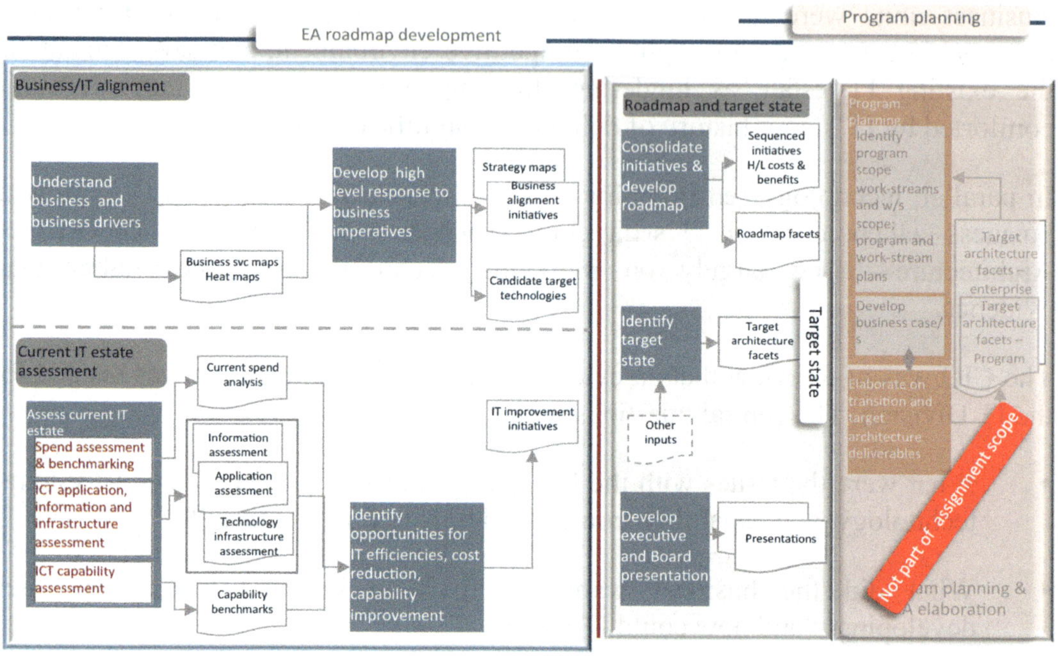

Image (9.1).

<u>9.2.1.1. Activities – Current State Assessment</u>

Task	Comments	Deliverables
Financial assessment	Several challenges: Historically, IT did not maintain its financial information in a manner conducive to this type of analysis. Accurate attribution was difficult. Historically, one of the business divisions performed a significant part of their IT work within their own division – this expenditure was not available for our analysis. Industry benchmark data was difficult to come by, since the enterprise did not fit neatly into an established industry segment. Hence the output was indicative, providing the CIO and senior IT managers with a very broad assessment of current ICT spend, and used as an internal IT	Spend indicators, ratios and comparison against industry; for example: % CapEx *vs* OpEx; % fixed *vs* variable costs; spread of IT spend across categories – staff, hardware, software, external services; IT spend as a proportion of company revenue.

Task	Comments	Deliverables
	report.	
Information assessment **Application assessment** **Tech infra assessment**	Qualitative, mainly through structured discussions with IT managers for each of these areas. Focused on current issues facing each area, and on identifying initiatives needed to improve the status quo.	For each area, an assessment report describing strengths as well as issues, and documenting at a high level the improvement initiatives.
IT capability assessment	A "business" services map for the IT division was initially developed and agreed with the CIO. Key capability areas were then identified, and, in association with the CIO's direct reports, an assessment was performed. A number of capability improvement initiatives were identified.	A business services map for IT A capability assessment report, describing: • The key capability areas and IT's rating against each on a scale of 1 (non-existent) to 5(excellent/ expert). • The identified capability improvement initiatives (typically process or skills related).

9.2.1.2. Activities – High Level Response to Business Imperatives

Task	Comments	Deliverables
Develop high-level response to business strategic needs	Understand the business strategic imperatives *via* • Review of their strategy and planning documents • Discussions with key senior and executive business management • Development and analysis of a business services map for the division. With key senior and executive business managers, develop a set of IT-based initiatives that respond to/	A business services map for the division; business services heat map (Section 9.3.2.1). Set of business/ IT-based initiatives (projects) to support the realisation of business goals.

Task	Comments	Deliverables
	address the business imperatives.	

9.2.1.3. Activities – Consolidation, Roadmap Development

Task	Comments	Deliverables
Consolidate and prioritise initiatives into a roadmap	A large number—over 100—were identified. The considerable task of grouping and structuring these was undertaken using a workshop based approach. • Duplicate elimination • Consolidation • Understanding precedence requirements, including the analyses/ platform/ appln/ capability structure (see Fig. **9.6**) • Preserving traceability • Uniform high-level documentation	A consolidated roadmap
Roadmap architecture implications	Key IT architectural considerations, for example reinforcing the need for a set of key platforms upon which applications can be built; recommending architecturally favourable options, for example for master data management, integration *etc.*); undertaken in parallel with finalising the roadmap	Architecture-based assessments and recommendations in the context of the roadmap
Assess IT's financial commitment	A considerable proportion of the IT roadmap (the business/ IT projects identified for each of the businesses) would be business funded. However, the shared elements of IT (the platforms, infrastructure improvement) would need capital IT budget (and associated OpEx). The three year financial commitment for	Estimate of CapEx and OpEx, based on the roadmap elements to be IT funded

Task	Comments	Deliverables
	IT in the context of the roadmap was estimated	

9.2.1.4. Activities – Assignment Outputs Including Executive and Board Presentations

Task	Comments	Deliverables
Finalise roadmap facets/ deliverables • **Overall roadmap** • **Business information systems plans** • **Technical stream roadmaps**	Delivery of the final output/ presentations The overall roadmap, plus two sets of views of the roadmap • The IT views • The business views Both views contain the same initiatives, but grouped along business and technical lines	Overall roadmap Business views • Information systems plan for each business division IT views: Roadmaps for • Application • Information management • Infrastructure • Capability improvement
Develop executive management and Board presentations	The planning/ roadmap content was suitably summarised and structured for the executive and the board	Executive presentation Board presentation

9.2.2. Key Enterprise-Level Artefacts

We can classify the artefacts were referenced in the Section "approach/process" above into the following types:

- Artefacts produced (and/or assist) primarily in *aligning* IT with business direction
- Artefacts produced (and/or assist) primarily in *representing* the direction
- Artefacts produced (and/or assist) in *establishing detail* of the direction

We would focus here on the key artefacts of the former two types. However, since these artefacts are not part and parcel of traditional enterprise architecture work and may not at first glance appear to be natural candidates for this tag, in Section "Zachman mapping" we map these to the Zachman framework.

9.2.2.1. Business Alignment Artefacts

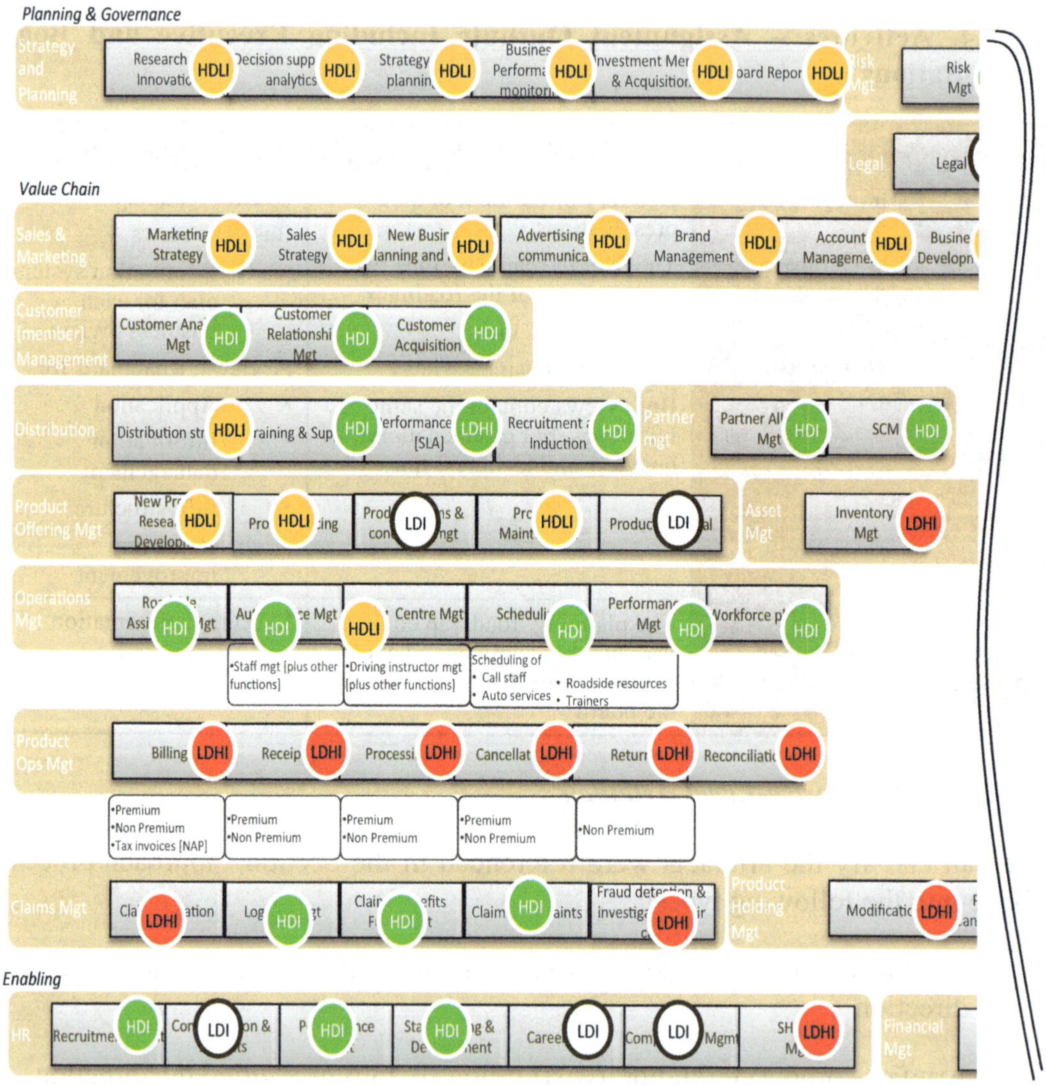

Fig. (9.1). Business services heat-map.

The business services map and the heat-map are key elements to developing a business-led framework for analysis and decision making on IT investment. The business services map is a high-level description of the various functions (services) performed by the business (Fig. **9.1**). Above, a mainly two-level map is shown (with some services being described at level 3), of one of the organisation's business units. Similar business services maps were derived for all business units. The heat-map differentially classifies business services into the typology shown in Fig. (**9.2**). The classification (discussed earlier in this eBook and reproduced below) identifies appropriate investment/support strategies for the different business service types.

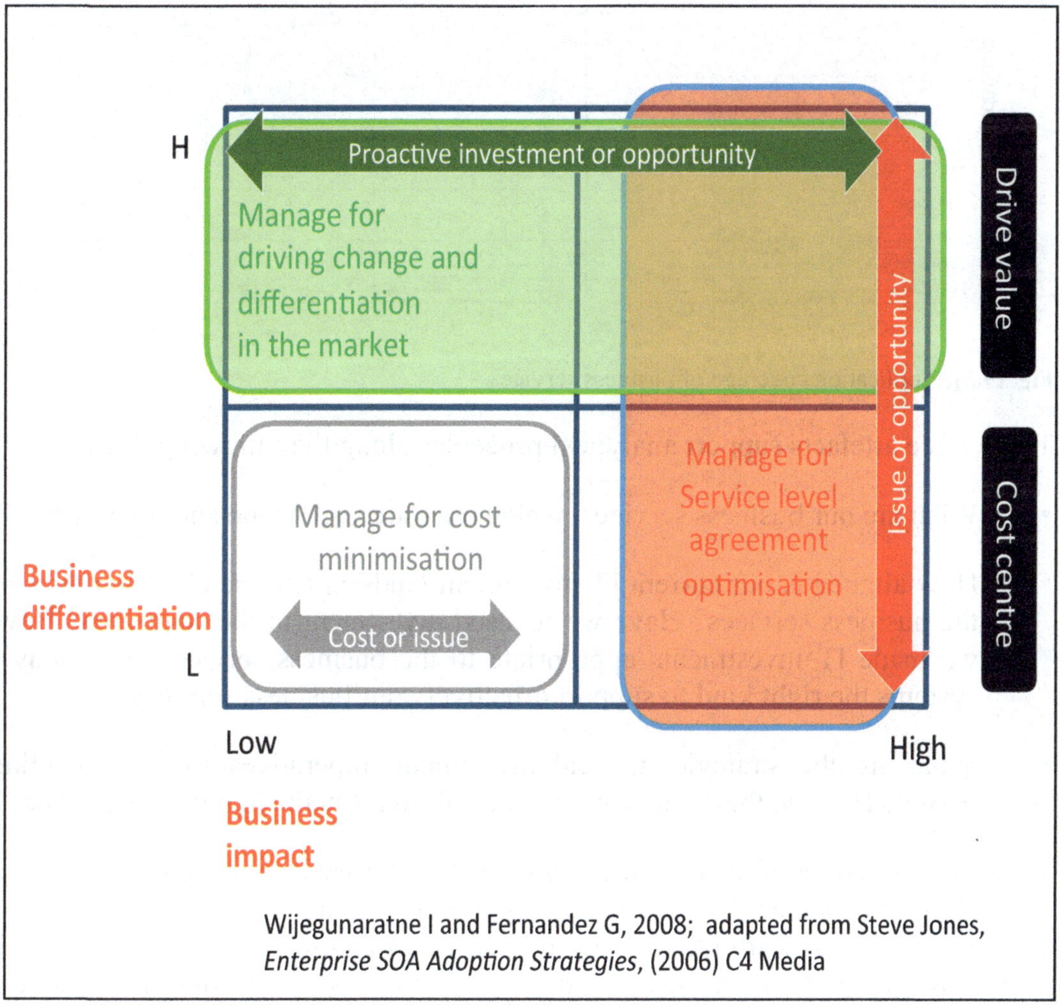

Fig. (9.2). Business services classification framework.

This matrix of existing applications intersecting with the (heat-mapped) business services shows application coverage of business services (Fig. **9.3**).

Fig. (9.3). Application coverage of business services.

These three artefacts support analytical processes along the following lines:

- What are our business services; which ones are high value and high impact?
- How aligned is our current IT investment landscape to the characteristics of the business services? Have we focused investment in the right area? Have we made IT investments appropriate to the business service? Are today's systems the right kind to support effectively our business services?
- What are the strategic/ tactical investment imperatives for the planning period? How do these translate into actual investments in business services?

An operating model of the organisation is the "necessary level of business process integration and standardization necessary for delivering goods and services to customers" [22]. An artefact closely related to an enterprise's operating model, shown in Fig. (**9.4**), is particularly useful in enterprises with multiple business lines. Grouping business services in this manner can tease out functional similarities among business silos, and consequently the potential to apply similar business processes and application functions: *i.e.* shared application service opportunities in a federated environment.

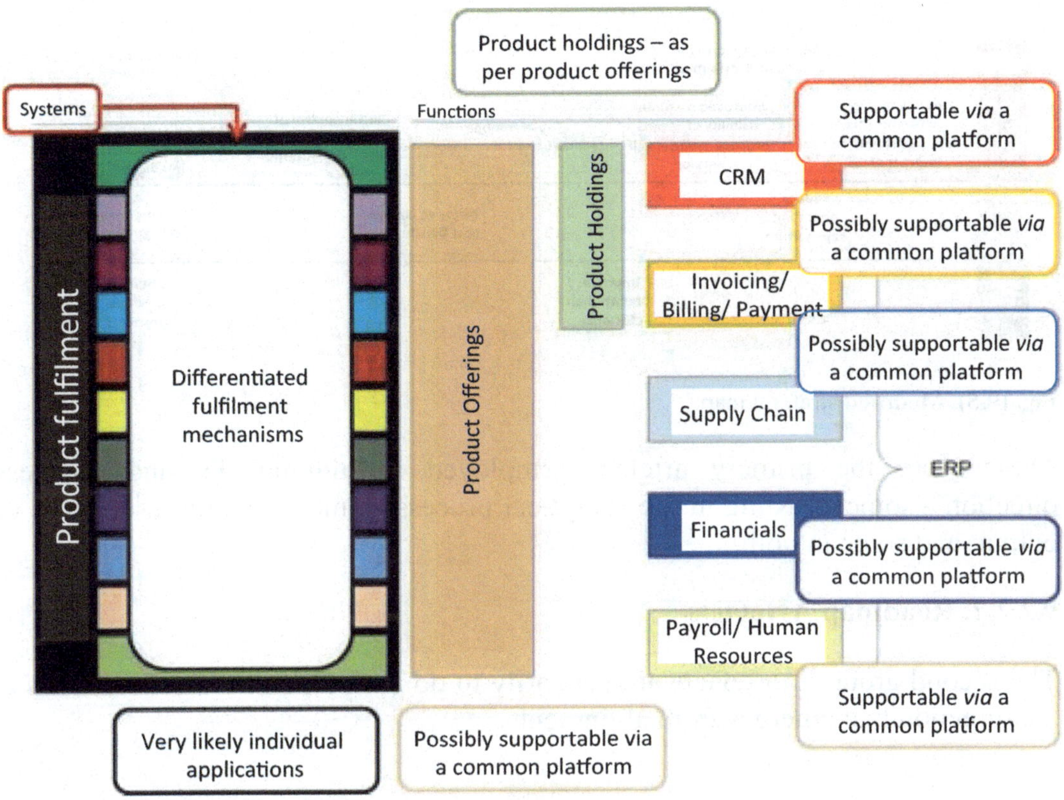

Fig. (9.4). Application coverage options.

Fig. (**9.5**) is a modified form of Kaplan and Norton's strategy mapping technique and output [23]. The middle row of this strategy map shows the strategies at Group level—the strategic goal "improve operational efficiency" is visible. The rows immediately above and below indicate the strategies of the Insurance business of aligned to the Group's strategy—*i.e.* reduce operating expenditure, achieve top-tier average claims cost. The next layer shows the Insurance/IT initiatives that align with the particular Insurance business strategies. Accordingly, this analytical technique enables the formulation of IT projects clearly aligned to business imperatives. As shown here, a clear traceability between IT projects and business/corporate strategy can be illustrated using this visual representation.

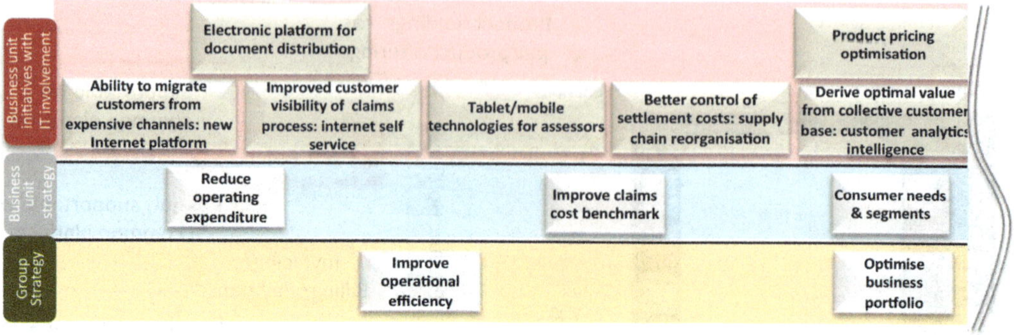

Fig. (9.5). Modified strategy map.

These were the primary artefacts employed in aligning IT and business direction—some assisting in the analytical process, some in the representation of output, and some in both.

9.2.2.2. Roadmap Artefacts

The second group of artefacts are primarily to do with representing direction; *i.e.* the direction that emerges from alignment.

Fig. (9.6). Roadmap structure: typical form of a set of initiatives.

The main artefact in this space was the roadmap, which was structured in the manner illustrated in Fig. (**9.6**). Note the classification of initiatives into categories: platforms enable applications to be built rapidly; initial analyses will be required on occasion for feasibility and due diligence before large sums of money are committed; and IT capability development will be needed to support the program of work and improve IT service levels. Hence, the structure depicted above represents relationships within any large transformation program.

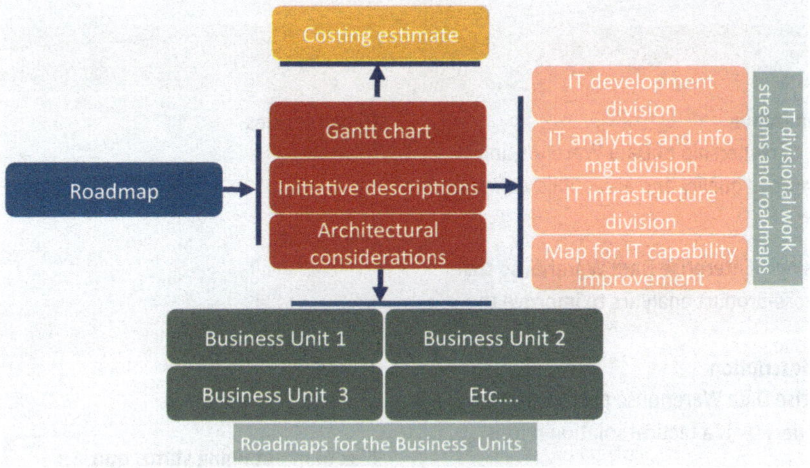

Image (9.2).

Roadmap Perspectives

In 'Roadmap perspectives' we show the different facets of the roadmap: the roadmap comprises a Gantt chart, initiative descriptions (with each initiative described to the extent shown in Fig. (**9.7**)), and (now!) technical / architectural considerations.

This content is organised along two convenient views (Image **9.2**), plus the IT costing forecast derived from the roadmap.

- An IT based view: those parts of the roadmap coming under the purview of each Senior Manager in IT (Applications, Analytics, and Infrastructure), plus a common capability improvement roadmap.
- A business division-based view (business information systems plans): the parts of the roadmap relevant to each business unit plus supporting material.

> That is, the business IS plans also contain the relevant alignment artefacts produced for that business: strategy map, heat-map, application coverage.

This arrangement facilitates the identification and allocation of ownership—for example the IT liaison manager of each business unit was happy to jointly own their business information systems plans with the IT account manager for that business. The ownership of the IT plans of course was assigned to each IT manager.

<table>
<tr><th>XX</th><th colspan="2">Move to a Single Analytics Data Warehouse</th><th colspan="2">Owner/s: IT</th></tr>
<tr><td colspan="2">Business Imperative
Reduce cost of ownership of Data Warehousing at xxxxx and improve quality and accessibility of data</td><td colspan="3">Dependencies
BI Strategy</td></tr>
<tr><td colspan="2">Outcome
XXXX has a single Enterprise Data Warehouse that allows for cross-product analytics to improve the ......</td><td colspan="3">Alignment</td></tr>
<tr><td colspan="2" rowspan="2">Functional description
•The Enterprise Data Warehouse project that is currently underway is a tactical solution that is.......</td><td colspan="3">Traceability</td></tr>
<tr><td colspan="3">Risk of maintaining status quo
Continued inability to properly analyse data across products to optimise pricing, marketing etc.</td></tr>
<tr><td rowspan="4">Technical description
•An Enterprise Data Warehouse can be built......</td><td rowspan="4">Indicative non-Functional requirements
•Rapid response times to complex queries
•Large storage volumes
•Metadata management
•Data quality management
•............</td><td colspan="3">Risk associated with implementing the initiative
May be seen as a panacea, when in reality, data quality at the source is still an issue</td></tr>
<tr><td colspan="3">Complexity
High</td></tr>
<tr><td colspan="3">Benefit
High – xxxx is currently hindered by its ability to analyse data across its multiple lines of business to improve pricing models, to optimise its distribution network and to understand its customers</td></tr>
<tr><td colspan="2">Estimated Duration</td><td>Estimated Effort</td></tr>
</table>

Fig. (9.7). Initiative descriptions.

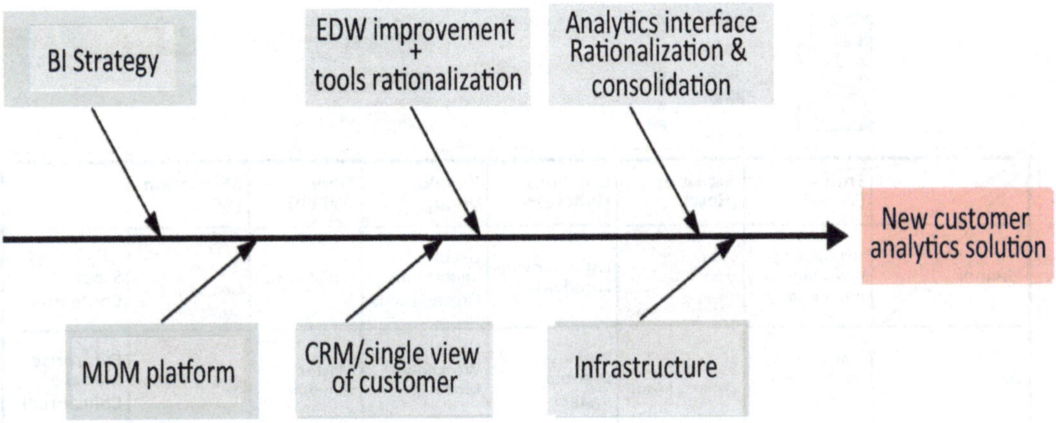

Fig. (9.8). Roadmap dependencies.

Another key feature of the roadmap process was that the dependencies were made extremely clear; most importantly the dependencies between the IT funded platforms and the specific business/IT solutions. The fishbone diagram (Fig. **9.8**) indicates how dependencies were illustrated in the presentations to management and executive staff.

Using the overall structure (analyses/platform/application/capability – shown in "Roadmap Structure"), the fishbone diagram, and the strategy map, we can show very clearly the chain of dependencies: the Group strategies, business unit strategies, business/IT initiatives, supporting IT platforms and the initial analyses. This chain of evidence was extremely beneficial in making senior business stakeholders appreciate the building blocks needed to deliver the end product, the systems that deliver their business benefits and realise their strategic goals.

9.2.2.3. Zachman Mapping

Since these artefacts are not found in a 'typical' EA exercise—where UML diagrams, data/object models, *etc.* are instead the norm—we have mapped them to the Zachman framework (Fig. **9.9**). The alignment artefacts are mapped to the higher level (*i.e.* mainly Owner, Planner perspectives) cells of the framework, and the roadmap exhibits to Master Schedule and Business Plan cells.

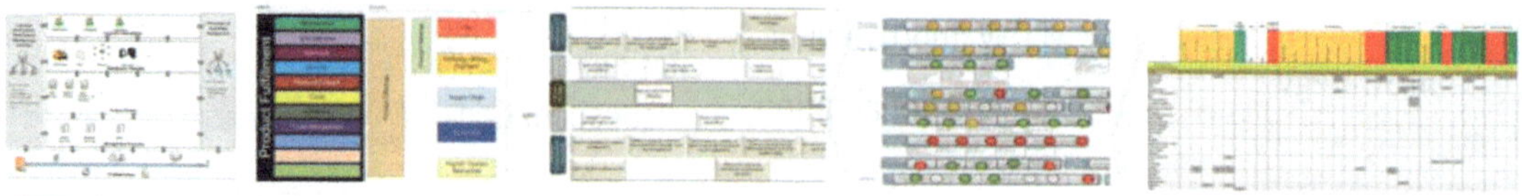

	Entities (What)	Activities (How)	Locations (Where)	People (who)	Time (When)	Motivation (Why)	
Planner	List of things important to the business	List of Core Business processes	List of Business Locations	List of important Organisations	List of events	List of Business Goals/ Strategies	**Objective/ Scope Contextual**
Owner	Conceptual Data/Object Model	Business process Model	Business Logistics System	Workflow Model	Master Schedule	Business Plan	**Enterprise Model Conceptual**
Designer	Logical Data Model	System Architecture Model	Distributed Systems Architecture	Human Interface Architecture	Processing Structure	Business Role Model	**System Model Logical**
Builder	Physical Data Model	Technology Design Model	Technology Architecture	Presentation Architecture	Control Structure	Rule Design	**Technical Model Physical**
Sub-contractor (Programmer)	Data Definitions	Program	Network Architecture	Security Architecture	Timing Definition	Rule Specification	**Components Out of context**
Functioning Enterprise	Usable Data	Working Function	Usable Network	Functioning Organisation	Implemented Schedule	Working Strategy	**Functioning Enterprise**

Zachman framework

Fig. (9.9). Mapping of alignment and roadmap artefacts.

Other Artefacts

The more traditional artefacts of EA—such as high-level application and interface diagrams, CRUD matrices, and high-level technical and functional descriptions of specific application platforms—were produced during the course of the assignment:

- High level 'as is' application/interface diagram: evidence of integration complexity (effort/cost)
- 'As is' and 'to be' technology stack: evidence of rationalization
- Technical and functional descriptions: used in elaborating upon the strands of the roadmap

Broadly speaking, these artefacts were produced for, or assisted in, either providing supporting evidence or in establishing the detail of the roadmap/direction.

9.3. Lessons

9.3.1. Evidence-Based Delivery

A key to the success of this engagement was that at the outset we deliberately assumed very little by way of IT solutions. Although there were major issues with the IT estate (which were common knowledge), that the new CIO inherited, we did not assume these either: we allowed these matters to emerge in the current state assessment. IT professionals often tend to jump prematurely to the solution space, usually assuming a technology solution. In this project too we observed this behaviour: for example a senior IT technologist was convinced that SOA was the 'answer', and had for some time been proselytizing SOA. We took the view at the outset that adopting SOA as a solution was premature, although indeed SOA may well become part of a solution. Rather, we let the assignment progress, let evidence speak for itself, and solution/s gradually unfold as the strategy roadmap progressed.

In the event, the shape of the output may well have surprised many in IT. A very strong common thread was observed within the many business/IT initiatives: the Business went for analytics as the solutions critically important to them. Channel and customer analytics were key issues, and Master Data Management emerged as a key enabler to better understand customer behaviour, to up/cross sell, to improve customer experience, and to promote brand awareness. The emphasis was on consolidating, cleansing, and unifying the individual pools of federated customer data. Integration's initial role—with SOA in an integration guise—was as an *enabler* for Master Data Management.

9.3.2. Stakeholder Management

Managing business and IT stakeholders is vital to EA success. The CIO's direct involvement and participation in the exercise in part paved the way within IT. As a general dictum however, EA teams undertaking this type of assignment must be conscious of sensitivities that exist in an assessment of current state, in terms of people, capability, cost, process, technology. An honest assessment—in most cases a self-assessment—needs to be elicited and building a trust-based relationship with IT stakeholders is crucial.

Equally, earning business stakeholder trust is essential. The new CIO's efforts in the background to this assignment were admirable: among other things he inherited damaged relationships with a few key business executives and the new CIO was very quickly able to repair them and build a position of trust. Consequently, the EA exercise benefitted greatly. Within the roadmap assignment, our ability to show *via* a Roadmap structure analysis/platform/application, fishbone diagrams and strategy maps very clearly the dependencies and traceability was an important factor in their buy-in to the overall roadmap. Due to underinvestment in IT in the past, there was a great deal of pent-up demand for business/IT solutions. However, because of these mechanisms, we were almost always on the same page with the business. Though inconvenient and painful, in the main the high-value business solutions were some distance away, because of the necessary building blocks needed first.

9.3.3. Conclusion

This assignment was contextualised firmly in business positioning, strategy, and direction. It was thus possible to deliver naturally, as part of the process, an IT direction aligned with business positioning and direction. Business buy-in flowed again naturally, as did business acquiescence of the IT costs. It was important for our timing not to be out of kilter with the business planning cycle—though starting a little late, we were able to deliver within the planning cycle and process.

As we have shown, the content of this exercise includes artefacts not typical in the EA domain. We have, however, shown their place and significance in this assignment, and also their home within an industry standard EA framework. Underlying these artefacts are skills in analytical processes accompanying these constructs, mixing creative and analytical thought processes, interacting comfortably with senior business managers and presenting outcomes to senior audiences.

The key constructs and the thrust of this exercise were to make big decisions and paint the big picture of how IT is to proceed—the approach, artefacts, timeframe and effort were all tailored to this end. The appropriate time for the detail of the architecture, using some of the more traditional architecture constructs and techniques, is to be developed after this alignment and direction setting is done, to elaborate upon the architecture of the direction that was set here.

To conclude, we demonstrate here how a successful outcome was delivered by embedding appropriate EA activity within the context of setting and aligning IT with its business direction, by using appropriate representational content plus underlying skills, and by making the timing congruent with business expectations.

9.4. Case Studies Two and Three

These case studies exemplify the different nature of EA engagements, and how they need to be considered 'on their merits', as the approach may be different for a short 8 weeks engagement as opposed to a 10 months project.[1]

9.4.1. Introduction

We start first by stating that whether it is apparent of not, any functioning enterprise possesses, if not an architecture, some kind of functional structure. Thus, initially the challenge of the Enterprise Architect in a functioning enterprise is to uncover this structure and represent it in a manner that stakeholders can comprehend. However, the task of accurately describing an enterprise and the way it works is a very complex, difficult undertaking. Indeed, given the sheer size, complexity and dynamic nature of modern organisations it may even be argued to be unfeasible. It is often too easy to forget that the real aim is to produce and demonstrate tangible benefits for the business. But if documenting the organisation in "excruciating level of detail" as espoused by Zachman [13] is not practical, what is the extent and depth appropriate for Enterprise Architecture?

The answer lies in that not all EA projects have the same drivers and goals. We agree with Doucet *et al.* [24] that EA encompasses any approach, large or small, to promote coherence into the current management practice of the enterprise. Hence, our 'purpose test':

I. The raison d'être for EA must stem from, and be kept aligned to, a business purpose.

II. The level and detail of the enterprise descriptions must be tailored to be sufficient for its intended purpose.

We here compare and contrasts two very different, successful EA exercises carried out by the authors as external consultants to two Australian-based multinationals:

---

[1]This material has been published previously in the Journal for Enterprise Architecture: "EA Heavy and EA Light: Two Examples of Successful Enterprise Architecture", I. Wijegunaratne, P. Evans-Greenwood, George Fernandez, Volume 7, Number 2, 2011. and presented here with permission.

- *EA heavy:* an engagement for an FMCG (Fast Moving Consumer Goods) company headquartered in Australia. The EA engagement was initiated by a direct report of the CIO and performed over a period of approximately six months by a team of ten staff working full time. Initially, the purpose was articulated as "The current architecture evolved through several years of acquisitions and business unit integrations (...) The result has been an extremely complex landscape with application and data duplication, process complexity and inefficiency (...) inhibiting flexibility, agility, and innovation".

- *EA light:* carried out in six weeks by a team of two external consultants, for an Australian financial services group, to build on existing business-as-usual *via* initiatives aligned with the strategic goals of the business. The main requirement was to build a chain of evidence connecting actions back to business drivers to align the IT project portfolio with the organization's overall business strategy.

9.4.2. The "EA Heavy" Project

The EA engagement was initiated by the IT division, by a direct report of the CIO. The IT stakeholders engaged a team of external consultants to carry out a collaborative EA exercise, with the engagement encompassing the entire Group. The assignment was performed over a period of approximately six months by a team of ten full-time staff.

Fig. (**9.10**) shows the sequence of steps for the EA Heavy project. The left hand side shows the initial phase to the process, including the development of the current logical, conceptual and physical models. The APQC process framework was used as the basis for the classification of business processes necessary to support the logical model. APQC is a taxonomy of business processes that makes possible analysis of organisational performance within an organisation and between organisations. The taxonomy is organized into twelve categories of business processes, five categories of operating processes and seven of support processes (shown in Fig. **9.11**). Each category contains processes representing the operations of a single business function within the organization, providing organizations with a framework for benchmarking each function, and monitoring its improvement.

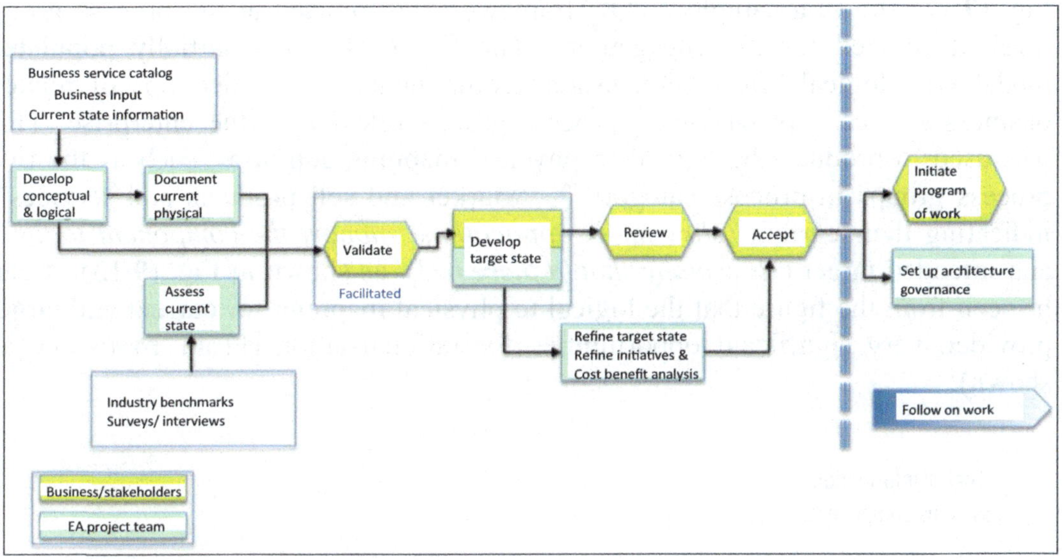

Fig. (9.10). Steps in the EA heavy approach.

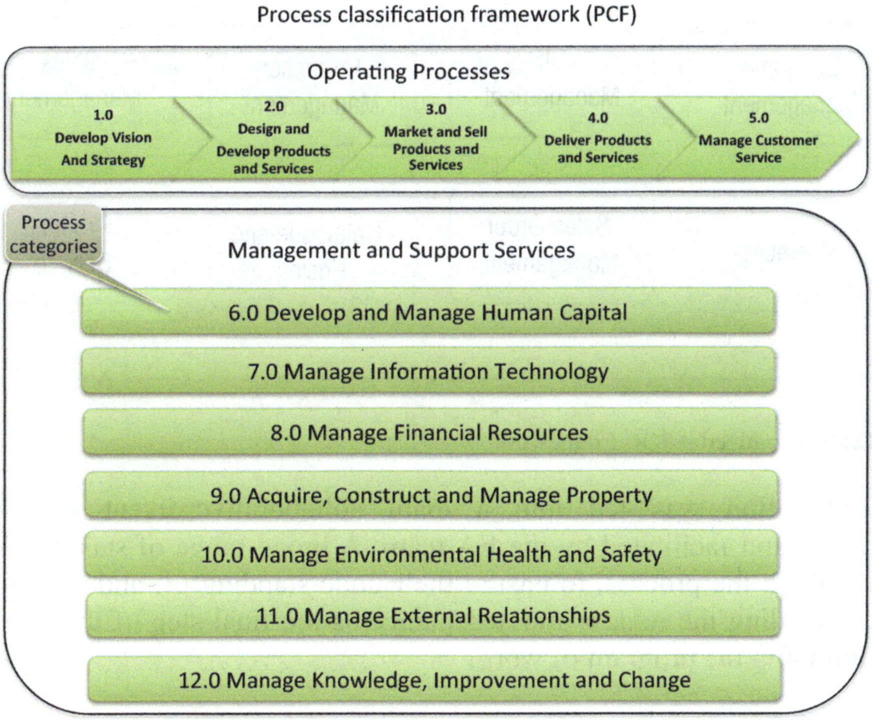

Fig. (9.11). American Productivity and Quality Center (APQC) framework. Reference framework in EA Heavy (http://www.apqc.org/portal/apqc/site).

Fig. (**9.12**) shows a sample APQC framework customised at the process group level, developed for the engagement. The figure shows a partially populated model with logical information system components—*i.e.* collections of related business services—provisioning process groups relevant to the enterprise. This was used to produce the logical to physical mapping activities, such as the two process groups in process category 3, "Market and sell products and services", indicating their current (*How many applications support the component today?*) and intended target (*How many should there be?*), as shown in Fig. (**9.13**). It can be seen from the figure that the logical to physical mapping for current and target provided very significant opportunities for rationalisation (From 14 to one as shown).

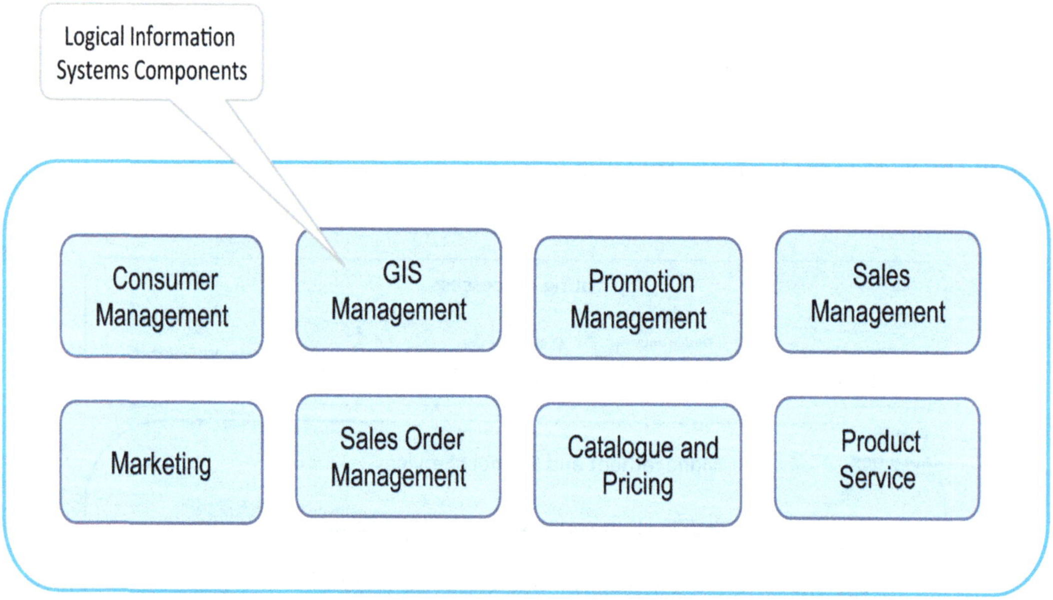

Fig. (9.12). Customized APQC Framework.

This information was fed into a main collaborative event involving the stakeholders and facilitated by the EA team. A broad range of stakeholders were involved along the process, to ensure their understanding of, and support of, the project, including the review and acceptance as the final step of the EA exercise before initiating the program of work.

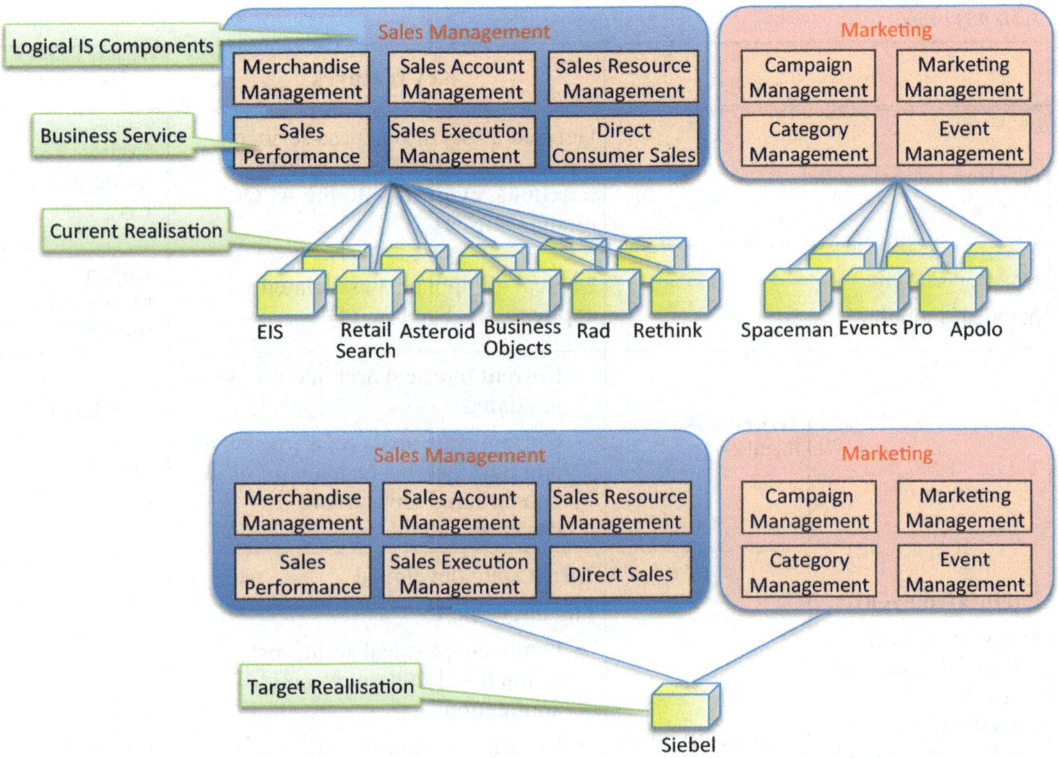

Fig. (9.13). Mapping of logical components to physical applications – current state and target state.

Table **9.1** shows our three step approach, also depicted in Fig. (**9.10**): a) initial work by the EA team; b) a facilitated event; c) first cut of the initiatives. The table classifies and summarises the activities, their features and their outcomes.

Table 9.1. Description of activities: significant features of the activities and their outcomes.

	Key features	**Outcome**
Context	Summarise business context: scope, mission, and objectives	EA context document
Develop current state analysis	In-depth assessment of the current IT estate. Assesses key aspects: *e.g.* numbers of servers and applications; functional coverage and non-functional behaviour, user/IT assessments and against industry benchmarks	Current state assessment

(Table 9.1) contd…..

		Key features	**Outcome**
Develop logical model		Defined as set of business services, representing discrete re-usable functions, mapped onto the APQC model. (Fig. **2**)	Logical model for EA.
Develop current physical model		Logical components associated with applications. See Fig. (**4**)	Current physical EA model.
Facilitated event Major analytical activity: facilitated by external consultants, where key business and IT work cooperatively with the EA project team	1. Validate inputs	• Current physical architecture is validated • Current state analysis is presented and implications (especially of the "do nothing" option) are communicated.	Validated current physical model.
	2. Develop target physical model	Target state developed The target state: • Duplicate physical solutions rationalised to do *via* a single application • Use of existing (underutilised) solutions expanded • Point solutions retired Bespoke or heavily customised solutions in non-differentiating areas such as Finance & HR retired. Customised APQC.	Target physical model for EA.
	3. Develop initial transformation roadmap	Develop first cut roadmap in terms of a list of initiatives, their precedence relationships and order of implementation.	
Refine deliverables		Target state plus first-cut roadmap refined.	
Package and present results		Appropriate packages of the deliverables produced, tailored to the target audiences.	

The target state, initially developed at the facilitated event, was refined along with the costs and benefits. The prioritised set of initiatives to move today's enterprise to the rationalised state—including a five-year transformation program—was accepted by the enterprise, and they are currently implementing the program.

9.4.3. The 'EA Light' Project

During a financial year, the lines of business of this financial services group released their new strategic goals, prompting the Information Technology department to review its established programme of work. The challenge was to find a method that would build on existing business-as-usual and top-line initiatives to align with the new strategic goals, and build a chain of evidence connecting actions back to business drivers. All this within a very short period of time to provide a tangible output that could be presented to the business executives.

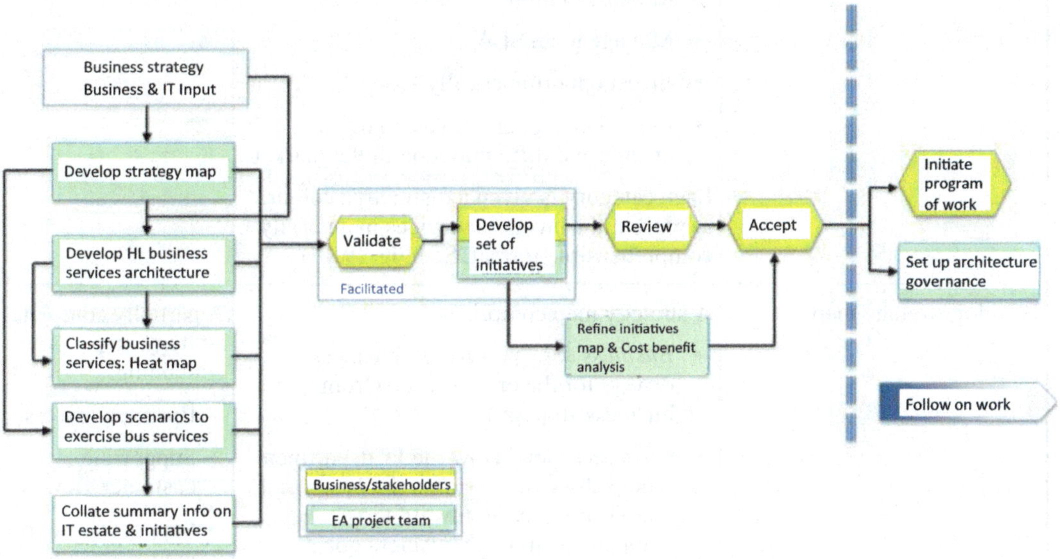

Fig. (9.14). Steps in the EA light approach.

The external consultants undertook the assignment, and (with assistance from IT and business stakeholders) delivered the required outcomes within a period of six weeks. Fig. **(9.14)** shows the main activities undertaken, and the relationships between them. The same three-step pattern of 1) initial work; 2) facilitated event and review; and 3) acceptance is shown in Fig. **(9.14)** and Table **9.2**. The table shows the different activities undertaken, their key features and their outcomes.

Table 9.2. Description of activities: significant features of the activities and their outcomes.

	Key features	Outcome
Develop high-level business services architecture (BSA)	At a high level, Identify the business services and how they interact. Big picture view of how the business operates. *Decompose just enough:* with level 0 being the context (the three businesses of the Group and how they interact in this case) maximum decomposition to level 3. Fig. (**9.16**) shows a sample deliverable.	BSA for the three businesses of the Group in scope for this study
Classify business services (heat map)	Business services classified based on business value into four categories, from less to most important: • Manage to minimize cost • Manage to an SLA • Invest opportunistically • Market changing – invest to drive change and differentiation in the market Each category is given a distinctive colour, to present the business services in an easily comprehensible format. See Fig. (**9.17**)	Heat map of Business services in BSA
Develop strategy map	A strategy map comprises: • *Business drivers:* Overall business drivers for the organization (from business strategy) • *Customer view:* How the IT department would show the business (its customer) that IT are moving toward the company's strategic business goals • *Internal view:* How the IT department would deliver the Customer view • *Actions:* The concrete actions that IT will undertake to realise the strategies in the internal view. *The actions are not identified at this stage of the process* The business view was identified from the business strategy, and the customer view and internal view developed. The initiatives are identified later. See Fig. (**9.15**) for an example	A partially complete strategy map containing: • Business drivers • Supporting customer view • Supporting internal view.

(Table 9.2) contd.....

<table>
<tr><th colspan="2"></th><th>Key features</th><th>Outcome</th></tr>
<tr><td colspan="2">Develop scenarios to exercise the business services</td><td>Scenarios developed to exercise the BSA.
• Business as usual (BAU) scenarios – exercising key E2E business processes
• Stretch scenarios: “stress testing” the BSA
Walking through a scenario exercises one or more services in the BSA. “What happens if” scenarios must be traceable to one or more of the business drivers.
Adequate coverage – mix between BAU and stretch, and traceability to the business drivers must be ensured</td><td>A set of BAU and stretch scenarios</td></tr>
<tr><td colspan="2">Collate summary information on IT estate & existing initiatives</td><td>List of existing initiatives
Use a lightweight survey to gather information on the existing IT estate
Intention: use for reference purposes at the facilitated event</td><td>List of existing initiatives.
Summary information on existing IT estate.</td></tr>
<tr><td rowspan="3">Facilitated event
An event, facilitated by external consultants, where key business and IT representatives work cooperatively to produce the outputs:</td><td>1. Validate strategy map, BSA, heat map</td><td>Validate the inputs
• Strategy map
• Business services architecture
• Heat map</td><td>Validated inputs</td></tr>
<tr><td>2. Exercise the scenarios to determine initiatives</td><td>In groups, walk through each scenario, exercising the relevant business services and understanding the consequences. Explore how you would change the IT estate to support different scenarios where additional IT support is needed, or where IT needs to be changed. When the IT estate is found deficient or wanting, a new initiative is created to rectify the problem</td><td></td></tr>
<tr><td>3. Classify and prioritise the initiatives to identify a three-year program</td><td>A first-cut road-map in terms of a list of initiatives (costed at a high level), their precedence relationships and order of implementation is developed out of this exercise.</td><td>Set of initiatives</td></tr>
</table>

(Table 9.2) contd…..

	Key features	Outcome
Refine the initiatives	The initiatives are scoped and costed (still at a high level) but in a little more detail.	Set of initiatives (refined)
Package and present deliverables	Final report is produced	Final report, + work products for the Strategy map, BSA, Heat map, Initiatives documentation in the selected EA tool

Several strategies and tools were used for this exercise, as inputs to a facilitated event. These are discussed further in the following sections.

- Strategy Maps were used to establish direct links between the business drivers and the actions that IT should carry out to deliver the goals.
- A 'just-enough' decomposition of a Business Services Architecture was developed, with a maximum decomposition to Level 3.
- A Heat Map, a classification of business services according to their value was produced.

9.4.3.1. Strategy Maps

The strategy map was based on the work of Kaplan and Norton [25], which we customised for IT purposes. Our map components are summarised in Table **9.3**:

Table 9.3. Strategy map components.

Construct	Description	Example (Fig. 9.15)
Business View	Business drivers	Depicts two of the overall business drivers sourced from their business strategy
Customer View	How the IT department would demonstrate to the business that the IT estate are moving toward the company's strategic business goals	Shows the "Customer View" for the two business drivers
Internal View	How the IT department would organise itself to deliver the Customer View	Shows the "Internal View" for the Customer View components
Initiatives	List the concrete actions that IT will undertake to execute on the strategies in the Internal View	Shows the initiatives to realise the "higher" components of the strategy map

In our conception of the Strategy Map for EA, the business is the customer of the IT department. The overall business drivers, part of the business strategy, sit at the top of the Map. Underneath, the Customer View expresses how the IT department will demonstrate to the business that they are moving to achieve these objectives. The Internal View is related to how the IT department will deliver the Customer View. Finally, the Initiatives lists the concrete actions that IT will undertake to execute the Internal View. Fig. (**9.15**) shows our Strategy Map for two of the enterprise business drivers.

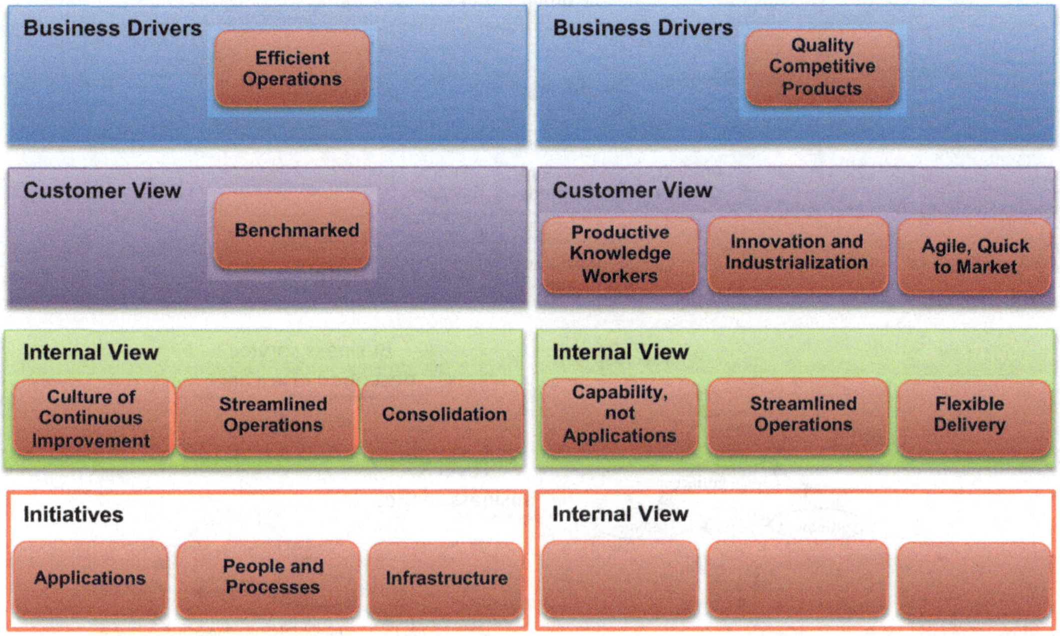

Fig. (9.15). Example strategy map.

Using a Strategy Map this way it was possible to establish a direct link between the strategic business drivers and the initiatives that will form part of the program of work for the transformation.

9.4.3.2. The Business Services Architecture (BSA)

Our Business Services Architecture (BSA) representation follows and extends the work of Jones [26]. The business services represent what the business does and delivers, and what is required to meet business goals. Where an application represents large areas of functionality across the business, the BSA worked with the business to align our understanding of the IT estate with the business activities it is intended to support. As such, it may becomc a clear language of communication between the business and IT.

Fig. (**9.16**) shows the decomposition of the funds management business. Following our premise of 'producing just enough', Level 3 decomposition was sufficient for the purposes of our exercise. The first indicates the process while the second shows the hierarchy of the business services.

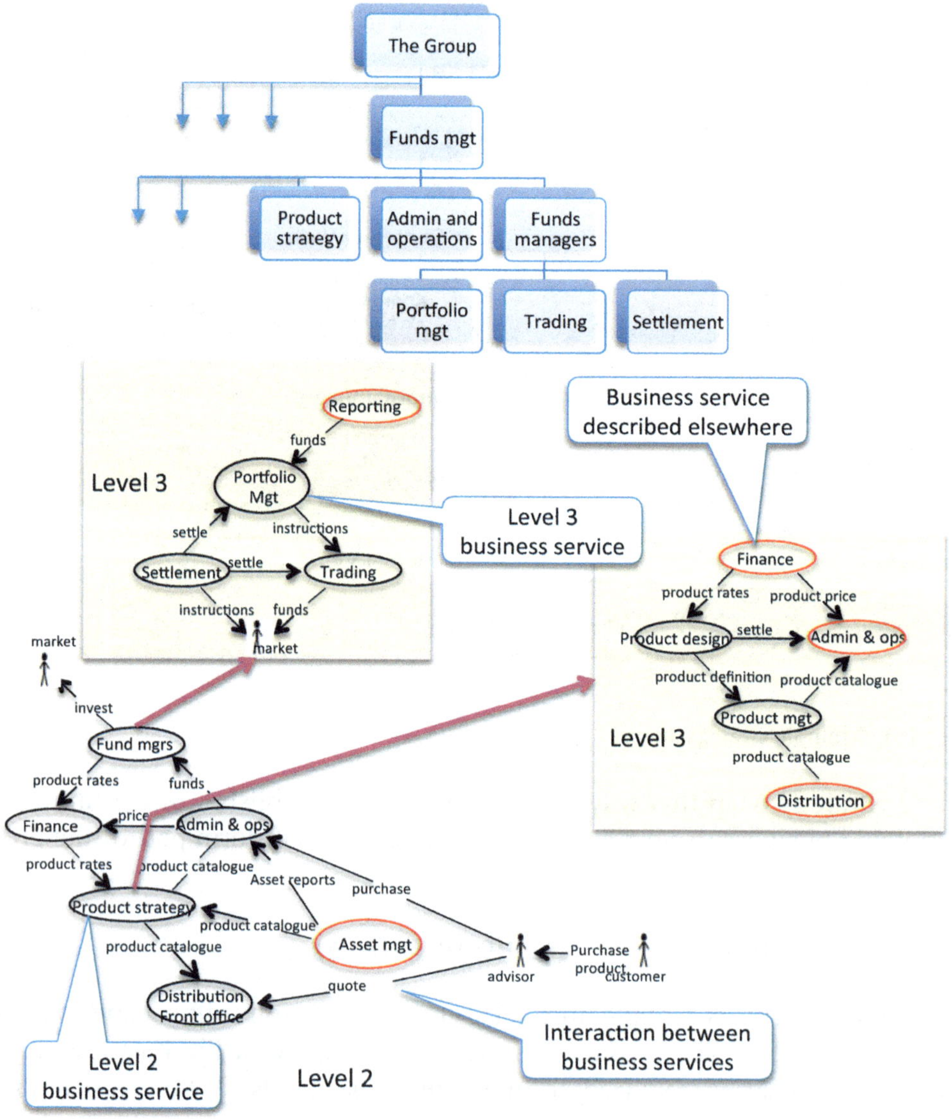

Fig. (9.16). Business Service Architecture – Level 2 and 3: funds management.

9.4.3.3. Prioritising IT Investments: Heat Map

There are several frameworks that can be used to prioritise investment in the IT estate, such as the one in illustrated in Fig. (**9.17**, adapted from Jones (op cit)). A four-quadrant classification is used here, stating Business Value and Business Impact. Investments priorities, from highest to lowest, are:

1) Market differentiation;

2) Return on investment;

3) Cost minimisation;

4) Service Level Agreement (SLA);

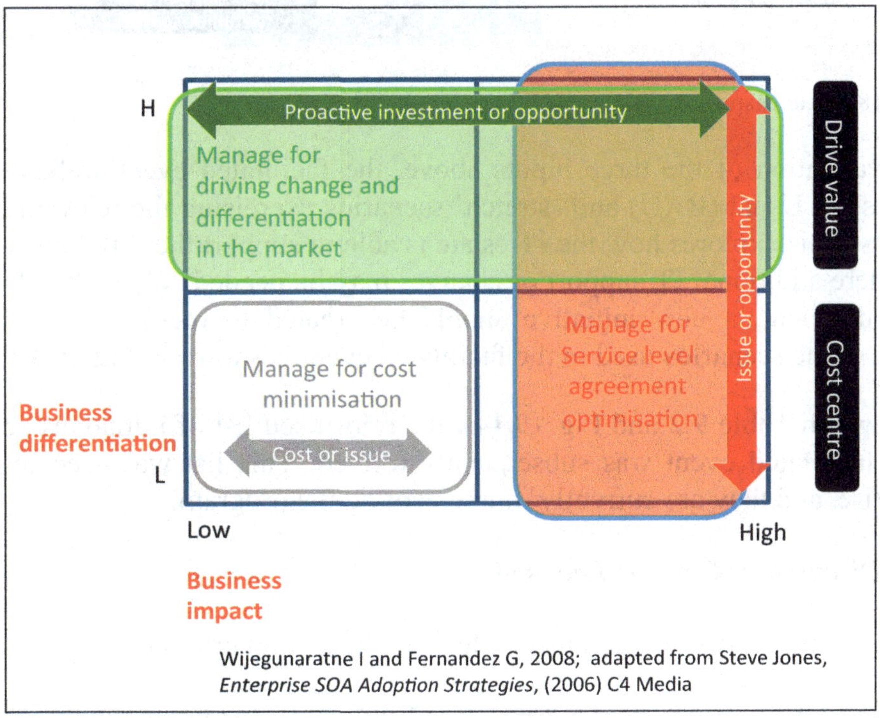

Fig. (9.17). Business value classification.

Fig. (**9.18**) shows the resulting investment Heat Map, showing in different colours the priority of investments according to the framework. As the first activity, these three input elements, Strategy Map, Business Services Architecture and Heat Map were validated during the facilitated event described in Table **9.2**.

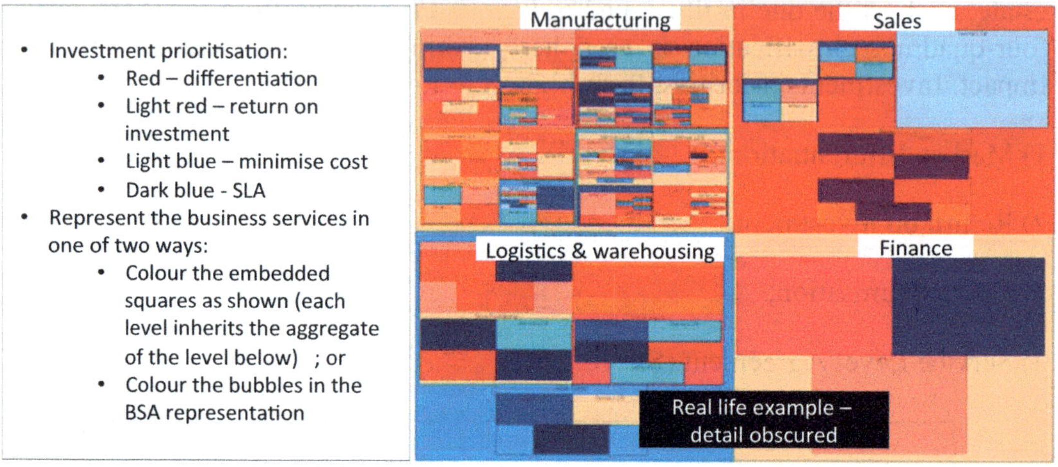

Fig. (9.18). Heat Map.

After validation of the three inputs above, the facilitated event walked through Business as Usual (BAU) and 'stretch' scenarios exercising the relevant business services. This explores how the IT estate is able to support the different scenarios, and where additional IT support or changes may be needed. When the IT estate is found deficient, a new initiative should be created to rectify the problem. A sample of the scenarios used in the facilitated event is shown in Fig. (**9.19**).

As shown in Table **9.2** and Fig. (**9.14**), the prioritised list of initiatives developed at the facilitated event was subsequently refined. This list was accepted by the enterprise, and they are currently[2] implementing the program.

9.4.4. Discussion: Lessons Learned

We argued previously for a "purpose test" with twofold criteria:

I. The raison d'etre for EA must stem from, and be kept aligned to, a business purpose

II. The level and detail of the enterprise descriptions must be tailored to be sufficient for its intended purpose.

---

[2]At the time of publishing this paper.

Examples: stretch scenarios	
Description	**Drivers**
Growth	
An acquisition results in having to integrate relevant business processes (elaborate on the processes) within three months	efficient ops
An acquisition results in transaction volumes (elaborate on the transactions) growing 400%	efficient ops
Due to increase in the mortgage business, the transactions (elaborate) are anticipated to double year on year for the next three years	efficient ops
A new office (elaborate on the types of business) needs to be established in NY. Needs to be done within three months. The projected business volumes are uncertain; IT needs to support the established offices, and be ready to provide services	Strong distribution capabilities, global scale
Innovation	
A knowledge work developes an innovative new risk management strategy. How did you identify, capture and industralise the idea?	Efficient operations, quality & competitive products
The business needs to place a new product (shared equity mortgage) in the market within 3 months.	Efficient operations
Risk	
A new mortgage competitor emerges on the market--little green men finance-- with a product 30% 'cheaper' than ours (over the life of the loan). How do we claw back our position?	Competitive products
Little green men finance can introduce a new product into the market in 1/2 the time we can. How can we make the business become competitive again?	Competitive products
A new law is passed with a 4 month implementaton deadline, requiring IT to respond by updating impacted systems if the business wants to avoid major penalties.	Efficient ops; compliance

Fig. (9.19). Scenarios.

The two case studies, involving two starkly different levels of detail, clearly illustrate the purpose test.

Lesson 1: Understand the business purpose

The purpose of the EA light exercise was *alignment*, of IT with the strategic goals of the business. The purpose was clear and well understood by the consultants and IT stakeholders. The challenge here was to move IT away from its technical comfort zone and into thinking of alignment in terms of answers to business objectives and problems. The mechanisms used to achieve this included the strategy map, which presented very clear traceability to the business objectives, and the scenarios that were exercised during the facilitated event, which were business scenarios that required an IT response (See also "Lesson 5").

The terms of reference of the EA Heavy were expressed in terms of the gains *via rationalisation*: "reduce complexity, improve flexibility and interoperability, improve service levels and lower the cost to serve." The challenge with EA Heavy was to:

- Produce evidence in support of the terms of reference—*i.e.* to show the cost to the business of the current, very complex IT estate.
- Properly communicate the message to develop a common understanding of the problem and generate momentum for solving it.

This was done through the current state assessment, which depicted the problem clearly and unambiguously, and then by communicating this to stakeholders both formally and informally (see below).

Lesson 2: Understand and deliver what business and IT stakeholders actually want

In both cases, the ultimate purpose *was to identify a set of initiatives according to the purpose of each exercise*. In the former, the initiatives would serve to align the IT division more closely with the strategic drivers of the business; in the latter the initiatives would rationalise and simplify the IT estate, yielding significant savings in operational expenditure. The approaches and the interim artefacts produced in the two exercises—albeit very different—nevertheless shared a common characteristic: they were only a means to the end of establishing the initiatives. The final form of the target IT estate was of very little interest to the senior business and IT stakeholders, as opposed to the benefits that the initiatives would bring: better alignment with business drivers in EA Light; savings through rationalisation in EA Heavy. In both engagements, the EA teams were keenly fixed on this goal, and avoided being seduced by producing artefacts along the way, unless they directly served a business purpose. To summarise, stakeholders need:

- Where the problem is not clear or commonly understood: present the problem and the do-nothing consequences articulated in clear, business (preferably dollar) terms.

- Establish a set of initiatives to achieve the goal/s (whether it is better alignment, cost optimization, *etc.*), and the benefits, also preferably expressed in dollar terms (see 'Lesson 3' below).

This is a lesson that EA practitioners should not miss. There are many examples of EA failures in which producing glossy diagrams of the target state ends up becoming the goal. This typically leaves business stakeholders cold; indeed, we argue that the technical artefacts of EA, in themselves, do no generate enthusiasm or support for the change initiatives that may be recommended.

Lesson 3: Communicate benefits in business terms

Management is understandably averse to releasing funds where the business benefit cannot be clearly perceived: so always couch the benefits in business terms. We agree with Lapkin "Define a value proposition specific to the enterprise, and articulate it in business terms" [12] and Strassman "Computer investments must show as enhancements to a business plan" ([27] pp 3). A benefit originating in IT should be couched in business terms, as clearly demonstrated by EA Heavy, where the team's brief was confined to rationalisation. The team worked with the business to streamline provisioning of the business services *via* a rationalised set of application functions and supporting infrastructure. However, any significant efficiency gain—as in this case rationalisation of a key set of business services from 14 different applications to one, or consolidating the server infrastructure—having a positive bearing on CAPEX/OPEX (Capital Expenditure/Operational Expenditure) is of interest to the highest echelons of the enterprise. By couching these in the right terms, in EA Heavy the extent of duplication and the current costs became clear, as did the very significant rationalisation opportunities and the gains these would bring. The team pressed the rationalisation message home to IT and business executives, using the savings dollar figures effectively to solidify support, acceptance and enthusiasm for a critical, significant transformation program with an estimated cost well in excess of $100 M over five years.

Lesson 4: Tailor effort to the intended purpose and management expectations

The two projects show a wide variation of effort:

- The EA light exercise was carried out in six weeks by a team of two external consultants.

- EA heavy was a far more substantial affair, involving the entire Group of the multinational; performed over a period of approximately six months by a team of ten staff—internal staff plus external consultants—working full time

Our measure of success is that the output was not only accepted, but it has been used to initiate programs of work. Therefore, both in scoping and designing an engagement, as well as in responding to an established scope definition, it is imperative to understand the purpose and tailor the effort and the output to stakeholder expectations and no more, to avoid the EA exercise losing momentum and support along the way.

With the engagement in progress, the EA team constantly communicated that they were delivering value for money by: (a) constantly reporting progress to stakeholders, including the percentage task completion of project management, and what it was being uncovered; (b) establishing credibility by 'brown bag' sessions on affiliated subjects; (c) most importantly, by facilitated events engaging stakeholders as active participants in key decisions.

Lesson 5: Leverage the richness of the potential EA space

There was a significant difference in starting assumptions for the two approaches. EA Heavy operated under terms of reference that channelled the project towards delivering a rationalised IT estate. Consequently, it was not possible to explore other solution spaces, such as how IT can support strategic business intentions. In the event though, we were able to show very considerable financial gains through rationalisation that, as described above, fuelled a large transformation program.

EA Light, on the other hand, did not start with any such assumptions. This enabled the team to explore a richer solution space, including BPO (Business Process Outsourcing) and SaaS (Software as a Service), to be able to deliver a more complete set of solutions—which may or may not involve technology installations—to the business challenges presented. Two slightly different points should be highlighted here:

- IT staff must be cognizant of non-IT aspects in EA. The natural inclination of IT staff and management is to think of an EA roadmap primarily in terms of IT application or infrastructure change. However, changes to the business architecture will be necessary for the enterprise to change position within the business landscape. We were cognisant of EA Light's terms of reference as the IT division's response to the business strategy. However, recognizing the natural bias amongst IT staff and management, an explicit attempt was made to step outside their familiar concerns.

- A holistic approach makes possible to explore a wider solution space and possibly develop a more appropriate—higher value—solution for the enterprise. The techniques used in EA light were tailored to explore this: for example, three categories were created for initiatives: application, infrastructure (the traditional IT ground), plus people and process, and the scenarios shaped to trigger discussion in this third area as well. Some of the 'softer' aspects were encapsulated in initiatives such as facilitated organizational learning, streamlining of internal IT processes, capturing internal knowledge and succession planning.

Capturing these softer aspects in current IT frameworks is a challenge. The Zachman framework offers slots—but not techniques—in its taxonomy to include them. However, research is starting to recognise and try to address these aspects within the strategy. For EA to become more than IT change, these non-technical aspects of the enterprise should be included together with the more tangible IT and process aspects. This is an important area for further research.

9.4.5. Conclusions

These two EA exercises deliver very important lessons, which can be summarised thus:

Follow the principle of parsimony:

- Carefully tailor the methodology used to the purpose of the exercise;
- Where possible, use existing artefacts, including non-technical artefacts, and only develop new artefacts when really required;
- Decompose, describe, illustrate, just enough for the purpose of the exercise;
- Work together with, and deliver to, the business;

- Always involve stakeholders in the process;
- Communicate the benefits in business terms, and clearly articulate the consequences of doing nothing, as the business will invest on a new IT function only if this clearly provides more benefits that the status quo;
- Produce a prioritized list of IT initiatives directly linked to enterprise drivers and business outcomes;
- Use the priority list above to produce the transformation program.

CHAPTER 10

Wrap Up

We have come to the end of this journey.

Fig. (**10.1**) illustrates the familiar disconnect in the strategic priorities for the Business and IT. Let alone pulling the ship in different directions, we sometimes don't seem to be on the same ship! And sadly the enterprise architect, as a key member of the IT "brains trust" driving IT's strategic priorities, is often found at the helm of this rift and discord.

Fig. (10.1). Disconnect between Business and IT.

Inji Wijegunaratne, George Fernandez & Peter Evans-Greenwood

Our aim in this eBook has been to show you, as the enterprise architect, how to heal the rift, and help IT support the business navigate the ship of the enterprise through today's treacherous competitive waters (Fig. **10.2**).

Fig. (10.2). The navigators.

In other words, at the outset, we said

> 'The position of an enterprise architect is a privileged one, but all too often this privilege is wasted by pushing a favourite technology barrow; taking refuge in visually appealing diagrams; or becoming the organisational change police. *How an EA adds value in his or her position is unanswered for many organisations'*

We hope that we have provided some useful answers to this challenge.

Let us reiterate some of the points we raised in the eBook, less by way of a summary, but more in the spirit of a wrap up.

Complacency

If you are not getting your message across as the EA, *it is in your own personal interest* to make it right. The situation is not symmetrical: the Business hold the purse strings, and as we said at the beginning, you, as the enterprise architect, after all are an overhead on an overhead function. Joining the dots from there is not rocket science.

Cycles

Enterprise Architecture as a discipline is seriously obese with frameworks and methodologies. The main thing we need to be in step with though, is the business cycle (Fig. **10.3**): very simply put, businesses plan, implement, and operate; they plan, implement their plans and operates the business as they plan and implement. Well, we as IT need to follow suit: IT must plan with the business, support the changes the business implements, while operating business as usual (BAU). The EA, as the standard bearer for IT, must ensure harmony between the two cycles, aligning IT's direction with that of the business in planning, elaborating on the plan so that the vision and the trajectory is clear, and helping keep the ship on an even keel during the journey through architectural governance.

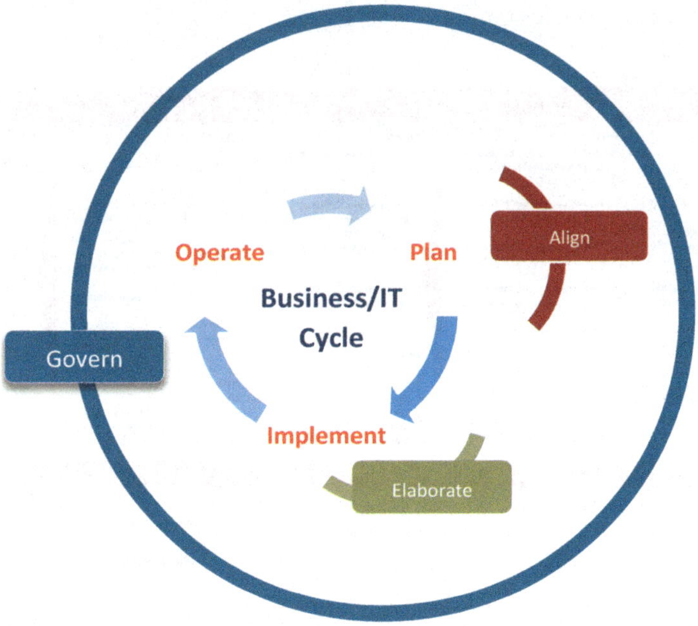

Fig. (10.3). The business and IT cycle.

How to align, elaborate, and govern was the main focus of the eBook (Fig. **10.4**). We would urge the reader not to look upon it as yet another framework, but simply as a useful heuristic: whether you like it or not planning, implementing and operating is how the enterprise functions; and aligning, elaborating and governing is how you organise yourself to support the enterprise. To put another way, none of these activities are architecturally contrived; align, elaborate, and govern fit naturally into the processes that keep the organizational wheel turning.

Moreover, you do just enough architecture to support these key organisational processes. You don't produce artefacts for architectural completeness, or simply because a framework mandated an artefact. If your journey is from Sydney to Singapore, you do not waste time drawing maps of the African shoreline. Time enough for that when you actually plan to travel around the Cape of Good Hope. By aligning your activities in this manner, you produce deliverables in line with the needs of the business cycle, not only that, you do something much more significant: you intertwine yourself with these business processes, starting with planning, so that IT/IS alignment and support with the business direction happens naturally. This is not easy, especially at the beginning when you may need to gain credibility, to change entrenched ways of working *etc.*

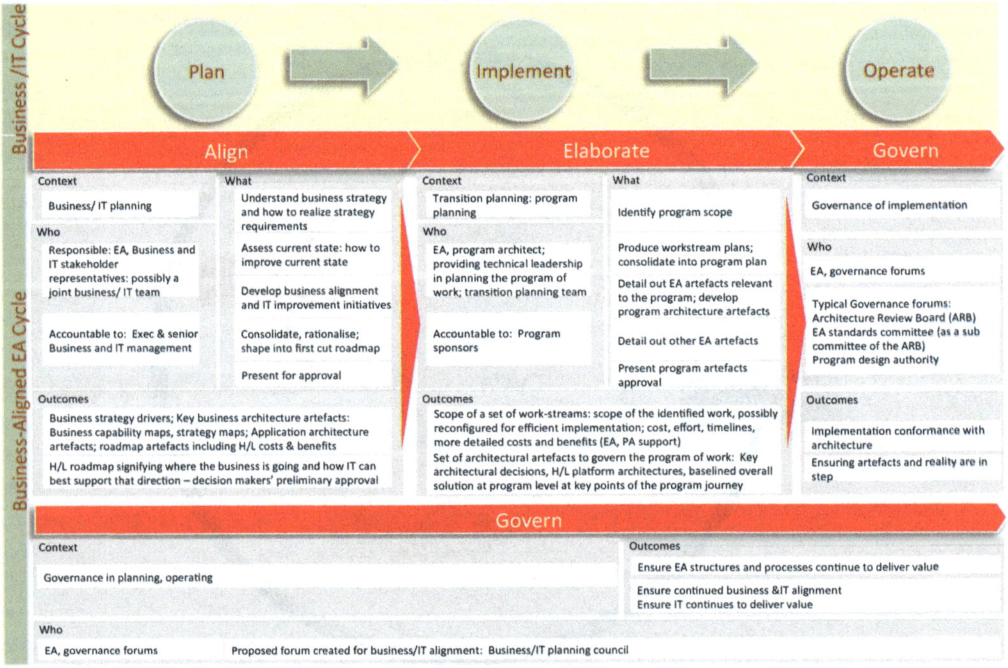

Fig. (10.4). Align, Elaborate, and Govern – a summary.

Communication

	Architecture Artefacts	Audience	Purpose	Communications attributes
Enterprise level	High level business architecture, strategy alignment, roadmaps	Exec/senior business management Exec/senior IT management Business staff IT staff	Understanding for persuasion buy-in Understanding for information	Presentation and messaging
Program level	Program architecture artefacts	Senior business and IT management Business stakeholders Program management	Understanding for Buy-in and acceptance	
Project level	High level solution architecture	Business stakeholders Project management	Understanding for Buy-in and acceptance	
	Solution architecture and solution architecture components	System designers System designers Programmers Testers	Understanding for design Understanding for construction and testing	Specification

Fig. (10.5). Communication attributes.

We must, as enterprise architects be very mindful of the purposes that our artefacts intend to serve. A key skill in aligning the imperatives and carrying the stakeholders with you is presentation. If you present badly, your output is unlikely to find favour with the audience: you cannot for instance, couch a deliverable intended for senior business management in the same terms as one intended for system designers; indeed, when put like this, it is obvious, a 'duh' statement. However, the number of architectural artefacts the authors have seen which actually tell the truth but are woefully inadequate to communicate to its intended audience is surprising. The above matrix (Fig. **10.5**) shows how the intended audience and the purpose of communication changes as we move from enterprise to project level artefacts. At the top, you need to make executive and senior management understand what you are saying and then to persuade them to your way of thinking. At the bottom you need to be dry and precise, because what you now produce is an architecture specification to guide designers and downstream IT staff.

Target states

We say in the example on "EA Heavy" and "EA Light" in Chapter 9:

> "The final form of the target IT estate was of very little interest to the senior business and IT stakeholders, as opposed to the benefits that the initiatives would bring: better alignment with business drivers in EA Light; savings through rationalisation in EA Heavy. In both engagements, the EA teams were keenly fixed on this goal, and avoided being seduced by producing artefacts along the way, unless they directly served a business purpose."

You must remember that especially to the Align stage stakeholders, the senior business and IT managers, what is important is the *outcome/s* that the target of the plans aims to provide: the *form* of the target, how it looks on an A3 sheets of paper or a PowerPoint presentation is far less important.

And see what happens as you move down the communication matrix shown above. A "target state", from being aspirational in a five year business plan, assumes a firmer shape as the objective of a one and a half year program of work, and becomes a concrete "thing" to deliver for each of the five individual projects of the program: the stakeholders, the required outcomes, and purpose the respective "end state" serves in each of these endeavours is different. Please shape your output accordingly, focusing on what your respective stakeholders actually need.

Skills

The role that we describe for the enterprise architect extends the realm of their responsibility beyond the EA's traditional patch.

From being a custodian of artefacts and a policeman, the EA's domain expands out into areas of high value (Fig. **10.6**). The EA is now at the vanguard IT's close association with the desired business direction, helping align business and IT imperatives; assessing IT's performance; taking technical leadership in shaping a program of work; helping in governing the enterprise's journey.

These responsibilities spill over some of IT's traditional role and responsibility boundaries. You will need to tread carefully, work with incumbent staff and create a niche as a trusted advisor to senior business and IT management.

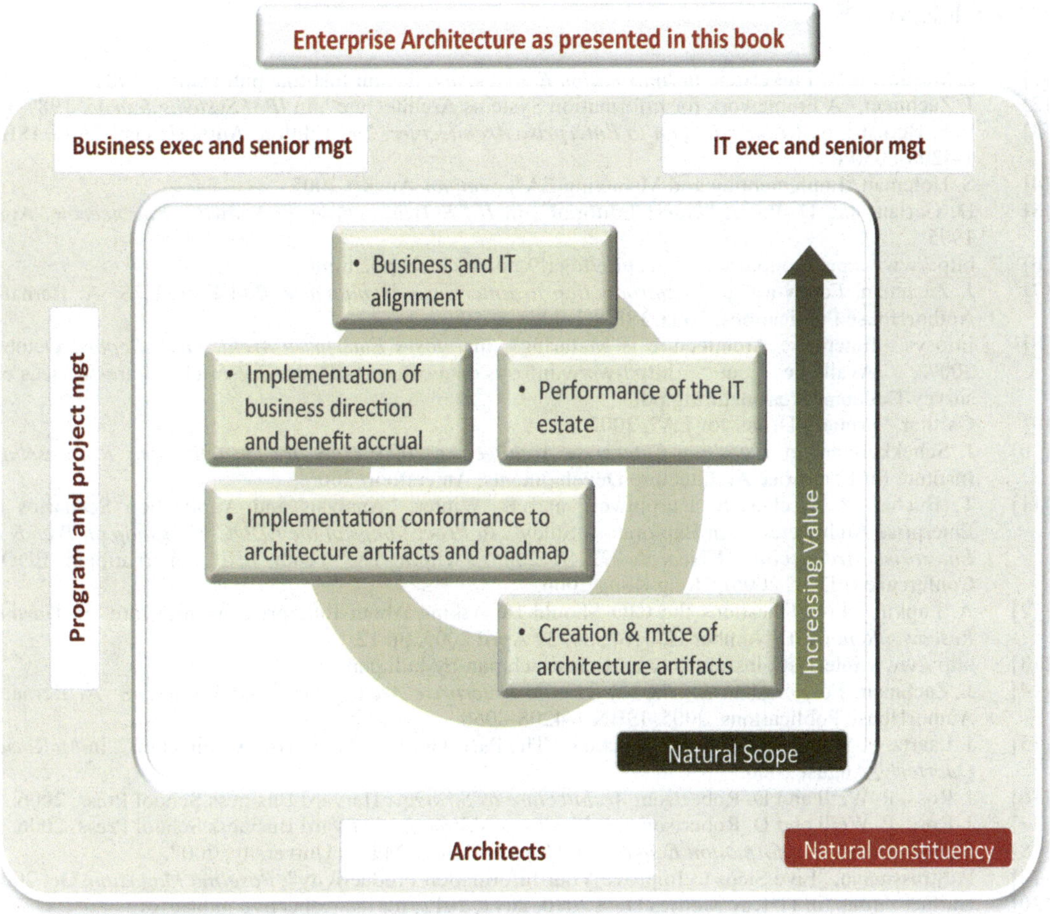

Fig. (10.6). Expanded role of the EA.

The EA must develop skills to be successful in these new areas of concern: Skills in business strategy, planning and business architecture, financial analysis, program planning, softer skills of consulting, stakeholder management, negotiation, and persuasion, the ability to rise above detail and see the big picture

Finally

Well, we have had our say. We can only hope that this eBook helps you in going forth and adding value….

REFERENCES

[1] J. Martin, and C Finkelsten, in *Information Engineering*, Savant Institute publication, 1981

[2] J. Zachman, "A Framework for Information Systems Architecture", in *IBM Systems Journal* 1987

[3] S.A. Bernard, in *An Introduction to Enterprise Architecture*, 2nd Edition, AuthorHouse, 2005, ISBN 1-4208-8050-0

[4] S. Holcman "Implementing and Managing EA", *Seminar* August 2005

[5] D. Garlan, and D. Perry, "Guest Editorial", in *IEEE Transactions on Software Engineering*, April 1995.

[6] http://www.opengroup.org/architecture/togaf9-doc/arch/chap02.html

[7] J. Zachman, Foreword to *An Introduction to Enterprise Architecture*, 2nd Edition, S. A. Bernard. AuthorHouse Publications, 2005. ISBN 1-4208-8050

[8] Infosys, "Enterprise Architecture is Maturing", in *Infosys Enterprise Architecture Report*, October 2007. Available at http://www.infosys.com/offerings/IT-services/architecture-services/ea-survey/Documents/ea-maturing.pdf

[9] Gartner, "Primary Driver for EA", 2007

[10] J. Schekkerman, in *Trends in Enterprise Architecture 2005: How are Organizations Progressing?* Institute for Enterprise Architecture Developments, Amersfoort 2005.

[11] T. Bucher, R. Fischer, S. Kurpjuweit, and R. Winter, "Analysis and Application Scenarios of Enterprise Architecture: An Exploratory Study", in *Proceedings of the EDOC Workshop on Trends in Enterprise Architecture Research (TEAR 2006)*, within The Tenth IEEE International EDOC Conference (EDOC 2006), Hong Kong 2006.

[12] A. Lapkin, "Five Questions the CIO Should Be Asking About Enterprise Architecture" in *Gartner Research Report*, ID Number G00167384, 29 April 2009, pp 12.

[13] http://www.intervista-institute.com/articles/zachman-by-kull.php

[14] J. Zachman, Foreword to *An Introduction to Enterprise Architecture*, 2nd Edition, S. A. Bernard, AuthorHouse Publications, 2005. ISBN 1-4208-8050

[15] J. Laartz, E. Sonderegger, and J. Vinckier, "The Paris Guide to Enterprise Architecture", in *McKinsey Quarterly*, August 2000.

[16] J. Ross, P. Weill and D. Robertson, *Architecture as Strategy*, Harvard Business School Press, 2006.

[17] J. Ross, P. Weill and D. Robertson, *Architecture as Strategy*, Harvard Business School Press, 2006.

[18] P. Strassmann, in *Information Economics Metrics*, George Mason University, 2007.

[19] P. Strassmann, "Five Steps to Improve Your Information Productivity", *Baseline Magazine*, Oct 2006

[20] Gartner Group, in IT Key Metrics Data 2010, 2011, 2012, for the respective industries.

[21] Kaplan and Norton, HBR, Sept-Oct 2000; HBR, Feb 2004.

[22] J. Ross, P. Weill, and D. Robertson, in *Enterprise Architecture As Strategy: Creating a Foundation for Business Execution*, Harvard Business School Press, 2006, ISBN 978-1-4221-4817-4

[23] R. Kaplan and D. Norton, "Having Troubles with your Strategy? Then Map it", in Harvard Business Review 2000 Sep-Oct, 78 (5), 167-76, 202

[24] G. Doucet, J. Gotze, P. Saha, and S. Bernard, *Coherency Management-Architecting the Enterprise for Alignment, Agility and Assurance*, AuthorHouse, Bloomington, Indiana, 2009, ISBN: 978-1-4389-9606-6

[25] R. Kaplan, and D. Norton, "Measuring the strategic readiness of intangible assets", *Harvard Business Review*, February 2004.

[26] S. Jones, *Enterprise SOA Adoption Strategies*, C4 Media, 2006.

[27] P. Strassman, *The Squandered Computer*, The Information Economic Press, New Canaan, Connecticut, 1997.

Inji Wijegunaratne, George Fernandez & Peter Evans-Greenwood

Index

Inji Wijegunaratne, George Fernandez & Peter Evans-Greenwood

Made in United States
Orlando, FL
04 November 2026

90200452R00129